THE UNTOLD STORY

of

EXPLORATION

By
LOWELL THOMAS

WITH ILLUSTRATIONS BY KURT WIESE

GARDEN CITY PUBLISHING CO., INC.
GARDEN CITY   NEW YORK

1937
THE GARDEN CITY PUBLISHING COMPANY

G 80
T45

PRINTED IN THE UNITED STATES OF AMERICA

PREFACE

THE genesis of this book has a direct bearing on its title, if you will permit me to tell it.

Ever since I was an urchin in a raw Colorado gold-mining region, exploration has fascinated me more than any other subject. In some of my subsequent years I was fortunate enough to travel up and down the globe quite a bit. But my luck never went so far as the accomplishment of any actual geographical discovery. Nevertheless it has always been to me the most absorbing of all topics.

So my next ambition was: "Until I can do some worthwhile exploring, why not write about what other men have done? I can have at least the vicarious thrill of following through their exciting records." The psychologists, I believe, would call that an escape motive.

So I conceived the idea of a book to be entitled *The Romance of Exploration*. A few weeks of research showed me that I had projected a job which only a thoroughly reckless, improvident or charitable publisher would issue. It would have entailed a survey of the entire field of geographical adventure and discovery from Sargon of Akkad down to Richard Byrd of Little America and Bertram Thomas of the Rub' al Khali.

Obviously, a formidable, extravagant tome. Sir Raymond Beazley, being the rare combination of profound scholar, great humanist and artist in words, took three great quarto volumes for his *Dawn of Modern Geography*. And that covers only the Middle Ages, ending just as the magnificent Prince Henry the Navigator is about to prepare the way for the Golden Age of Discovery.

Professor J. N. L. Baker took 543 pages to set forth the bare outlines of the subject in his *History of Geographical Discovery and Exploration*. It is today and will remain for ages to come a monumental and invaluable work. In it Dr. Baker gives you the principal achievements of practically every traveler who has done anything important. In such a compendious work he was naturally obliged to confine himself to facts without any highlights of character and drama.

While I was meditating this, there burst from the presses of Macmillan and Company a volume called *A History of Exploration, from the Earliest Times to the Present Day*, by General Sir Percy Sykes, K.C.I.E., C.B., C.M.G., Gold Medallist of the Royal Geographical Society, author of *A History of Persia, Ten Thousand Miles in Persia*, etc. It turned out to have all the charm and gusto that you might expect of a man who is not only a distinguished British Proconsul, but a humanist and also himself an explorer and a fascinating writer to boot.

Right on top of that another brilliant work was published, Leonard Outhwaite's *Unrolling the Map*. Technically speaking, Mr. Outhwaite had a new approach. In a series of vivid, flashing sketches he not only told the history of exploration but gave us incisive, marvelously succinct insights into the character and drama of the famous explorers.

Having read these enviable books, it became obvious that it would be absurd to try to compete with them or to rewrite them. A rewriting of such works would be no more than a rehash.

Meanwhile, however, I had occasion to observe that there were absorbing and romantic figures in the history of exploration which my predecessors—and betters —had been obliged either to skip or to pass over with a few words, in their compendious surveys of the entire field. Covering, as they did, one field of human effort throughout some forty centuries, they could hardly stop off by the wayside to dramatize individual romances such as the love story of Lapérouse or the manner in which Will Adams, the shipwright's apprentice, became the favorite of the Shogun Iyeyasu and a Samurai with two swords.

So there, it seemed to me, was my field. And hence the title, *The Untold Story of Exploration*. The explorers I am going to talk about have been deliberately chosen because other historiographers have not written about them so much. To my mind, some of them are even more glamorous, more extraordinary, than those who were more famous.

To the works mentioned above I am considerably indebted. Likewise to *The Ancient Explorers*, by M. Cary and E. H. Warmington and the monograph on Pytheas by Sir Clements Markham, to Sir Raymond Beazley's biography of Prince Henry the Navigator and Clennell Wilkinson's *Dampier;* to numerous issues of the *Geographical Journal*, the *Proceedings of the Royal Geographical Society* and the *Journal of the Royal Central Asian Society;* to the *Reisebuch* of Hans Schiltberger and the autobiography of Ulrich Schmiedel; to the monographs by Major Kenneth Mason and General J. T. Walter on the Pandits; to Major Stephen Gwynn's biography of Mary Kingsley and various books mentioned in the text.

LOWELL THOMAS.

Clover Brook,
Pawling, N. Y.
August, 1935.

CONTENTS

EXPLORERS BY LAND

EXPLORERS BY SEA

ILLUSTRATIONS

EXPLORERS BY LAND

I

THE FIRST CHINESE PIONEER

I

THE FIRST CHINESE PIONEER

IMAGINE a scene one day in 138 B.C. at the court of the great Han Emperor, Wu-ti. The Son of Heaven is not surrounded by grave, venerable graybeards. He has combed his dominions for the brightest young aggressive officers and councilors. Himself only eighteen years old, he has inaugurated the Golden Age of Youth in the Middle Kingdom.

The young ruler is talking to his courtiers about the silk trade. It is an index of his peculiar and precocious sagacity. The fabric woven from the product of the worm that feeds on mulberry leaves is the principal source of his people's prosperity.

"My lords, we must find more markets for our silk," declares the Son of Heaven. "China has lived within itself too long. We must expand; we must sell to other peoples."

"Majesty, we are hemmed in," observes a minister of state. "To the south are lawless, masterless robber tribes who would seize all our caravans. On the west and northwest lie the Hiung-nu (the Huns). They would not let our caravans through either."

"True," agrees the Emperor. "The Hiung-nu understand nothing but fighting. The only way to convince them is to conquer them."

"Are we then to wage war upon them who are numerous as the sands of the Gobi?"

"Yes, when the time is ripe," replies the Emperor sharply. "But we shall not fight alone. Who are the worst enemies of the Hiung-nu?" he asks.

"The Yüé-chi," several courtiers answer in chorus. "But they were defeated and driven out of their lands by the Hiung-nu."

"Exactly," says Wu-ti. "All the more reason why they must be anxious for revenge. This is what we shall do: we shall make an alliance with the Yüé-chi. Together we can annihilate the Hiung-nu. Now, my lords, whom shall we send to carry this offer to the king of the Yüé-chi?"

A strapping young officer strides forward eagerly.

"O Son of Heaven, permit me to do this thing!" he pleads.

"You, Chang K'ién?" says the Emperor in a questioning tone. "What makes you think you can carry through such an undertaking? You may have many tens of thousands of *li* * to travel, over desert and mountains, to a far, strange country. Indeed you will go thousands of *li* before you even find out whither the Yüé-chi have gone since they were driven from their

* According to some geographers the *li* at that time was the equivalent of about three land miles.

own lands."

"Majesty, I am a man of the mountain country," the young man urges. "Your Majesty will remember that I come from Han-chung, in the Tsinling Shan, in the south of the province of Shensi, the province of your own august family. You must know that we of Shensi are hardened to long journeys. And we can find our way anywhere in the dark."

Wu-ti thinks for a while and looks around on the faces in his court. Some of them are sneering at such adolescent presumption. Others are scowling jealously. It happens that the youthful Emperor knows this Chang K'ién from his own native province quite well. Most of the ruling dynasties of China originated in Shensi. They are a hardy lot, the men of Shensi, especially those from the mountains in the south. Intelligent, too. That is why Wu-ti sent for his young neighbor to come to court in the first place and appointed him a *lang* (yeoman officer) in his household. In his two years of service there Chang K'ién has shown a remarkable capacity for getting along with people.

"He is discreet and likeable, energetic and trustworthy," reflected the young monarch. "And what a physique!"

The result of all these cogitations is that Chang K'ién is appointed the first ambassador to the remote King of the Yüé-chi, "somewhere in Asia." And by that appointment he also becomes the first of the Chinese explorers. At least, he is the first to be recorded in the most ancient of the ancient history of his country. He does not know what a prodigiously long journey he is undertaking, nor how many exciting adventures are to happen to him. Neither does he dream of the extraordinary expansion of China that his mission is destined to bring about. His master does, however.

While the new ambassador is getting ready for his travels, let us take a glance at the character of that master. Wu-ti undoubtedly is a genius, one of the great men of all time. When he ascended the throne in 140 B.C., at the age of sixteen, he found himself ruling over a country that had been isolated for centuries, yet was in constant fear of invasion by barbarous neighboring peoples. The position of the crown was not strong. Powerful feudal lords, jealous of each other and jealous of their overlord, dominated the various provinces, fought amongst each other and frequently defied the central authority.

Wu-ti astonished the country from the beginning of his long reign. His first action was a swift and unexpected series of decrees that smashed the power of the feudal lords almost at one blow. To start with, he banished them from court and sent them home to their provincial seats. Then, to prevent them from using their local feudatory powers to conspire against him, he assigned special resident councilors, men he could trust, to watch them. Next, in place of the haughty

[6]

graybeards whose words had been law in China, he surrounded himself with intelligent young men of humble origin. All these were deadly thrusts at the old aristocracy. They amounted, in fact, to a revolution from the top. His subsequent step showed still further sagacity. He insured the reduction of the great fiefs belonging to the dukes and local kinglets by revoking the law of primogeniture. By this means, when a great landowner died, his estate was divided up amongst all his legitimate sons.

Thus he set about consolidating his own authority. Thereupon we find him as described above, getting ready to free his country from her isolation, paving the way for the expansion and intercourse with other nations that are to make her richer and greater than ever. We may ask: "How does it happen that a youth still in his teens has so much vision, such statesmanship?" The only possible answer is that Wu-ti is a freak of Nature, virtually born in the possession of uncanny wisdom.

He sends his young ambassador on his way to the king of the Yüé-chi in considerable state. There are a hundred men in Chang K'ién's retinue. Among them is T'ang-i-fu, a Tartar. He has been an hereditary slave in the household of the T'ang-i family. His services have been loaned for this expedition partly because, being a Tartar, he knows something of the ways and language of the fierce Hiung-nu. But he is also invaluable, as Chang K'ién is to find out, because he is one of the crack bowmen of the kingdom. Many centuries before the period which we are considering, the art of archery reached in China perfection never since surpassed. The weapon they use is a far better instrument than the longbow subsequently used by the Welsh with such devastating effect at the Battle of Crécy. It is a composite bow, which the Chinese invented, made of sinew and horn as well as wood. The inner surface is sheathed with plates of horn which not only add to its power but protect and preserve the wood. Unlike the wooden bows of the Flemish and British, the Chinese bow lasted forever and was handed from father to son as an heirloom. Many of them were beautifully ornamented and polished.

So let us follow the adventures of Chang K'ién as related by Ssi-ma Ts'ién, "the Herodotus of China"— also the court astrologer. The first stage of the journey, to the Chinese frontier, is easy for Chang K'ién. He goes by way of Lung-si, now Kansu. He first has to traverse what is known today as the Richthofen range, so-called after one of the greatest of all European explorers in Asia, the Baron von Richthofen (probably an ancestor or collateral forbear of the famous Red Knight, Germany's brilliant war ace). Even this preliminary stage would stagger an ordinary man. But Chang K'ién, as we have observed, was born in the heart of the Tsinling Shan, and mountaineering comes naturally to him.

When he reaches the limits of Lung-si his job has only just begun. He is now about to set foot on soil that does not belong to his Emperor. We must remember that at this time practically nothing is known in China about the lands outside the Empire. The deadly, hostile Hiung-nu are believed to be occupying the territory to the west and northwest. But the exact extent and location of their outposts are a complete mystery.

That mystery Chang K'ién solves in short order. Hardly has his little band crossed the border and reached the northern slopes of the Nan Shan than they hear the trampling of hundreds of galloping hoofs, to an obbligato of wild yells and a shower of arrows. Bow in hand, spear in socket, a regiment of mahogany-faced, shaggy, black-haired horsemen surrounds the ambassador and his retinue. Resistance is hopeless. Already several Chinese lie dead and wounded on the ground. Now, as through the centuries to come when their name strikes terror throughout Europe, the Huns observe the maxim of shooting first and asking questions afterwards. Barely a day's march from the confines of his own country, Wu-ti's envoy with all his companions is a prisoner of the Hiung-nu. His mission seems a failure before it has really begun.

What can the captives expect? The usual practice of the Huns is to massacre the wounded and make slaves of the rest. But one of their customs saves the life of Chang K'ién. The cream of the loot and all the captured who appear to be persons of importance are the personal perquisite of the Great Khan. So the ambassador to the Yüé-chi is sent to the *ordu* (camp) of the Shan-yü. The name of this potentate is Lou Shang. It is he who, some twenty years before, finally crushed the Yüé-chi. We obtain a fair idea of his sweet disposition from the fact that he now drinks his favorite tipple of cosmos (kumyss) out of a drinking cup fashioned from the skull of his defeated enemy. On the whim of this ruffian depends the fate of our Chinese explorer.

No young man could find himself in a worse jam. The Huns despise the Chinese, not with a comfortable, patronizing contempt, but with savage hatred. The chances are about 500 to one that the visitors will be used to make sport for a Hiung-nu holiday, possibly as targets in an archery competition. The presents intended for the king of the Yüé-chi have of course been confiscated. The beautiful silken clothing and precious fabrics of the captives will probably be used for carpets in the traveling huts of the barbarians. It is a cruel ordeal for a young envoy utterly without experience. He explains his presence in those parts. The archer, T'ang-i-fu, serves as interpreter. In this crisis, Chang K'ién has recourse to a curious expedient, an expedient that he subsequently finds exceedingly valuable all over Asia. He tells the truth.

"My Emperor, His Sacred Majesty, has sent me on a mission to the Yüé-chi," he says simply. He does not add that the purpose of the mission was to make an offensive alliance against the Shan-yü. But he has told enough to make the Great Khan burst into a roar of laughter.

"What folly is this?" he exclaims. "Why, the Yüé-chi are to the north of us. How can China send ambassadors to them?" Therein the chieftain of the Hiung-nu is somewhat mistaken, but he does not know that. However he continues:

"What would the king of China do if he captured ambassadors that I sent to some other nation?"

"He would receive them with courtesy and respect their dignity and persons," replies Chang K'ién boldly.

"Hm-m-m," grunts the Shan-yü, scowling meditatively at the Chinamen. Then he proclaims the order: "Take them away. See that they are fed—and well guarded." The spearmen of the Great Khan hustle the prisoners out. But as they are so doing, a pair of luminous black eyes look with something more than interest on the handsome, keen face and magnificent body of the Chinese envoy. And even an envoy of the great Emperor Wu-ti may be excused if he returns the glance. A smile from a pretty girl is something to return with gratitude, even if she is a barbarian princess. In fact it may be exceedingly useful in such a predicament.

Here the reader may protest: "What's this? The Pocahontas story again?" As a matter of fact, yes. It is definitely recorded by the historian Ssi-ma Ts'ién that

Chang K'ién does marry a princess of the Hiung-nu.
What is more, she follows him in all his wanderings.
Unfortunately we have no details of their courtship.
But we may reasonably infer that it is a stroke of luck
for him in more than one way. Naturally, it helps to
make his life among the Hiung-nu more pleasant and
comfortable. A captive envoy, presumably a spy, from
an enemy nation is one thing. The husband of a princess of the blood royal is another. Chang K'ién lives
among the Huns for ten years. Of course he is still a
prisoner, under close surveillance. But his existence is
interesting. He has none of the luxuries of the Chinese
court, none of the civilized conversation or intercourse
with artists and men of learning. But the young man
from Han-chung is of tough fiber. Also he has a keen
curiosity and learns much about the strange tribes that
hold him captive. He acquires information about their
customs, their history, their technique in warfare, their
resources. He also makes shrewd observations of their
terrain, their sources of supply, the strategic points in
their territory. All this knowledge, stored up in his
brain, becomes later of priceless value to the Chinese
general staff.

We are still in the year 138 B.C. But we can contrive
a pretty accurate picture of the customs and conditions
that Chang K'ién finds at the *ordu* of the Shan-yü. All
we have to do is to read the book of Friar John of Pian
di Carpini, the envoy of Pope Innocent IV to a later

Great Khan at Karakorum in 1246. Fourteen centuries elapse between the capture of Chang K'ién and the journey of the medieval monk. But there is no reason to believe that any change takes place in the habits of the fighting, predatory nomads of Central Asia during those fourteen hundred years. Says Friar John:

"Their habitations be round and cunningly made with wickers and staves in the manner of a tent. But in the midst of the tops thereof they have a window open to convey the light in and the smoke out. Their walls be covered with felt. Their doors are made of felt also. Some of these tabernacles may quickly be taken asunder and set together again and are carried upon beasts' backs. Others cannot be taken asunder but are stowed upon carts. And whithersoever they go, be it either to war or to any other place, they transport their tabernacles with them. They are very rich in cattle as in camels, oxen, sheep and goats."

This is particularly interesting because it shows why the Huns—and later the hordes of Genghis Khan—are so extraordinarily mobile. Not merely the army can move overnight, but the entire nation. In fact, the nation is the army. All such information gathered by Chang K'ién is to prove eventually of great value to the Chinese military intelligence service. What he learns of Hun politics and their relations with the surrounding nations also turns out to be extremely useful.

For the ten years that he lives among the Hiung-nu,

as a kinsman by marriage and as an unusually truthful fellow, the Great Khan trusts him, but not too much. When the young Chinaman's Hun princess bears him a male child, his position at the court of Lou Shang becomes still more favorable. He is taken along on some of the military expeditions of the Hiung-nu, which adds still further to his education. But all the time he is surrounded by a watchful bodyguard. However, he is treated with such consideration that he is able to retain possession of the token of authority entrusted to him by the Emperor Wu-ti. And it is manifest that he, during all this exile, never forgets his mission for one single moment.

It is a great pity that we do not know the details of his escape at the end of those ten years. We may readily believe that he never could have accomplished it without the help and ingenuity of his Hunnish Pocahontas. All the circumstances indicate that a loving woman's wits and guile are at least partly responsible. Consider the difficulties of getting away from the clutches of a nation in which every man is born to the saddle, with an inexhaustible supply of horses and swift camels for pursuit, people who can read tracks in the sand as we can read a book, and who know every route from waterhole to waterhole in the desert, every mountain pass. In the face of such obstacles even the cunning of a mountaineer must be of little avail without inside help. And such inside help most likely is afforded by the Hun princess.

We may also imagine the attitude of the Great Khan when Chang K'ién's escape is reported to him. He is not as furious as he might be when the first officers sent out in pursuit of the fugitives returns empty-handed. We have to remember two facts. First, the Shan-yü has grown attached to the strong, candid young envoy from China. Secondly, the man who fashioned a drinking vessel out of the skull of a defeated king is obviously one of brutal, saturnine humor. We can almost hear him roaring:

"Let him go. Shall we waste our good horseflesh and camels just to punish an ungrateful guest? Fools! The deserts will punish him for us."

Therein the great Shan-yü is not quite as wise as he thinks he is. The youth from Shensi, now a robust young man in his thirties and at the height of his strength, has learned a great deal during his captivity. He has realized that the Great Khan was mistaken when he said the Yüé-chi had fled to the north. He marches west. He marches "for several tens of days." With him are not only his princess wife and his son but the doughty T'ang-i-fu, the superb Tartar archer. The Tartar's skill with the bow brings down enough game to keep the party well fed during their long trek. Across deserts they go, passing Barkul and Turfan. For thousands of *li* they travel south of the Ak-tagh mountains, south of Lake Ebinor until they have the formidable task of traversing the northern slopes of the Tien Shan, the "Celestial Mountains." Finally they reach the country of the Ta-yüan, to be known later as Ferghana.

This is an experience like that of the Israelites upon reaching a land of milk and honey after forty years of wandering in the Arabian deserts. For the Ta-yüan are not only an orderly and a peaceful but also a most hospitable people. For more than ten years the travelers from China have been encompassed by perils from man, beast, earth and climate. And here they find themselves in a lovely, fertile country, surrounded by friendly folk. Not merely friendly but respectful.

"You come from China?" they ask. "Doubly welcome! We have heard of your country, of its wealth, of the wonderful things you produce. We have tried to get into contact with you for years. It is wonderful to see you. Our king wants to see you. Is there anything we can do for you?"

What a reception after ten years' captivity among the Hiung-nu, a desperate escape and months of hazardous traveling! Chang K'ién is edified to find himself in the midst of an organized civilization. The Ta-yüan are expert cultivators of the soil. They grow wheat, many fruits and make excellent wine. That of itself is a novelty to the newcomers, for up to this time China knows nothing of the fermented juice of the grape. Many of the Ta-yüan dwell in walled cities and well-built houses. Though they are peaceful, they are not soft nor decadent. They have well-trained armies of archers on horseback. When T'ang-i-fu shows them the skill of a crack Chinese bowman they are able to appreciate it for all it is worth.

To realize fully what Chang K'ién has achieved by reaching Ferghana from China in the year 128 B.C. you ought to look carefully at your map. (Take a good atlas of Central Asia. Then check up with map no. 2 in *A History of Exploration* by Sir Percy Sykes and also the map at the end of Sir Aurel Stein's *On Central-Asian Tracks*.) It is a prodigious, heroic piece of exploration, particularly when you consider the epoch. It enables the envoy of Wu-ti to make a tremendous addition to the knowledge of the Chinese geographers of his time. For instance, he estimates that all the rivers west of Khotan flow west and feed "the western sea." All those east of Khotan flow east and feed the Salt Lake (Lop Nor), the outlet of which flows underground. He also places the source of the Yellow River near the Khotan. (Some of this is not precisely accurate. But it is remarkably close, considering the period.)

So we have Chang K'ién being escorted to the court of the ruler of the Ta-yüan. There he relates his adventures. The King of Ferghana nods sympathetically.

"And you are still determined to continue?" he asks, with raised eyebrows.

"If your Majesty pleases," replies Chang K'ién.

"Where do you wish to go?" then questions the ruler of the Ta-yüan.

"If it is not asking too much," answers the courteous Chinese, "I would that you have some one conduct me to the country of the Yüé-chi. If I should succeed in reaching that country, upon my return to China my king will reward you with untold treasures."

"Since you have come this far already you might—possibly—succeed," observes the Ferghanian. "It shall be as you desire. My lord prime minister, see that the envoy of our cousin, the King of China, has safe conduct over our postal roads to the borders of the land of the K'ang-kü. As for the rewards, young man, we of the Ta-yüan will be sufficiently recompensed by friendly relations with your illustrious country. The audience is ended."

The words of the King of Ferghana tell us a great deal. "Postal roads?" The phrase sounds amazing. But it is established beyond reasonable doubt that they exist and function smoothly when the first Chinese envoy arrives in Ferghana.

So the next stage of Chang Kien's journey is not only easy but comparatively luxurious. Swift riders of the Ministry of Posts and Roads are sent ahead to warn the postmasters of his approach. Everywhere he is accepted at his face value—His Excellency the Envoy Extraordinary and Ambassador Plenipotentiary of His Imperial Majesty the Emperor of China. (Quite a difference from being a captive in the hands of the lawless Hiung-nu.) So he reaches the country of the K'ang-kü in such state as becomes his exalted mission.

Here he reaches a kingdom that once was a province of the invincible conqueror, Alexander the Great. To the historians it is better known as Soghdiana. It was formerly ruled by the scions of a Greek satrap, one of the Macedonian's generals. Another interesting and novel adventure for an officer of the distant Son of Heaven! But the Soghdianians have degenerated since the firm hand of Greece relaxed over them. As Chang K'ién finds them, they are a nomad people, cattlemen, cattle rustlers. Though they can muster some eighty or ninety thousand mounted archers, they are under the suzerainty of the Yüé-chi on the south, of the Huns on the east. But Chang K'ién has ample experience to enable him to get along with even these wild and uncongenial tribesmen. He uses the same expedient that he has employed to such advantage with the Hiung-nu: he tells the truth. So much so that we learn "for years to come, Chang K'ién's name becomes a guarantee of good faith." Not a bad record to have set up in twelve years of traveling!

It is this policy that gets him through the territory of the K'ang-kü—him, his wife, his son and the archer T'ang-i-fu. Perhaps some of the rest of the original hundred who left China with him in 138 B.C. are still with him. But we cannot say so with any certainty. In this respect the annals of his journey are skimpy. At any rate, after many months he finally reaches his destination, the court of the king of Ta-Yüé-chi.

The country in which Chang K'ién now arrives was known three hundred years before as Bactria, a part of the wide-flung dominions of Alexander the Great. The Yüé-chi conquered it when they migrated after their overwhelming defeat in 160 B.C. by the Hiung-nu. To the Chinese it is known as Ta-hia. Centuries later still it is part of Bokhara. The Yüé-chi capital, at the time of Chang K'ién's visit, is in the northern part of the valley of the Oxus. (At least, this is what scholars have inferred from the historical writings of China's Herodotus.)

In finding this capital, Wu-ti's ambassador has accomplished an extraordinary feat. As we have already observed, he had only the vaguest idea where it was when he was sent out by the Son of Heaven. He has traversed lands concerning which only conflicting and irresponsible rumors had reached the court of China. In the words of a later epic, he has "carried the message to Garcia," but after years of captivity and wandering. And he has come among a singularly interesting people. They are entirely different, not only from the Chinese and the Huns, but from all other surrounding races. All students of modern times agree that they are partly of European stock. Strictly speaking, they are Indo-Scythians. At first their manners and customs were similar to those of the Hiung-nu. They were nomads, cattlemen, fighters. For many years they successfully and comfortably occupied the oases of the great Gobi. It took three heavy defeats by the Huns to drive them south and west to Bactria, where they are now living and prospering. (They are destined to extend their dominions about a hundred and twenty-five years later. During the first three centuries of the Christian era their maharajahs rule over a strong, powerful empire which includes the Punjab and the regions to the west of the Indus.

The descendants of the Yüe-chi are to be found in Central Asia today. If you will consult Sir Aurel Stein's *On Central-Asian Tracks*, you will see photographs of hillmen who, if you gave them a shave and a bath and a suit of occidental clothes, would pass unnoticed in any café of New York, London, Marseilles or Berlin. As Sir Aurel points out, they have the physical features of the *Homo Alpinus* type, which is today the most prevailing type in Europe and America.)

So we perceive that the people whom the persistent, indomitable Chang K'ién has found at last are our own kinsmen, in a remote fashion. The ruler who greets the Chinese envoy is the son of the king out of whose skull the Hunnish Great Khan fashioned a drinking cup. Obviously, a fellow of stern mettle. Under a lesser man his people would have perished. But, after three crushing and humiliating defeats, he has contrived not only to keep them together, but to create a new kingdom. He has goaded and driven them until they have kicked the descendants of the Macedonians out of most of Bactria. He has restored their military strength so that Chang K'ién estimates it at 200,000 archers, including cavalry.

The ambassador from Wu-ti is received with the utmost friendliness by the king of the Yüé-chi. Indeed, he remains in those parts for an entire year. On one occasion, at least, he joins a military expedition of these Indo-Europeans to the west, a campaign, apparently, to consolidate the conquest of Bactria, exterminating or driving out the remaining outposts of the Greeks.

While in Bactria, Chang K'ién puts in considerable time gathering information about the outlying countries. He learns about Parthia, which the Chinese call An-si, also Chaldaea, Syria and India. He sees several articles in Bactria which he perceives to be of Chinese origin. Upon inquiry he finds that they have been bought in Shön-tu (India). That, he hears, is a civilized country inhabited by people who have fixed abodes. In other respects their social manners and customs are much similar to those of Bactria. However Shön-tu is a low-lying country, with a damp, hot climate. Its soldiers use elephants in warfare, riding into the thick of battle on their backs and shooting down their enemies. Thus we observe that the information gathered by the first Chinese traveler is remarkably accurate.

Incidentally, he also gets reports on a new and young nation far away to the west whose power is growing rapidly. He calls it Li-kan. To Chinese of a latter period it is known as Ta-tsin. As the great Roman Empire it is destined to become one of China's best customers, especially for silk, thanks to the exploits of Chang K'ién.

Thus his visit among the Yüé-chi is fruitful. Unfortunately, however, in his main object he fails. The king will not even consider the idea of leaving his comfortable new home in Bactria to go back east and look for trouble.

"As you see, we have here a rich, fertile country," he points out. "We are but little troubled with robber neighbors. We are just recovering from our last wars with the Hiung-nu. No, my friend, we will fight when we have to, but we are not going to cross deserts and mountains to seek a war. Our people are changing their ways somewhat and determined to enjoy a peaceful life. Return to your august monarch with my profound compliments and tell him we have put all thoughts of revenge out of our heads. Your quarrels with the Hiung-nu are now too far removed from us."

The Yüé-chi ruler gives the Chinese envoy safe-conduct and many invaluable presents, mostly seeds and cuttings of plants unknown in China. From the

Ta-yüan he has already received some of the superb horses for which their country is famous. Thus Chang K'ién starts on his return journey, still accompanied by his wife and child and the trusty archer, T'ang-i-fu. He chooses a slightly different road home, partly for the sake of surveying an alternative route across Central Asia, partly to escape the lands of the Hiung-nu. He wants to visit the country of the K'iang (Tangutasn). He elects to go south of the Tien Shan and, by way of the Tarim basin, traverses the eastern end of the Takla-makan, which in his time is not yet the fearsome desert it is today. The Chinese party passes the great salt marshes of Lop Nor and makes for the Nan Shan, hoping to enter China by crossing that range.

But Chang K'ién's troubles are not over. He has selected his route with cunning. The Nan Shan mountains are south of the Huns' territory. Nevertheless, just as he is almost within sight of home, a raiding party of the Hiung-nu comes whooping through a pass and once more the ambassador of the Son of Heaven is a prisoner of his master's deadliest enemies.

We can imagine the sardonic grin with which the Great Khan receives the runaway whom, as a kinsman by marriage, he had treated so unusually well. It is rather astonishing that all the recaptured fugitives are not instantly executed. Perhaps the Shan-yü is turning humane in his last years. And, no doubt, he is inter-ested to hear all about Chang Kien's adventures. However, the envoy, his princess and his archer are imprisoned and this time watched more carefully.

The second captivity lasts more than a year. It is ended by nothing but sheer luck. The Shan-yü, being of a ripe old age, dies. Himself a strong, ruthless man, he evidently has failed to perceive that his eldest son and heir is a weakling. Immediately upon his death a younger son attacks the rightful successor to the throne and defeats him. His usurpation is successful. But naturally this political upheaval is not accomplished without a terrific internecine fight. In the confusion Chang K'ién escapes, again with his wife and little son and his invaluable T'ang-i-fu. What is more, he is able to sneak away with the horses, the gifts, the seeds and plants that he has collected on his wanderings.

So one day in 125 B.C. the great Emperor Wu-ti has the surprise of his life. A strange-looking fellow dressed in outlandish costume begs for an audience. The slaves at the gate do not know him, the lords-in-waiting do not recognize him.

"He says his name is Chang K'ién, Majesty," they announced, "but surely Chang K'ién is long since dead."

"Chang K'ién always told the truth," observes the wise Son of Heaven with a smile; "bring him in."

It is a weird quartet that presents itself to the eyes of the beautifully dressed, incredulous, imperial court. Can that tall, bronzed, travel-stained person, clad in the raiment of the barbarians, be an imperial ambassador?

[25]

And who is the obviously foreign woman with him? She looks like a female of the Hiung-nu. And the little boy? If this is Chang K'ién, where are the hundred silk-clad companions who went with him thirteen years ago, as befitted the dignity of a Chinese ambassador? Wu-ti and his courtiers stare and wait. They observe that the stranger and his lone male attendant execute properly the ritual prescribed by Chinese etiquette for such an occasion.

"O Son of Heaven, live forever!" says the tall stranger in the cultivated tongue of a Chinese gentleman while the court gasps in amazement. Then he continues quietly, "Your Majesty's servant, Chang K'ién craves permission to give an account of his travels."

Wu-ti does live for a long, long while, but he lives through few such sensational scenes. He had indeed given up his ambassador to the Yüé-chi for dead long since. The person now making obeisance before him is a man well past thirty, a hardened, seasoned, vastly different individual from the eager youth who left for the west thirteen years ago. We must remember that in these thirteen years he has had no opportunity to communicate with his sovereign. Not even the return of Odysseus to Ithaca was more dramatic than the homecoming of Chang K'ién. It is easy to believe that the Emperor sits up all that night and for several nights thereafter listening to the copious and careful report of his envoy. Practically all the information he has gathered in his wanderings is news to the Chinese government. It is as important to the geographers as to the general staff. What he tells about the customs and wealth of the peoples he has visited awakens the Emperor's keen sense of the chances of extending his country's foreign trade. But it is with considerable trepidation that Chang K'ién reports the failure of his mission to the Yüé-chi.

"Tut, man, we are sure you left nothing undone," Wu-ti reassures him. He is delighted with the agricultural specimens and the horses that his returned envoy has brought with him. Among the new products he introduces are the sesame, garlic and coriander, as well as the grape vine. The Son of Heaven shows his appreciation in concrete form. He appoints Chang Kien to be T'ai-chung-ta-fu, which means Imperial Chamberlain. He rewards the archer T'ang-i-fu with the title of Föng-shï-kün—The Gentleman Attending the Embassy.

But this is by no means the culmination of Chang Kien's career. More troubles are lying in store for him —disgrace and also greater distinction. Meanwhile, however, his return is like a spark that kindles the activity of China. We learn from Ssi-ma Ts'ién that upon hearing Chang K'ién's report, the Son of Heaven reasons thus:

"The country of Ta-yüan and the possessions of

Ta-hia and An-si [Parthia] are large countries, full of rare things, with a population living in fixed abodes and given to occupations somewhat identical with those of Chinese people, though having weak armies. They place great value on the rich produce of China. The possessions of the Ta-yüé-chi and K'ang-kü, being of military strength, might be made subservient to our interests by bribes. Thus they could be gained over by the mere force of persuasion. In this way a territory 10,000 *li* in extent would be available for the spread of our superior Chinese civilization by communicating through many interpreters with all those nations holding widely different customs."

So the Emperor approves one of Chang K'ién's recommendations, which is to send ambassadors to India by the southerly and southwesterly routes through Shu. Wu-ti dispatches four expeditions, one by way of the Upper Yangtze. All these missions fail ignominiously, though one of them approaches within 1,000 *li* of the "elephant-riding country" (Indo-China). It also brings back the first information to the court concerning the Tién country (Yünnan) "whither the traders of Shu surreptitiously export the produce of China." The failure is due to the numbers of "landless, lawless, masterless tribes" who intercept the expeditions, killing and capturing some of the envoys. The effort to penetrate south and west from China through those barbarians is abandoned, for the time being, as too expensive.

However, in 123 B.C. Wu-ti starts his first important military enterprise. He sends his crack general, Ho Kü-Ping, across Eastern Turkestan. It is a dramatic moment in China's history. Hitherto the Middle Kingdom has been on the defensive against the threatening Huns. But now, suddenly, comes a spear-head thrust into the heart of the aggressor's strength. Chang K'ién is attached to the staff of Field Marshal Ho as Chief of Intelligence. His knowledge of Hiung-nu territory, of their pasture grounds, enables the Chinese army to live comfortably off the country. The expedition is supposed to be a cavalry reconnaissance in force. But Chang's eleven years of captivity at the *ordu* of the Great Khan bring a sensational fruit. His familiarity with Hun customs enables the Field Marshal to surprise an enemy camp and inflict an overwhelming defeat. Of itself the victory is valuable enough but into the bargain its moral effect throughout Central Asia is electrifying.

For his share in this triumph, Chang Kien is elevated to the rank of Marquis of Po-wang. But the higher they go, the further they fall. In the following year he makes a bad blunder. General Li Huang is dispatched with an army to attack the Huns on a new front. He joins battle at Yu-pëi-ping, about eighty miles northeast of where Peiping is today. The newly appointed Marquis of Po-wang is present as commander of the household troops, which are held back of the line as reserves. At a crucial moment in the battle he fails to bring up those reserves quickly enough. As a result, General Li is defeated with considerable loss.

Though Wu-ti knows how to reward achievement he is ruthless in punishing a blunder. At the first report of this disaster he sentences Chang K'ién to death. Eventually, remembering the man's really great services, he commutes his sentence, inflicting a heavy fine, stripping the Marquis of his rank and titles and reducing him to the rank of a common soldier.

However on the western fronts one brilliant success after another attends the armies of the Son of Heaven. Marshal Ho Kü-Ping drives the once indomitable Hiung-nu back further and further. The Khan of the Western Huns surrenders outright and does something unknown in the traditions of his race: he tenders his allegiance to the Han Emperor. Marshal Ho and his colleague, Wei Tsing, inflict blow after blow. In 119 B.C. they smash even the Khan of the Eastern Huns so badly that he is forced to retire to the lands north of the Gobi.

Thereupon Chang Kien enters into the picture once more. Though degraded to the rank of a common soldier, he has plodded along, obtaining a few minor promotions, until he is able to obtain audience with the Emperor. Out of the knowledge obtained during his captivity under the Hsiung-nu, he suggests a plan for securing the allegiance of the Wu-sun, a tribe tributary to the Huns. The details of the plan are involved and will not be retailed here. But it is, particularly, Chang's familiarity with the politics of the Hun tribes that enables him to make this suggestion. He shows how the Huns can be further weakened by diplomatic means.

"That sounds like a good idea," is the Emperor's comment. "Perhaps you have been punished enough for an error of judgment."

So once more he appoints Chang Kien a commander in his bodyguard and sends him on a mission to the K'un-mo, prince of Wu-sun, with 300 men, 600 horses and "of oxen and sheep, myriads." He also entrusts him with presents worth millions, gold, jewels, and priceless silks. Under his authority are several subordinate envoys who are to be sent to Ferghana, Soghdiana, Bactria, Parthia and India. So once more we see the unquenchable Chang K'ién starting out as Envoy Extraordinary and Ambassador Plenipotentiary of the Son of Heaven.

He reaches the *ordu* of the Wu-sun without serious impediment, thanks to the recent victories of Marshal Ho. But at the first interview with their prince, the K'un-mo, he encounters an official snub. The precious gifts are laid out, but the Wu-sun look upon them with a supercilious eye. Thereat Chang K'ién shows his mettle. He issues a sharp challenge.

"If the king of the Wu-sun does not pay due respect to these gifts which have come from the Son of

Heaven," he declares brusquely, "they will be with-drawn."

At which, says the record, the K'un-mo rises hur-riedly from his chair of state and makes a profound obeisance. But even after that, Chang K'ién has no easy task. He has arrived among the Wu-sun at a critical time. Politics are sizzling in a dispute over a succession to the crown. The nation is divided into three parties. Fortunately for him, the Chinese Ambassador has on his side the king, who controls the majority. Chang K'ién dispatches his assistant envoys to the western kingdoms he visited ten years before and even to Parthia, India and Chaldaea. What is more, he sends a courier back to the court of China who takes with him, not only a herd of horses, but several of the Wu-sun. They re-turn presently, their eyes popping out as they tell the K'un-mo about the greatness and wealth of China. The outcome is that Chang K'ién accomplishes the object of his mission to the K'un-mo. The king of the Wu-sun sends him on his way home with not only an escort, interpreters and presents but a request for an alliance by marriage with the family of the Son of Heaven.

The work of his subordinate envoys is equally fruit-ful. They return bringing representatives from the Ta-yüan, from Ta-hia, from Parthia, even from far-off Syria. All of them visit China and go back to their own homes with glowing accounts of the power and magnificence of the Son of Heaven.

In short, Chang K'ién, by diplomatic means, supplements and multiplies the work of penetration accomplished by Wu-ti's victorious generals. The influence of China spreads over Central Asia. The Emperor establishes the first silk route to Europe, with the Parthians as the most important middlemen. He builds a line of frontier outposts which, as Sir Aurel Stein has proved, are a fore-runner of the *limes* which later protect the trade routes of the Roman Empire. Shortly after the end of the second century B.C. China's silk is selling on the banks of the Tiber for its weight in gold.

Not all of this happens during the lifetime of Chang K'ién. But it is all directly due to his heroic journeyings, the hardships and imprisonment that he suffered and the intelligence he brought to bear on his job. He dies, about 115 or 114 B.C., in full enjoyment of honors he has richly earned. For, upon his return from the land of the Wu-sun, he is appointed Foreign Minister, a job for which his experience and hardly acquired knowledge have amply equipped him, also one of the Council of Nine, the Emperor's supreme advisory body. So the *lang*, who rose to be a noble Marquis and was degraded to the rank of a common soldier, ends his life in a blaze of glory.

Surely this stout fellow from the mountains of Shen-si was properly designated by his sovereign as Ta-hing— Great Traveler.

II

THE BAVARIAN MARCO POLO

II

THE BAVARIAN MARCO POLO

A NEW and awful danger confronted European civilization toward the end of the fourteenth century. It had barely recovered from the staggering blow of the Black Death, the devastating plague that had changed the course of history as an earthquake may drive a river into a different channel. But the new menace was even more terrifying. The Turk was hammering at the gates of Constantinople. Under the Ottoman chiefs the janizaries, as fearless as they were cruel, had become almost irresistible. Already they had overrun Asia Minor, occupied the Holy Land and Egypt and shut off the essential trade routes to India, China and the Spice Islands. And now they had a foothold in Europe itself.

In those days the European was not conscious of being European. But he was intensely conscious of being a Christian. Europe was Christendom. In all the countries it contained there was an abundance of fighters as brave, though not quite as ruthless, as the invaders from Asia. And they had generals of experience and ability. On the battlefields of France the Welsh longbow had proved itself a most formidable weapon. But whereas the Turks were one united, single-minded, sternly disciplined force, the Christians were split by local jealousies and the selfish vanities of their princes. In vain one Pope after another pleaded desperately for unity against the Moslem enemies of the Cross. Through the lack of it every Crusade had failed.

In 1389 a man of blood and iron named Bajazet (or Bayazid) became the first Ottoman Sultan. He got there because his father had been assassinated on a victorious battlefield. Whereupon Bajazet had murdered his elder brother, whose skill had brought about the victory. Christendom had a brave and pious leader in the Emperor Sigismund I, who was also King of Bohemia and Hungary. But for nine years Sigismund's resources and energies had been strained to the utmost in the attempt to suppress the rebellions of his contumacious Magyar subjects. Bajazet took advantage of the distraction to push his standards right up to the banks of the Danube. The peril was obvious to even the most selfish of the Christian rulers and barons. Pope Boniface IX preached a new Crusade. From all over Europe the knights came flocking to the banner of Sigismund. The French contingent was led by John the Fearless of Burgundy. For once, it seemed, Christendom was united against the Paynim.

In the contingent from Bavaria was a lordling named Leinhart Richartingen. He brought with him as his page or esquire a fourteen-year-old boy named Johannes Schiltberger. This stripling was of fairly good family. Some of his kin were of the burgher class. One or two of his forebears had been marshals to the Dukes of Bavaria. Hans, as his name is usually abbreviated, left his home to help drive out the Turk in 1394. He marched and fought in the campaign that resulted in Sigismund's recapturing Widdin. Quite an experience for a lad barely fifteen! He was part of an army that had finally made the Cross triumphant over the Crescent after so many years of humiliation. Sigismund pushed the Turks back along the line of the Danube towards the Black Sea. And in 1396 he laid siege to Nicopolis.

"This becomes serious," exclaimed Bajazet. He had left the campaign on the Danube to his lieutenants and was encamped outside Constantinople. He raised that siege and sent to Asia for re-enforcements. With an army of 140,000 janizaries and at the speed that had earned him the nickname of "Lightning," he swept down on Sigismund outside Nicopolis. There, on September 28, 1396, an old story was repeated. The Christians had too many generals, the Moslems had only one and that was Bajazet himself. Sigismund's army was destroyed. Many of the "flower of Europe's chivalry" perished. All prisoners over the age of twenty were slaughtered, a gentle Turkish custom. If you imagine fifteen-year-old Johannes Schiltberger as a non-combatant in this decisive battle you are wrong. He was wounded three times, but captured alive. A sweating, frothing janizary was swinging a crimson-stained scimitar at the boy's neck, with a cry of "Allahu Akbar!" At that moment a young Turkish prince rode up with his retinue. It was Soleiman, eldest son of Bajazet.

"Halt!" he cried. "Didn't you hear the order that no captives under twenty are to be executed?" The janizary grumbled, but lowered his weapon and looked around for another wounded prisoner to murder. Soleiman commanded his men to bring the youngster to the sultan's tent.

"You promised the Mameluke Barkouk of Cairo to send him a Christian slave as a present," suggested the prince.

"But that one is damaged," growled his father. "The unbelieving young dog can't walk. What's the good of a slave who can't walk?"

"He'll be all right in a couple of weeks," replied Soleiman. "He isn't badly hurt, just flesh wounds in his legs. They'll soon heal. Then we can make a True Believer of him, for the glory of Allah and his Prophet."

"Well, if he recovers, we can use him as a dispatch runner. He looks as if he might be a fairly speedy pup," said the Sultan.

So that Bavarian lad, barely sixteen years old, became a slave in the wandering court of Bajazet. We may well imagine how utterly lost and wretched he felt, his homesickness for the little estate on the Isar, near Munich. Probably he saved his life by making the profession: "Allah il Allah, Mahmoud resoul illah." He never admitted it in the story that he subsequently told of his wanderings. But it is highly improbable that he could have survived so long among the Moslems, even as one of the humblest of slaves, without at least pretending to be converted to Islam. Perhaps it would have been nobler in him to have been staunch, upheld the honor of Christianity and had his throat cut. But if he had, the world would be the poorer by a fascinating tale of adventure and travel. For, though he did not know it at the time, Hans Schiltberger's destiny was to take him for the next thirty-two years wandering all over Asia, seeing many towns, countries and other sights on which no European had set eyes until then. It enabled him to bring information from strange places concerning which the geographers of Christendom had been either in the dark or utterly misled.

He was not an educated fellow. During the Age of Chivalry many of the nobility considered reading, writing, poetry and such pastimes as fit only for monks, clerks and ladies. They were beneath the honor and dignity of a fighting man. King Henry II of England was actually conspicuous among the sovereigns of his day because he did not despise learning. The great Prince Henry of Portugal, Henry the Navigator, was almost a disgrace to his family because he abandoned a promising career at arms to devote his life to the study of navigation, geography, mathematics and astronomy.

So it is not surprising that a well-born Bavarian younker should have been allowed to go to the wars unable to read or write. However, he was intelligent and observing. Thanks to that, his countrymen benefited by some exceedingly interesting accounts of Asiatic kingdoms and peoples. At times he was too credulous. The professional story-teller has always been a famous institution throughout Asia—and then as now, a large proportion of his stories were tall stories. Johannes Schiltberger heard them and believed them. In later years he frequently got those tall stories mixed up with the truth. What he saw himself was accurately related. But when he undertook to describe places and races he had not seen, he so mingled fact and fancy that for centuries the scholars were bewildered. However, we must remember that the more famous Marco Polo committed the same error.

For three years Schiltberger ran his legs off carrying messages for Bajazet. He served as an errand boy during the second siege of Constantinople, on raids and battlefields throughout the Balkans. The victory at Nicopolis had put a large part of that peninsula at the mercy of the Turks. After a couple of years, apparently, the eighteen-year-old Hans was promoted. That is, he was ordered on longer errands and trusted on horseback. Bajazet sent him with an expeditionary force that went to Egypt in 1399. The Mameluke Abu Saadat Faradj was the legitimate successor to the throne

of the Sultan Barkouk at Cairo. But a rival claimant had
obtained the support of several emirs and took the field
against Faradj. Bajazet supported Faradj. All of which
matters nothing to us now except that it enabled Hans
Schiltberger to see more of the world. As a dispatch
rider to the Osmanli troops he then saw service on
several campaigns in Asia Minor. Thus he visited Ico-
nium in Karamania and Sebaste in Cappadocia, places
that were mere legends to the folks back home on the
banks of the Isar. He went as far north as Samsun on
the shore of the Black Sea. He crossed the Upper
Euphrates to the land of the White Tartars. He rode
through Pamphylia and Cilicia. To be sure, he was
an exile and a slave. At the same time it must have
been a marvelous experience for a youth who, until
he went crusading, had never been further away from
home than Freisingen or Munich.

In six years his term as a captive of the Ottoman sultan came to an end. Bajazet, the "Lightning," met a
better man than himself. His ambitions had crossed
those of Timur the Lame, otherwise known as Tamerlane. That one caught the Turks at Angora in 1402
and smashed them. He captured Bajazet and kept him
prisoner until his death.

Throughout the centuries there has been much argument over *Timur i Lenk*. He has been called the
Destroyer, principally because his armies overran and
conquered such a prodigious portion of the earth. But

he was undoubtedly greater than the Osmanli he crushed at Angora. For one thing, Timur was well read. His father and grandfather had been students by inclination rather than fighting men. And although the great Mongol was called a Destroyer he was also a builder. He made his capital at Samarkand, a beautiful city, though today it is half ruins, half modern gimcrack architecture. He established a fine university there. He encouraged literature, the other arts and sciences. Bajazet and the rest of the Ottomans considered such things effete and idolatrous.

There is a legend that Timur carried Bajazet all over Asia with him in an iron cage. It was even made the subject of one of Racine's most famous and pathetic tragedies. To be sure, it would have been nothing less than Bajazet deserved. But owing to the adventures of Hans Schiltberger, that legend has been rejected. For, though the battle of Angora ended the Bavarian's slavery to Bajazet, he had merely changed masters. He now entered upon a more interesting servitude. Though he didn't know it and probably didn't appreciate it, he was beginning the most important period of his life. He was to visit regions traversed by no European except the Polos and many that not even the famous Marco had approached. Schiltberger's new owners took him on the march all over Central Asia. He accompanied Timur's army in the invasions of Armenia and Georgia. In the book dictated by Hans after he

A FROTHING JANIZARY WAS SWINGING A CRIMSON-STAINED SCIMITAR
AT THE BOY'S NECK

returned home he recorded the fact that Bajazet was dragged along, too, until he died. But it is significant that he made no mention of the iron cage. So in that respect at least the legends have been unfair to the character of Timur.

At the date of the battle of Angora our young Bavarian had reached the age of twenty-one. He was now thoroughly familiar with the ways and customs of Mohammedans, so it was not difficult to accommodate himself to the wishes of his new masters. He saw service on an expedition to Abkhase in the Caucasus. After that he saw the lower valley of the Kur and Aras. The plain of Karabagh was the favorite winter camp of all the Tartar generals and there the army rested several months. Thence it marched south of the Caspian. Hans was taken across the River Araxes and the nine kingdoms of Persia to Timur's capital, Samarkand. He saw the rich cities of Ispahan and Herat, the luxuries of Persian satraps. The Lame Destroyer, of course, was now ruler over most of the territory that in Marco Polo's day had paid allegiance and tribute to Marco's friend Kublai Khan. At Samarkand, Timur rested for a while, attending to affairs of state, playing chess and organizing his resources for his next campaign. For he had one yet unsatisfied ambition. His power did not extend over China. He wanted particularly the highly civilized, cultivated country where the mulberry trees nourished the silkworms, whence came the most precious fabrics, the priceless paintings, the exquisite porcelains. Timur was not merely lusting for possessions. Not that he despised them, but he also was anxious to educate his Mongol hordes. He desired the art and culture of old China. Furthermore he was tired of paying tribute, even though it had grown smaller every year, to Peking.

While the Lame Destroyer was getting ready for his march on Cathay, an embassy arrived from far Castille. Though Timur was a devout Moslem, his behavior towards the Christians after the battle of Angora had been conspicuously politic and a contrast to that of Bajazet. The Turks were a bigoted and puritanical lot, somewhat like the Wahabis of Arabia today under Ibn Saud. The ruler of Samarkand, on the contrary, was by way of being a liberal Mohammedan. So King Henry III of Castile and León sent one of his most distinguished nobles, Ruy Gonzalez de Clavijo, of Madrid, as ambassador to the court of Timur. He made a notable journey, by way of Trebizond and Tabriz, past Mount Ararat. He saw the great caravans carrying silks from China, pearls and gems from Ormuz, spices and other precious goods from India. He passed through Nishapur and admired the elaborate post and courier system created by the Mongol emperor. He arrived at Samarkand, as Sir Raymond Beazley says, "when Tamerlane was just completing those princely buildings which make it still the cynosure of Central Asia." The Spanish ambassador was in time to see one of the great festivals that Timur organized for traders from all over the continent. He met "princes from the ruby country of Badakshan and the sapphire land of Ferghana." Clavijo, who was educated as well as intelligent, wrote a most entertaining account of his travels. Among other things it shows what a wide gap must have existed between the fanatical puritanism of the Turks and home life in the court of Samarkand. Clavijo gives us a picture of Timur's sultana vainly pressing wine upon him with her own hand. Meanwhile courtiers were falling down all around her. Mistress and retainers alike seemed to believe that there could be no jollity without drunken men.

However, we are not telling the story of Clavijo, but of the slave, Hans Schiltberger. And here's a problem: the Bavarian must have been in Samarkand when the noble grandee of Madrid arrived. It is a point that seems to have escaped the attention of Beazley, of Sir Percy Sykes, of Professor Baker and all the other scholars. Apparently the Caballero, Ruy Gonzalez, did not observe any German runner around the court of Timur. At any rate he did not mention him in the narrative of his journey. Neither did Schiltberger say a single word about the coming of the Spanish ambassador. We can only guess at the explanation and your guess is as good as mine. If Hans had really wanted to return home, wouldn't he have made himself known to the envoy of the Most Catholic King and begged to be smuggled out in his retinue? He might have done so and Clavijo might have refused, either because it wasn't safe or because he was ashamed of his fellow Christian as an apostate and a renegade. But if so, why didn't he at least mention him when he returned home? The answer probably is that Timur did not want to lose his Bavarian slave runner and sent him somewhere out of town on a mission. Clavijo was in Samarkand only two weeks.

Whatever happened, the exile of Hans Schiltberger was to last for twenty-four more years and to show him far more of the distant places of earth than the Spaniard ever saw. Soon after Clavijo's embassy started back to Madrid, Timur set out on his last expedition. In the middle of winter, he crossed the ice on the Syr-Darya and penetrated no further than a place called Otrar. There he died in 1405. Unlike his great predecessor, Genghis Khan, the Lame Destroyer left no heirs with the capacity of carrying out his dreams of dominion. His heir, Shah Rokh, abandoned the march on Peking. Timur's great courier system enabled news to travel fast through his empire. The funeral ceremonies were hardly over when word came of a rebellion in the far-off provinces of Mazanderan and Armenia. Tribes that had been kept quiet only by the fear of Timur broke loose and started fighting amongst

[48]

themselves. Incidentally the uprisings kept Clavijo's embassy on their return journey detained in Tabriz for six months. It was no time for the Mongol successor to think of fresh conquests. Shah Rokh led his army west, taking with him the German runner, Hans Schiltberger, whom he had inherited with other possessions from his father. So Hans took part in the war between the Turcomans of the Black and the White Sheep. (They surely had picturesque names to describe the ferocious tribes in those regions! The fiercest of them all were the Tartars of the Golden Horde.) Shah Rokh died and Hans, with the rest of Timur's vast possessions, passed into the ownership of Miran Shah. The latter, who was Timur's elder son and legitimate heir, had been deposed by his father because he was a sadistic maniac. He had a capacity for only one thing, destruction. But it did not extend to the destruction of his enemies. Kara Youssouf, Chief of the Turcomans of the Black Sheep, overthrew Miran Shah. So Schiltberger became the property of Abou-Bekr, son of Shah Rokh. Abou was a pretty weak carbon copy of his grandfather, but he was a fighter after a guerilla fashion. The Bavarian runner's life for the next few years was one of irregular warfare, raids on Irak, Kars and Erivan. At the last place Hans had opportunity to pass considerable time among the Armenian Catholics. In his book he recorded many interesting observations about their doctrines, customs and ritual. This is the one passage in his memoirs that throws any doubt on the idea that he must have professed Mohammedanism in order to survive.

All this was just a prelude to a more important departure in the life of Schiltberger. It is impossible to keep any accurate track of dates. He was constantly on one campaign or another. He survived them all because, as a slave, he was not permitted to bear arms and take any part in the actual fighting. But he lived in the midst of racial wars of which there are few other written records. A local potentate named Ydegu enters the picture. He had long been a thorn in the flesh of Timur. He was a wily politician, always changing sides. When the ruler appeared in force he always made his submission. The moment the conqueror was beyond the mountain range, Ydegu was stirring up trouble again. His own territory was not so important, but he was a sort of regional king-maker. Upon the death of Timur and Shah Rokh and Miran Shah, Ydegu came to the front once more. He offered the command of the Tartars of the Golden Horde to Tschekre, a feudal chieftain on the staff of Abou-Bekr. The latter was only too glad of this solution of a vexing problem. "Go, my lord," he said to Tschekre, "and I will send with you my grandsire's favorite slave and runner. Likewise four other slaves captured from the Unbelievers."

Thus Schiltberger was sent on one of the most interesting of all his travels. With Tschekre he traveled through the Khanates along the western shores of the Caspian Sea. They were bound for the almost unknown land of Great Tartary. Out of this journey Hans brought back the first and for a long time the only information possessed by geographers concerning that region. One hundred and fifty years were to elapse before the epoch-making journeys of Antony Jenkinson. From Schiltberger's time until the power of Moscow reached the Caspian, one century and a half later, "this country drops almost wholly outside the ken of Christian politics, trade or travel." Tschekre and his retinue passed through Derbent and the Iron Gate, thence to Northern Daghestan. They stopped at Astrakhan and Khiva. North of there they joined forces with Ydegu and proceeded with him to a colossal enterprise: the conquest of Siberia. For two months they traveled on sledges, "drawn by huge dogs almost the size of donkeys." European Russians had not yet become conscious of Siberia. Hans, in the train of Tschekre and Ydegu, traversed the provinces now known as Tomsk and Tobolsk. He afterwards mentioned having seen wild beasts the names of which he could not tell because no such animals were known in Germany. Tschekre and Ydegu conquered as far as Great Bolgara. Thereupon they returned to Great Tartary. They occupied the province later known as the Khanate of Kazan. Here they escaped defeat only by the help of a division of Tartar Amazons, led by a revengeful princess. This part of Schiltberger's narrative would be incredible but for what we know about the regiment of Russian woman soldiers in the Great War.

After the conquest of Siberia—we don't know how soon—Tschekre died. Dates are vague, but the Schiltberger who left Bavaria a boy of fourteen must by this time have become a grown man in his thirties. He was still a slave and fell into the hands of Manshuk, formerly a counselor of the dead Tschekre. Evidently Manshuk conspired against the successor to Tschekre. At any rate, he fled, taking Hans and the four other ex-Christians with him. They traversed the kingdom of Kiptchak, crossing the River Don and visiting the cities of Tana, Solphat, the capital of Kiptchak, as well as Kyrkye and Sary Kerman. The Bavarian got a glimpse of Urganj on the bank of the Oxus. He was at Sarai, the seat of the Great Tartar kings, also at Tana-Azov, from which galleys full of fish sailed to Venice and Genoa. (The fish must have been sturgeon, otherwise the galleys would have been doing something more absurd even than the proverbial carrying of coals to Newcastle.) After much wandering, Manshuk and his followers reached the then great city of Kaffa in Crimea. There they remained five months. It was still an outpost of Christendom. Roman, Greek, Armenian and Syrian Catholics lived amicably side by side with Jews and Mohammedans. Further south was Chufut Kale, a famous Jewish fortress surrounded by flourishing vineyards.

Again a question arises: Why didn't Hans and the other four Christians walk out on Manshuk? There were three Christian bishops in Kaffa: a Roman, an Armenian and a Syrian. Couldn't the slaves have run to any of these prelates and demanded help and a safe-conduct back home? Kaffa, to be sure, was under the sovereignty of Great Tartary. But Manshuk himself was proscribed, a refugee from the stronghold of the Tartar power. Again, your guess is as good as mine. I suspect that Hans, though he never would admit it, was enjoying his travels. At all events, he kept going. Manshuk took him south to Egypt, where he was present at the marriage festivities of the daughter of the Sultan Boursbai. As that magnifico ascended his throne in 1422 we now have some idea about dates. Schiltberger saw enough to grasp the true position of the Mameluke sovereign, "that strange lord of Heathenesse, who could not be King-Sultan unless he had been sold." The Bavarian, moreover, was the first European traveler to discern that the legendary Prester John was not an Asiatic king, but the Negus of Abyssinia.

Manshuk's next wanderings took Hans back to Asia Minor. Whether it was on this journey or on his rovings in the train of Timur, Schiltberger undoubtedly saw the ruins of Babylon and visited Bagdad, Ctesiphon and Damascus. He devotes no fewer than eleven chapters to an extraordinarily accurate discourse on Mohammedanism, its history, doctrines and legends. In this part of his narrative you will also find the first mention in European literature of the use of carrier pigeons.

And he accomplished another feat that sets him quite apart, though few people realize it even today. He was the first European to penetrate into the Holy Places of Arabia: Mecca and Medina. Many writers have given the credit for this achievement to Sir Richard Burton. But as a matter of fact Ludovico di Varthema of Bologna did it in the sixteenth century and the Bavarian slave, Hans Schiltberger, preceded him by almost 100 years. His descriptions of the architecture of "Madina," of the decorations on the tomb of the Prophet Mohammed, are too accurate and detailed to have been faked or written from hearsay. Furthermore, everybody in Europe at that date believed that the tomb of the Prophet was at Mecca.

Schiltberger has another rare exploit to his credit. Trekking by way of Syria and Palestine, he crossed the Hejaz. For instance, he describes a bird for which there was then no name in the German language. We now know it to have been the pelican. And he gives such a vivid account of the arid, sandy wastes of Arabia and Persia that he must actually have been there. Likewise of the "Giant's Shinbone," a natural bridge spanning a ravine between two mountains. This has been identi-

fied. It is to be found in the neighborhood of Kerak
and Shaubek, on the regular caravan route to the Hejaz.

Hans and the other Christian slaves returned with
Manshuk by sea to the Crimea. Thence they jogged to
the Caucasus, the "great forest inhabited by seventy-
two languages." It is a fact that no fewer than seventy-
two different races populated that district. Schiltberger
wrote with great indignation of the slave traffic in the
Caucasus, observing that the denizens sold even their
own children into slavery. He also furnished a shock-
ingly accurate picture of the strange marriage customs
of the Georgians and Alans.

Manshuk apparently had his mind set on returning to
Tartary. He got as far as Circassia. But the ruler of
that country was a feudatory of the Great Khan, who
soon received word of Manshuk's arrival. The Tartar
overlord promptly sent word to Circassia: "Out with
Manshuk." So the former counselor of Tschekre had
to keep moving. He went to Mingrelia, by way of
Abkhase and Soukhoum. There Schiltberger and his
mates saw their opportunity to escape and return home.
One suspects they had come to the conclusion that there
was no more fun or novelty to be had in the company
of Manshuk. "We five Christians agreed that we should
go to our native country from the land of the infidels,
as we were not more than three days' journey from the
Black Sea. All five of us escaped from the said lord
[Manshuk] and came to the chief town of the country

[Batoum]. There we begged that we should be taken across the Black Sea."

But they could find no ship's master who would take the risk. So they rode along the shore, having evidently taken the precaution to steal horses from the abandoned lord Manshuk. When they reached the mountains they saw a "kocken." This was a vessel round at both stern and bow, used in Euxine and Mediterranean navigation. The kocken was "about eight Italian miles" at sea. They lit a signal fire. A skiff put off from the kocken. As it approached the shore the five slave refugees rushed towards it, waving and yelling: "We are Christians, save us." But the skiff's crew were cautious fellows. They had to have it proved to them. Schiltberger and his mates were not taken aboard until they had recited the Credo and the Ave Maria. However, their troubles were not over. The kocken was sighted and chased by three galleys, manned by Turkish pirates. Helped by a favoring breeze, the Christian vessel slipped into the harbor at Amastris, now called Amasserah. The Turks hung around outside the harbor several days, then went on their predatory way. The kocken put out once more, but a storm blew the ship all the way back to Sinope. After eight days there they weighed anchor again. This time they were "one month and a half on the sea without being able to get back to the land." Schiltberger's sense of time was extremely vague, so you can divide those six weeks by two and still allow for a voyage of unusual length on the Black Sea. However, it must have been a hard ordeal, because they ran short of food and would have starved but for finding snails and crabs on a rock in the middle of the waters, on which they lived four days.

Finally the five were landed at Constantinople. They were promptly taken before the Greek Emperor, John VIII, Paleologus. He received them sympathetically, heard their story and sent them to the palace of the Patriarch. There they were kept three months, for no apparent reason. At the end of that time the Emperor sent them in a galley to Kilia, the fortress at the mouth of the Danube. Schiltberger separated from his companions. It gives us a fair idea of the period to learn that, instead of going straight home, he went by way of Poland, Silesia and Saxony. He was taken north by a band of merchants to a place then called White City, now Byelgorod. Thence they journeyed by easy stages through Wallachia. Hans fell ill there and lay on a sick-bed for a couple of months. He then went to Cracow and to Meissen in Saxony. From Meissen he rode to Breslau, the capital of Silesia, and home to Freisingen by way of Regensburg.

At last back on the banks of the Isar! He had left home a fourteen-year-old boy. He returned a travel-worn veteran of forty-six. It is good to be able to record that he came to be not without honor in his own country. Duke Albert III of Bavaria made him his

Chamberlain and Captain of the Body-Guard. He wrote his memoirs, the language of which proves amply that they were dictated because he could not write himself.

Hans Schiltberger undoubtedly was a slave and may have been a renegade to save his head. But few men in the history of exploration or, indeed, the history of the world, had such a rich and full volume of adventure.

III

THE FIRST ROBINSON CRUSOE

III

THE FIRST ROBINSON CRUSOE

ONE afternoon in the spring of 1445 a boat is lowered
from a Portuguese caravel anchored in the Bay of Arguin and rowed to land. A young man steps out on the
shore of West Africa, burning hot under the fiery sun
of the tropics. The boat's crew then shove off and
row back to their ship. Presently the caravel, with her
two consorts, weighs anchor and sails away on a northwesterly course.

If you were watching you might wonder what all
this is about. Is the young man a mutinous member of
the crew, marooned as a punishment? To understand
the spectacle it is necessary to go back a few hours and
eavesdrop on a conference of officers aboard the largest
of the three caravels, the flagship of the commander of
the little squadron. That commander is Antam Gonsalvez, one of the doughtiest of the captains of the
Infante Don Henry of Portugal, known to the world
as the great Prince Henry the Navigator.

"How are we to obey the orders of His Highness?"
asks the impatient Gonsalvez. "There are not settle-
ments here, nor so far as the eye can see. All very well
for him to say: 'Civilize and make Christians of the na-

tives.' But how can we civilize and convert what we can't find?"

"The Infante is hard to please," replies another captain. "Did you not bring back the first captives to his court? And the first gold?"

"Surely," says Don Antam, who had been knighted for the exploit in question. "But he is dissatisfied because we do not bring back more news of this land and its people, under what law or lordship they live."

Then up speaks a young esquire from the Infante's household. His name is Joan Fernandez.

"With your permission, Don Antam," he suggests, "if you will put me ashore and let me live here a few months I may be able to obtain some information."

Some of his elders laugh aloud. Antam Gonsalvez frowns and shakes his head.

"That would be no task for a youngster," he replies. "And I can spare no men to go with you."

"I want no men with me," the young esquire answers eagerly. "I would go alone."

"Absurd!" is the chorus of comment from all the captains.

"Give me leave," pleads the young esquire. "I can speak some of these African tongues. I was for more than a year a captive on the northern coast. I know how to make friends with these peoples."

Eventually the young man has his way. And thus begins the great adventure of the man whom Sir Raymond Beazley describes as "the pattern of all the Crusoes of after time."

As Joan Fernandez starts his trek inland, let us leave him for a few moments and take a quick glance into the court of his master, the Infante, at Sagres.

Don Henry of Portugal, Duke of Viseu, Duke of Coimbra, Lord of Covilham, Governor of the Algarves and Grand Master of the Order of Christ, was the most enlightened prince of his time. He might have been a great and famous general. When he was barely twenty-one he led the attack on Ceuta and captured that important seaport from the Moors. Until then he had been merely the third and least important son of King John of Portugal. But his campaign in Africa proved him such a brilliant soldier that his kinsman, King Henry V of England, offered him an important command. The Emperor of Germany tendered him the supreme leadership of all the imperial armies.

Personally, you would have said he was born to a life of adventure on the battlefield. He was brawny, broad-shouldered, large of limb, blond and blue-eyed. His physical strength was prodigious. But for the greater part of his life he made no use of it. To the sore disappointment of his father, he declined all political and military offers. Instead, he retired at the age of twenty-four to the court he had founded at Sagres, atop what is now known as Cape St. Vincent, the old "Sacred Cape" of the Greeks and Romans. There he built and equipped the most modern observatory and laboratory the science of the times could afford. He sent for geographers from Genoa, map-makers from Venice, the keenest Arabian mathematicians, the most learned Jewish astronomers. And thus he set himself to collecting and improving the geographical knowledge of his day, combining the lore of the Arabs with that of Christendom, all the sciences that contribute to geography.

The near-by port of Lagos, once a naval arsenal, had declined into a fishing village. Prince Henry rebuilt and enlarged the arsenal and thence he sent out one expedition after another. He made but few discoveries himself. But at Sagres he became the teacher and master of explorers who made invaluable additions to modern knowledge and who really began the "Golden Age of Discovery." That is why, though he seldom put to sea after 1418, he earned the name Prince Henry the Navigator.

He knew it was necessary to find a new way to Asia. The Turks, closing down on Asia Minor, were already blocking the trade routes to the East. In fact it was only a question of years how soon they would capture Constantinople. Don Henry was sure that India, far Cathay and the isles of spice could be reached by sailing around Africa. None of his captains ever accomplished it, though they pushed the map of the known world beyond Guinea and south of the Gambia. But it was Henry the Navigator who made possible the exploits of those who came after him, Bartholomew Diaz and Vasco da Gama, the re-discovery of America, the ventures of the Cabots, of Amerigo Vespucci and their successors. "The whole onward and outward movement of the great exploring age was set in motion by one man," says Beazley.

Such was the master of the young esquire, Joan Fernandez, whom we left all alone on the shores of the Bay of Arguin. Here the long desert coast of the Sahara bends towards the rich country of the south. And here, three years after the adventure of Joan Fernandez, Prince Henry built a fort which rapidly became the trading port for a rich European commerce, "one of the first steps of modern colonization." But when the young Portuguese was put ashore there the place was utterly barren.

So it was a rare piece of good fortune that he did not have far to hike before he encountered a wandering band of Berber shepherds. What was more, they were friendly and he was able to address them in their own language. They accepted him, gave him shelter in their tents and shared their sparse food with him. But when he brought up the question of accompanying them on their wanderings, they balked.

"Inland in the desert are tribes who are not such as we," said the sheikh gravely. "Some of them are not friendly. If we brought an unbeliever into their midst it might go hardly with you—and with us."

But Joan Fernandez was not to be put off so easily. "I have seen the people of the desert, O Sheikh," he urged, "when I was a captive far to the north. Brave men always can understand one another."

"But you could not come with us in that raiment," observed the sheikh, looking at the heavy broadcloth and velvet suit, the tight collar, the high leather boots with sword, pistol and dagger which were the customary apparel of a Portuguese nobleman on active service.

After a long argument the sheikh yielded. But he made Fernandez strip off his cumbersome European clothing and dressed him as one of his own tribesmen.

Thus for seven months Don Henry's young esquire traveled over the Sahara. His name is not among the most famous ones of exploration. But actually his exploit was as extraordinary as that of the great Sir Richard Burton four centuries later. More extraordinary still, when you consider the age in which Joan Fernandez became the first European to acquire knowledge of the Mohammedan wanderers of the desert. .

Incidentally, the information he brought back to his prince was corroborated in 1795 by the more celebrated Scottish surgeon, Mungo Park. He found a country without any grass except on the banks of the rivers and wells. "Hills and mountains, all of sand," he reported, "and no trees save the 'fig tree of Hell' [palma Christi], or thorns and in some places, palms." He also observed that the Berbers "make war with the negroes more by thieving than by force, for they have not so great strength as these last."

For all his obscurity through the centuries, Joan Fernandez was a man of the same caliber as Burton, as the famous Doughty (author of *Arabia Deserta*), as Lawrence of Arabia and as Bertram Thomas, the man who crossed the Rub' al Khali. That is proved by his ability to make friends with the wild men of Islam.

Somewhere in the interior of that country was the stronghold of a potentate of considerable importance, named Ahude Meyman. The friendly sheikh asked Fernandez whether he would like to meet this magnifico. Naturally, the young explorer jumped at the offer. So they put him on a camel and for three days he traveled without water. The Moors, he remarked, found their way across the wastes by observing the winds and the flight of birds. On the journey he saw ostriches, deer, gazelles, partridges, hares, swallows and migratory storks. When he returned to Portugal, men called him a liar because he declared that, contrary to the general opinion of the time, ostriches hatch their eggs in the same manner as other birds. His statement, of course, was correct. He wasn't the first—or last—traveler to be given the lie by arm-chair naturalists. But his report of white camels that could go 50 leagues in a day—150 of our miles—is evidently an error on the part of his chronicler.

Fernandez found Ahude Meyman, a courtly, black-bearded, richly robed chieftain, to be a man of substance. He had a retinue of 150. "Men of rank," said Fernandez, "possess abundant gold here which they bring from that land where the negroes live [the western Sudan]. The principal traffic of the region is in slaves, gold, hides, wool, butter, cheeses, dates, amber, musk, resin, oil and the 'skins of sea-wolves.'"

The Berbers among whom he sojourned were of the great Azaneguy tribe. Four times that family had come over to Spain to help the Moors in the wars with Christendom.

"Yet these Moors of the west are quite barbarous," he found. "They have neither law nor lordship. Their food is milk and the seeds of wild mountain herbs and roots. Meat and bread are both rare luxuries and so is fish for those of the upland. But those of the coast eat nothing else. For months I have seen those I lived among, they, their horses and their dogs eating and drinking only milk, like infants. 'Tis no wonder they are weaker than the negroes of the south with whom they are ever at war, fighting with treachery and not with strength. Only the rich men keep good swift horses and brood mares. They are bigoted, ignorant worshipers of the abominations of Mahumet."

Now when Antam Gonsalvez left Fernandez on the shore he undertook to return and pick him up some seven months later. That, he calculated, was about the time it would take him to execute Don Henry's orders,

[68]

JOAN FERNANDEZ DID NOT HAVE FAR TO HIKE BEFORE HE EN-
COUNTERED A WANDERING BAND OF BERBER SHEPHERDS

to sail back to Lagos, refit his ships and retrace his course to the Bight of Arguin. So at the appointed time the intrepid young explorer made his way, with his friendly Berbers, to the coast.

He had quite a while to wait. Naturally, it was impossible to make an exact rendezvous, hitting both the right time and spot for the meeting. Fernandez could not camp on that barren shore indefinitely until the caravels hove in sight. Here is the story of his rescue, in the simple, graphic words of the historian who knew him personally:

"He came down to that shore many times to see if he could have sight of the caravels and I can well believe that this was his principal care. And it happened that those in the caravels, seeking to fulfill the orders of their chief captains, made sail to the Isle of Arguin, of which it appears that they had no knowledge."

Evidently Antam Gonsalvez had stopped off on his way down the African coast to make a raid. And so he had delegated the job of picking Fernandez up to his sailing master, a novice in those waters. The chronicle relates further:

"The caravels passed on past the Isle of Arguin and went cruising up and down for two days until they came to another land beyond. And a little more than an hour after they had cast anchor, they saw a man who stood on the land over against them.

"Quickly one caravel made ready to go and see who

it could be. And making sail toward him it was not able to go in as far as it wished, because the wind was off the land. And Joan Fernandez, seeing the hindrance that the caravel received, resolved to go along the shore, hoping that the ships would be there. And so he went a way until he saw the boats.

"When he shouted, those on the ship were glad. They thought he was some Moor, come to treat for the ransom of captives."

When the Portuguese took Moorish prisoners, it was the custom to take them to Sagres, hold them for a while, then carry them back to Africa and trade them, on the basis of one Moor for some four or six or eight negroes, depending on the condition and estate of the Moor to be ransomed. It is small wonder that Don Antam's officers aboard the caravel mistook the man on the beach for a Moor. He was dressed in flowing, Berber robes. Even at that distance they could observe that he was tanned as dark as any Moor. They lowered a boat and as they drew near they began to hear his words.

"Ahi! That is no Moor," they exclaimed. "He speaks our own tongue!"

There was reason aplenty for astonishment. Antam Gonsalvez had left a Portuguese of noble rank on that shore. The man waving frantically was apparently a native. The chronicle continues:

"When they understood his speech they were more

glad."

What a dramatic meeting that must have been! We can think of Stanley, arriving at Ujiji in 1871 with the now famous sentence: "Dr. Livingstone, I presume." We can picture the scene up north in 1884 when young Commander—subsequently Admiral—Schley rescued Adolphus Washington Greely and the other few survivors of his tragic expedition. So we may also imagine the feelings on both sides when the crew of that Portuguese caravel in 1445 found that the waving figure whom they had believed to be a Moor turned out to be their own countryman, the daredevil young esquire who had gone on that apparently foolhardy escapade. We can gather an inkling from the sober, restrained words of the chronicler:

"And I consider what must have been the appearance of that noble squire, brought up as he had been on the food you know, to wit, bread and wine and flesh and other things skillfully prepared, after living seven months in this fashion where he could eat nothing but fish and the milk of camels and drinking brackish water and not too much of that and living in a hot and sandy land without any delights."

"If I marveled before at the endurance of Joan Fernandez," continues the historian, "little less do I marvel at the affection which those who dwelt there came to feel for him. For I am assured that when he parted from the men among whom he had lived those seven months, many of them wept with regretful thought."

It is clear from old Azurara's language that the revelations of Joan Fernandez were fully appreciated by the ruler of the court at Sagres. We can judge their value by the fact that three and a half centuries elapsed before any other European brought home any news from those parts of the Sahara. That was Mungo Park who was destined to perish in his attempt to widen the scope of human knowledge.

Joan Fernandez survived to go on other expeditions. One year after his great adventure he went with Gomez Pirez to the Rio do Ouro. And in 1447 he accompanied Diego Gil to Meça, a city in the province of Sus, one of the principal places in the Empire of Morocco. We also find records which indicate that he took part in an expedition to Ethiopia.

It is an amazing coincidence that the name of the first Robinson Crusoe, as Beazley terms him, should have been Joan Fernandez. He was neither kith nor kin to Juan Fernandez, the Spanish pilot who, one century later, discovered the islands off the coast of Chile which now bear his name. It was on the principal Juan Fernandez island that Alexander Selkirk was marooned and lived alone four years and a half. And on Selkirk's adventure Daniel Defoe based the book, *Robinson Crusoe*, which some people consider the greatest novel ever written.

But even before Selkirk's adventure an Indian of the

Mosquito tribe had the same experience. He had been captured by the buccaneer Watling and taken along on his thieving expeditions. It was the custom of Pacific Ocean explorers, buccaneers and others to put in at Juan Fernandez to refit and provision their ships. Watling anchored there in 1681. The Mosquito Indian—by another coincidence named Robin—was ashore hunting goats in the woods. Watling took alarm at the approach of a fleet of Spanish warships. He weighed anchor quickly and sailed away, leaving Robin on Juan Fernandez. The Indian had with him nothing but a gun, powder and shot and a knife.

In March, 1684—three years later—another squadron, in whose company was the buccaneer-explorer Captain Dampier, made a landfall at Juan Fernandez. And there, waiting on the beach, was the castaway Robin. They found him in comfortable circumstances. When he had used up all his ammunition he sawed the barrel of his gun into small pieces. Out of these he made harpoons, lances and fish-hooks. With them he procured him an ample supply of food. He had built himself a hut, lined with goatskins and clothed himself in skins.

The goats had been brought to the place by Juan Fernandez himself, to whom the islands had been awarded by a Spanish royal grant. When the Spaniards learned that the goats had become a source of fresh meat for English buccaneers and other intruders they tried to destroy them. They landed a number of fierce dogs on Juan Fernandez, expecting that these would devour the goats. But the latter, quite simply and easily, escaped to the mountain tops whither the dogs could not pursue them. And so "the dogs it was that died."

As for Alexander Selkirk, some of the things he actually did are particularly interesting by contrast with the episodes in the great novel which they inspired. Those facts belong more properly in the story of William Dampier, the Buccaneer Who Became a Great Explorer. So, as we are going to consider Dampier subsequently, we will leave Mr. Selkirk for the present.

But we can't help having a considerable curiosity about the islands discovered by Juan Fernandez, the Spanish pilot whose name is almost a duplicate of the hardy and skillful Portuguese explorer Joan Fernandez. Is anybody living today where Robin, the Mosquito Indian and after him Alexander Selkirk, demonstrated so amazingly what one lone man can do when he is thrown upon his own resources?

The answer is Yes. As we have observed, the Spanish Viceroy in those parts gave the islands to Juan Fernandez. Their owner tried to make a home there for a while but apparently found it too lonely and unprofitable. Juan abandoned his little empire and for many years it was visited only by buccaneers, by vengeful Spanish captains in search of the buccaneers, and by explorers. For instance, in 1616 the largest Juan

Fernandez island became a welcome stopping-off place for the history-making Dutchmen, Jacques Le Maire and William Cornelis Schouten. They had just accomplished one of the most important but today seldom-discussed feats in exploration: they had discovered a new route from the Atlantic to the Pacific Ocean, the strait that today on all atlases bears the name of Le Maire. They had done it, not by accident, but by design. The all-grabbing King of Spain had forbidden the ships of all other nations to enter the Strait of Magellan. So the adventurous Dutchmen not only found a safer but a shorter route. And the islands of Juan Fernandez were their first landfall in the Pacific.

Actually they were for many years a sort of no man's land. When the days of explorers, buccaneers, privateers and just plain simple pirates were over, the sole visitors to the islands were fishermen from the coast of Chile and Peru. Since Juan Fernandez had abandoned his property the title lapsed to the government of Chile. For a while the principal island was a Chilean penal colony, a sort of Devil's Isle. But in 1855 the prisoners were transferred to Punta Arenas.

Some years later the islands of Juan Fernandez were leased to a private citizen. This happy individual, whose name was Von Rodt, paid the Chilean government a rental of $1,500 a year. At the latest report there were 60 human inhabitants, 100 head of cattle and 7,000 goats. Their numbers undoubtedly are vastly more today. The government's tenant makes a profit of about $2,000 a year out of the lumber alone and still more out of the lobsters, seals and fishes that abound in the surrounding waters. The inhabitants are not only peaceful and orderly but hard-working. And the incumbent of Juan Fernandez has reported: "In picturesque beauty and wildness, my little kingdom leaves nothing to be desired."

Such is the place where Robinson Crusoe had his unforgettable adventure, the place discovered by the man whose name was almost identical with that of the first Crusoe, Joan Fernandez.

IV

A GERMAN CONQUISTADOR

IV

A GERMAN CONQUISTADOR

A TYPICAL family row was going on in the household of
the good citizen Schmiedel in the town of Straubing on
the right bank of the River Danube. Young Ulrich
Schmiedel, the second son, was in open rebellion. His
older brother Thomas, a sober, steady fellow, had given
his parents nothing but satisfaction. With Ulrich,
however, they could do nothing. They had cherished
such great plans for the lad. With Thomas to carry on
Papa Schmiedel's business, it was their ambition that
Ulrich should enter a learned profession. He would
have none of it, he just was not the type. A stout,
strapping young man, his head was filled with dreams
of adventure. He had heard of the conquests of the
Spaniards in Peru and Mexico, of the great Portuguese
captains who had shown the way to the Isles of Spice.
He wanted to go where they had gone or even, if possible, where they had not gone. For book learning he
had no use. Only a smattering of the classics stuck to
his brain. He wanted to learn by seeing things for
himself. No wonder he had brought distress to that
solid burgher's family in the Bavarian town on the
Danube.

One day in the spring of 1534 the rich banker Sebastian Neidhart of Nuremberg arrived in Straubing on his way either to or from Vienna. Calling at the home of his friend Schmiedel, the shrewd man of affairs soon perceived the tension in the family. Presently the story was told to him. He looked the young man up and down.

"*Na!* That may not be so serious," said the great man, soothing the ruffled feelings of the family. "He isn't built for the counting house. Nor yet for a priest nor an advocate. "*Sag' einmal, junger Mann*, how would you like to go on a venture to South America?"

The young man's immediate enthusiasm almost blew the good Sebastian Neidhart out of his seat of honor on the family sofa.

"South America!" he exclaimed. "Would I like it? When can I start? Where? How? Tell me, Master Councilor, do you mean it?"

"Well, not tonight, young man. Just hold your horses," replied the banker. "But you ought to start soon. The Emperor is sending out an expedition to the province of the Río de la Plata under the Adelantado Don Pedro de Mendoza. Don Pedro will build a capital and establish a government there for His Imperial Majesty. Thanks to ahem—certain favors we were able to render His Majesty, he has graciously permitted Jacob Welzer and your humble servant to send a ship laden with our worthy Nuremberg goods to trade for the Indians' gold and silver. Heinrich Paime will sail in charge of our cargo. And we need some good stout German lads to protect it. The Emperor, God save him, is well disposed toward us. But sometimes his Spanish subjects when they are far enough away—! Enough of that. *Na*, Papa Schmiedel, what do you say? And what does the boy's mother say?"

What could they say? By June of that year young Ulrich Schmiedel, with his parents' blessing, was in Antwerp. But not until the first of September, thanks to contrary winds which had delayed his departure, did Don Pedro de Mendoza, in command of 14 ships and 2,650 men, leave the coast of Spain astern. Of this assorted personnel, 2,500 were Spaniards and the other 150 were Bavarians, Flemings and Saxons.

It may seem somewhat astonishing to read of Germans and Netherlanders being allowed to accompany a Spanish expedition. It certainly could not have happened under the dour, bigoted Philip II. But his father, the Emperor Charles V, was a totally different kind of monarch. Though a Spaniard, he was born in Ghent. As a boy he had Flemish tutors. When he ascended the throne he had Flemish ministers, Flemish councilors, Flemish and German bankers. The great European bankers of the day were the Fuggers of Prague, the Welzers of Nuremberg, the Schetzen of Antwerp. Of these the Fuggers are today the best known. We read about the Welzers far less often. But they were rich enough and powerful enough for Charles to have given them the entire province of Caracas for their own property. Sebastian Neidhart was an associate of the Welzers.

The River Plate, to which our young friend Ulrich was adventuring, had been discovered in 1516 by Juan Diaz de Solis. The armchair geographers had ventured the guess that it was the mouth of a passage leading from the Atlantic to the Pacific. Magellan spiked that rumor in 1519. He sailed up the estuary and tested the water. It was fresh. So the River Plate could not possibly be the long-hoped-for channel to the Western Ocean.

In 1527 Sebastian Cabot sailed 'way up the river, then up the Paraná to its junction with the Paraguay. That made him the first European to see the edge of the Gran Chaco, the region over which Bolivia and Paraguay have just finished their ruinous war. But he saw something more important still to the Europeans of that day. He encountered Indians of the Chaco wearing silver ornaments. That indicated the presence of mines of the precious metal. His report caused considerable excitement at the court of the Emperor. So in 1528 the pilot Diego Garcia was sent south to take possession of the Río de la Plata. Thereby he founded the claim of the Spanish crown to a province reaching, roughly, from thirty-six degrees South to latitude twenty-five, clear across to the Pacific Ocean. It took in not only part of what is now Argentina but all of what is now

Uruguay, with slices of Brazil, the Chaco and Chile. In 1531 the Portuguese established a factory, as trading stations were called in those days, at San Vicente, near the site of the modern Santos, to which they were entitled by the Treaty of Tordesillas. This seemed to be a direct threat at those rumored silver mines. That was why Charles V sent out those fourteen "great ships" under Don Pedro de Mendoza, on one of which was our keen young German friend, Ulrich Schmiedel. The great Emperor had given his Adelantado the instructions of a statesman. He was not equipping an expedition for plunder and loot. He told Don Pedro to "take it easy," build as he went, establish a solid government, colonize and found a dominion which should be of everlasting value to Spain. We shall see how those instructions were carried out.

Ulrich had his first taste of excitement and romance when the fleet reached Palma in the Canaries. They stayed there four weeks. It was long enough for Don Jorge de Mendoza, a young cousin of the Captain-General's, to fall in love with the daughter of a well-to-do burgher of Palma. Don Jorge had been assigned as a staff officer to the German ship owned by Welzer and Sebastian Neidhart. The rich man of Palma would never consent to his daughter's marrying an adventurer bound for remote, wild places. So, on the eve of the fleet's departure, Don Jorge and twelve companions promoted an elopement. The young lady was perfectly willing. The enterprising Spaniard took not only the girl and her maid but all her clothes and jewels as well. He hid her aboard the Welzers' vessel. So far so good for the cause of romance. Unfortunately a storm broke almost the moment the German ship got outside the harbor. She had to put in again. Heinrich Paime took the opportunity to go ashore, whether to get another drink of Madeira wine or more fresh vegetables we don't know. He was about to spring to solid ground when he espied a greeting party of thirty armed and angry men and they were not there to bring him a drink of wine. There was a skirmish. Paime was almost captured, but he made his escape and got back to his ship. But the Palma soldiers gave the alarm, and four shots were fired from the cannon in the fort. One of them brought down the German craft's mizzenmast and killed a seaman. The next thing the visitors knew, the commandant of Palma and the civil judge came aboard. They demanded the head of young Don Jorge on a charge of abducting a virgin. The young lady came to the front and proved that she had not been kidnaped. She came of her own accord and she defied anybody to separate her from her lover. She would marry him or know the reason why. He was of noble blood, so what obstacle could there be? This was disconcerting to the civil and military authorities of Palma. However, the German factor did not want a serious expedition to be jeopardized by the presence of a

FOR MONTHS ON END THEY HAD A PEACEFUL AND OFTEN ENJOYABLE
JOURNEY

woman aboard. It was no trip for a honeymoon, so he put the ever-loving Don Jorge and his bride ashore and left him to the mercy of the girl's parents. Schmiedel tells of this romantic episode with real gusto.

Don Pedro and his fourteen ships arrived in the estuary of the Plate River in 1535. He anchored first off San Gabriel Island and disembarked his men on the north shore in the territory of the Charuas. The natives promptly fled, setting fire to their huts. Mendoza then crossed the river and built a town of mud-huts on the site of what is today the rich, gay and brilliant city of Buenos Aires. Ulrich tells us it was so called because of the "*guter Wind*" (good wind) that so constantly blew there.

It is interesting to observe that Germans thus had an important share in the founding of Buenos Aires. To-day, both in the city and the surrounding province, there are large colonies of Teutonic origin, German banks, German ranchos, German factories.

Ulrich soon had his first experience of battle, murder and sudden death. It came about through a ruthless treatment of the natives all too typical of the conquistadors. Charles V had given Mendoza particular instructions to be humane towards the Indians. But the Adelantado was a sick man long before he reached the River Plate, and unable to enforce his own orders. His lieutenants, brave and formidable caballeros, were also callous and cruel. They looked upon the Indians as something less than human. Some Spanish theologians debated seriously whether American aborigines had souls. Our young German friend seems to have adopted the point of view of his Spanish officers pretty quickly. He became as loyal—and towards the natives as callous —as any Iberian man-at-arms. In the narrative he wrote later he expressed no horror of the Spaniards' cruelty. If he shared their hardships without complaining, he also shared in the loot.

The first fight was against a nomadic tribe called the Quirandis. They had treated the newcomers with the utmost hospitality. For two weeks they fed the invaders from their small store of provisions and their meager catch of fish. This much was admitted by Schmiedel. Some of the Spaniards abused the friendship of the Quirandis, seizing forcibly what was not given to them and interfering with the women. The natives did not attempt any vengeance. They just struck camp and withdrew. The move was serious enough, since it left the Spaniards without any source of supplies. They were not resourceful enough to find their own game and fish and did not know which plants of the country were eatable. So Mendoza dispatched a judge with a guard of two men-at-arms to find out why the Quirandis had suddenly let them down. The natives received them with a shower of stones. They returned to Buenos Aires, badly beaten.

By Spanish standards this called for reprisals. Don

Diego de Mendoza, the Captain-General's brother, took 30 horsemen and 300 foot, one of whom was Ulrich Schmiedel, on a punitive raid. According to Schmiedel they met a force of 3,000 Quirandis, but there is fair reason to believe that the young Bavarian was not so good at figures. There was a pitched battle in which the Spaniards lost 7 officers, including Don Diego, and 20 men. But the natives, armed with bows and arrows and bolas, could not stand up to the withering attack of even the clumsy European firearms of the period. Schmiedel tells us that they killed one thousand of the Quirandis, another guess open to question. In his account of this fight Ulrich gives the first description of the bola, the heavy stones tied to a rope by which the South Americans felled their enemies and brought down their running game. This unique weapon was adopted and improved by Spanish cowhands and is still in use among the gauchos of the plains.

The river where this battle took place is now called the Rio de la Matanza. The victory may have been good discipline, but it did not accomplish much towards solving the food problem for the new city of Buenos Aires. About the only loot captured was the fishing tackle left behind by the Quirandis. The entire expedition suffered from hunger. Three ounces of flour a day and one fish every three days were the rations for each man. Whoever craved more was at liberty to catch it himself if he could. Schmiedel relates all these

[87]

hardships without any suggestion of a whine. Don Pedro had split up his forces into fighting men and workers, but upon emergency the workers had to drop their tools and take up arms. He laid out the site of Buenos Aires carefully and built around it a mud wall "half a pike's length high." The Governor's residence also had some pretensions as a building. But the men were so weak from lack of nourishment that what they put up one day fell down the next. Ulrich tells one rather horrible episode that Spanish historians have doubted. But he describes it quite circumstantially. Starvation was so near that three Spanish soldiers stole one of the horses, killed and ate him. They were suspected and "put to the question," that is, tortured. They confessed, whereupon they were hanged in public. Then, says the German narrative, some of the starving survivors in the dead of night cut pieces off those hanging corpses and ate them. He also tells us that one Spaniard devoured the remains of his dead brother.

Whether this was true or not, Don Pedro perceived that his position on the bank of the Plate was impossible. So he had seven small "barquentines" constructed. In them he sent a foraging party of 350 men up the river under the command of Jorge Lujan. Schmiedel relates, with naïve pathos, that "as soon as the Indians were aware of us they wrought us the utmost knavery (*Buberei*) possible by burning and destroying all their victuals, as well as their villages, and running away."

After five months of futile raiding, Lujan's detachment returned to Buenos Aires practically empty-handed. While they were gone one half the garrison had died of starvation. All this time the conduct of the conquistadors had made such an impression upon the native South Americans that four tribes united in one big endeavor to wipe the invaders out once and for all. Twenty-three thousand strong, they swooped down upon the adobe city. Had they had the patience to conduct a long siege they could easily have exterminated the Spaniards to a man. But in South America as in the North, the Indians never showed the inclination or ability to beleaguer and wear down a fortified town. As it was, they practically destroyed the city, as a habitable place, with the incendiary arrows they fired. Most of the huts in Buenos Aires had thatched roofs, only the residences of the Governor and principal captains being tiled. The Spaniards beat them off, but not before the tribes had burned four of their "great ships" to the water's edge.

In his weakened condition, Don Pedro now turned over the command of the expedition to Don Juan de Ayolas. The deputy Captain-General mustered his men and found that he had 560 effectives left out of the original force of 2,560 that had sailed from Seville in 1534. He left 160 as a guard upon the few remaining great ships, with provisions sufficient to last them one year, provided they rationed themselves to four ounces of flour a day. "*Wollte einer mehr essen, so mochte er's suchen.*" (If any man wanted more it was up to him to find it.) The rest, Schmiedel among them, Ayolas led up the River Paraná in eight "barquentines." The ailing Don Pedro went along for a while, though he was practically a dead weight and a responsibility. After a few months, Ayolas sent him back to Buenos Aires. There he took two of the great ships and sailed for Spain. He died on the voyage. There was a report that he and several other officers were taken violently ill after eating his pet dog. Before he died he kept his promise and left instructions that two relief ships should be equipped and sent out to the Plate at the expense of his estate. Thus Don Pedro gave his life for his great adventure, on which he had also spent a large part of his fortune. On his deathbed he dictated a report to Charles V, who promptly sent a relief squadron under Don Alonso de Cabrera to Ayolas with reenforcements and provisions for two years.

Meanwhile Ayolas had reached the country of the Timbus, losing 50 of his men on the precarious journey into uncharted regions. The Timbus came to meet them in small fleets of dugouts. Evidently no word of the menace in those conquistadors had reached that tribe. They were friendly and, when Ayolas presented the chief, Chera Guazu, with a few worthless gimcracks, made the newcomers welcome to all they possessed. The Spaniards reveled in fresh game, fish, vegetables. It was none too soon, for they were almost at the last gasp of their endurance. Compared to what they had gone through, it must have been heavenly. The country was rich in food resources, the natives amiable. Also they were first-rate hunters and provided a copious supply of victuals. Ayolas took the opportunity to rest and recuperate his men. Schmiedel tells us they remained there four years, but we have already observed that the Bavarian was not awfully good at figures. However, it is certain that they stayed among the Timbus until the relief expedition under Alonso de Cabrera arrived. (Obviously Ayolas had sent couriers back to the abandoned site of Buenos Aires to let the captain in charge there know his whereabouts.)

Upon the advent of Cabrera there was a council of war. With the 200 replacements from Spain, the force now numbered 550 effectives. They decided to leave 150 men in the country of the Timbus. These built a fort near the site of the modern Santa Fé, with small outposts throughout the district. They were instructed to keep as strict a government over the natives as their small numbers permitted. The other 400 sailed and rowed up the River Paraná under the joint command of Juan de Ayolas, Alonso de Cabrera and Don Domingo Martinez de Irala. They went to seek the junction of the Paraná with the Paraguay, of which they had heard, also of a country in which maize, manioc, manioc wine and sweet potatoes were abundant. On the way they discovered a small lake and "came to a river flowing inland." There Schmiedel saw and shot his first boa constrictor, which earned the invaders the gratitude and admiration of the natives. For weeks and months on end they had a peaceful and often enjoyable journey. All the tribes were friendly except one, which attacked in war canoes but was beaten off after a few rounds of gunfire.

They reached the Paraguay finally and there encountered the Carios. These were a warlike people with rudimentary ideas of military engineering. They implored the Spaniards to move on and let them be. They offered an ample supply of provisions "and to let us go on our way in peace. But this did not suit the plans of Don Juan de Ayolas." He gave battle. The Carios retired into their fortress and then got a taste of what it meant to be besieged by soldiers who understood the principles of siege work. It lasted three days. The Carios capitulated. Among the spoils were six women for the commander-in-chief. Every common soldier was allotted two women to do his cooking and mend his clothes. Ayolas made a treaty with the Carios which obligated the natives to help build him a fort and to provide him with auxiliaries in any fights with other tribes. The fort was called Nuestra Señora de Asunción, the name by which the town is known today. The Spaniards had rowed, sailed and marched 400 miles to reach it. Ayolas left a garrison of one hundred men at Asunción and continued up the Paraguay with the remaining 300. Strangely enough, there are no reports of mutinies on this expedition. Ayolas quite unashamedly was looking for the fabulous silver mines of South America, and his men were heart and soul with him.

Alonso de Cabrera seems to have dropped out of ken somewhere on the march. At any rate, one hears no more of him. But when Ayolas reached a mountain that he christened San Fernando, he split his forces. He left a detachment at Mt. San Fernando under Domingo de Irala. The rest of his men, together with a force of 500 native auxiliaries, he took upcountry looking for the region of the Guaycurus, where there was supposed to be silver in abundance. At this point we come to a tragic interlude. Ayolas left explicit orders with Irala. The latter was to wait at Asunción five months. If Ayolas did not return before that time he was to return to Santa Fé and thence to Buenos Aires, there to await orders from Madrid. At least, that is the story told by Ulrich Schmiedel. In his account we can see how the Bavarian transfers his loyalty from one commander to another. Irala, according to Schmiedel, waited as long as six months at Asunción. By that time supplies were running low. Furthermore, rumors reached Asunción that Ayolas had lost half his men from starvation and that the survivors, with their captain, had been surrounded and massacred by the Indians. At least, that is what Irala told his command. Two Payaguas, who were captured by the Carios, were tortured and confessed the truth. Thereupon the men at Asunción elected Irala captain-general and went south.

Some Spanish historians have another version of the affair. According to them, Irala deliberately deserted Ayolas and left him to be murdered in order that he might have sole command, a story partially borne out by Irala's subsequent conduct. But the narrative of the German man-at-arms is clear, circumstantial and plausible. Whatever happened, Irala returned from Asunción to Santa Fé. There he found a war on his hands with the formerly friendly Timbus. Three of the men left in charge had murdered a Timbu chieftain. The tribes jumped upon the sparsely manned posts and almost annihilated them. Irala fought his way out and got back to his great ships anchored off the site of Buenos Aires. He met there a caravel with news that a relief ship from Spain had reached the island of Santa Catalina. Schmiedel and six others, under Don Gonzalo de Mendoza, were sent in a galleon to urge the captain of the relief ship to make haste. But the galleon was wrecked in the estuary of the River Plate. Schmiedel and five of his companions saved their lives by clinging to one of the masts and had to walk most of the way to Buenos Aires.

Irala then took the desperate measure of burning his great ships and also what was left of Buenos Aires. He sailed upriver again, all the way to Asunción, to await orders from Madrid. The idea evidently was that Asunción was more favorably situated, geographically, for the profitable exploiting of the Spanish provinces in South America.

Meanwhile something had happened in Madrid of which Irala had no knowledge. When Charles V received news of the death of the Adelantado, Don Pedro de Mendoza, he was being considerably bothered by a man from Xerez named Alvar Nuñez, Cabeza de Vaca. This importunate fellow had already gone through untold hardships and adventures. He was the first European to travel clear across North America. He had lived five years among the Indians. He had marched from Florida to the Gulf of California and thence down into Mexico. And now he was back, looking for more trouble. "Oh, well, if he wants employment, let's send him to the Río de la Plata. There must be precious metals down there and this pestilent wanderer seems to be mad about some mysterious City of Gold. He'll either find something or die. In any event, your Majesty will be rid of him." So said one of Charles's cynical councilors. But the Emperor, as usual, issued more statesmanlike instructions. Cabeza de Vaca was to proceed to Buenos Aires and rebuild the city. Having established order in that region, he was to advance up the Paraná, consolidating his positions on the journey and, if possible, rescue Don Juan de Ayolas. If Ayolas were still alive, he was to hand over to him the supreme command of the province and return home. If Ayolas were dead, Cabeza de Vaca was to become Adelantado and Captain-General. So the insatiable adventurer sailed from Cádiz with 2 great ships, 2 caravels, 400 men and 30 horses. (In all expeditions to the Americas, horses were extremely important. The awe inspired among the natives by the sight of armored men astride those beasts was second only to the destruction wrought by European firearms.)

When Cabeza de Vaca arrived off the island of Santa Catalina he lost his two caravels, though all the men aboard escaped. But the news he encountered there discouraged him still more from taking the roundabout route by water to Asunción. He sent his nephew by sea to Buenos Aires. The nephew returned to report that the town had been burned to the ground. So Cabeza de Vaca broke up his two great ships, which were crocks and already quite unseaworthy. Then with his 400 men, he undertook the terrifying march across country to the junction of the Paraná and Paraguay rivers. It was a devastating trip, through almost impenetrable jungle, over mountains, streams and rivers, and it was accomplished with a force of men utterly untrained to woodcraft and to preserving their own lives by living off the fruits and game of the wilderness.

There were no paths, no signposts, few trustworthy guides. He had to feel his way, to navigate, as it were, overland. It took him six months to make 500 miles and he lost 100 men on the march. But he reached Asunción, to the astonishment of Irala, who expected his re-enforcements to come up the Paraná River.

The first thing Cabeza de Vaca learned was that Ayolas surely had perished. "In that case, caballeros," he said, "by order of His Most Catholic Majesty, I take command." "*Ah, si, Señor?*" replied Irala and his lieutenants with the utmost politeness, "and you have His Majesty's written word for that?" The new Adelantado could show no letters patent from Madrid. At least that is what we learn from the German chronicle of Ulrich Schmiedel, always the loyal follower of his immediate boss. It was only natural that Irala should resent being thus superseded after all he had achieved. "But," adds the naïve Bavarian, "they became friends, dividing the command between them." The truth probably was that Irala and his gang did not seriously doubt that the claims of the new commander were genuine. The latter spoke with authority and was obviously a warrior of substance and experience, although they spread a false report to the contrary among their followers. They decided to knife him in other ways.

This much is to be inferred from artless old Ulrich Schmiedel's narrative. For he tells how Irala sent a detachment down the Paraguay to hang the chieftain of a friendly tribe, saying that such were the orders of the new Captain-General. Schmiedel admits that the murdered chief was entirely innocent of any offense, and he intimates that Cabeza de Vaca knew it. At any rate, the outrage provoked an immediate war of retaliation. The Spaniards won, inflicting terrific losses upon the Indians. But the episode aroused the country against the invaders and made their exploration so much the more difficult. It was part of the scheme of Irala and his fellows. Cabeza de Vaca had brought instructions from the Emperor that there was to be no unnecessary fighting, no ruthless slaughter of the natives. Charles V wanted to establish one peaceful dominion across the seas. Irala and his like sneered at such an idea. What was the profit in talking peace in the wilderness among savages who knew neither God nor Madrid? It was all very well to talk about peaceful dealings in the Escurial Palace. This was on the Paraguay, not the Guadalquivir.

Cabeza de Vaca made himself unpopular in other ways. He wanted discipline, law, order. The same law for the treatment of Indians as for Christians. With loyal officers, those principles would have helped him to establish a real colony in South America then and there. But to Irala he was talking nonsense and his ideas were a nuisance. On the other hand, the intelligence of Alvar Nuñez was manifestly diluted with a lack of tact. As Schmiedel puts it: "All the officers and soldiers hated him for his perverse and rigorous carriage towards the men."

Much as they disliked him, Cabeza de Vaca drove his mutinous conquistadors to explorations and discoveries from which their greed and stupidity had hitherto stopped them. They had been looking for silver. He was bound for nothing less than the legendary Golden City of Manoa. He had looked for it in vain through Florida, through Texas and Mexico. So it must be here, amid the jungles of South America. He left a garrison at Asunción and proceeded up the Paraguay. He discovered the Isle of Paradise. He reached Candelaria, where Juan de Ayolas had perished. On the journey Ulrich Schmiedel had his first sight of crocodiles, tapirs, emus and other fauna of that continent. The expedition got to Lake Gaiba and there Cabeza de Vaca founded the town of Los Reyes.

But the exploits of that great explorer have been told in too many other narratives. After all, we are concerned principally with the adventures of the young Bavarian from Straubing and his view of those historic events. Cabeza de Vaca returned to Asunción a sick, weary and disappointed man. He stayed indoors. The soldiers were told that he did so "more out of pride than weakness." Meanwhile Irala and his accomplices were biding their time. Alvar Nuñez had sent a minor expedition out from Los Reyes under Don Hernando de Ribera with certain explicit instructions. Ribera got

as far as what is now San Luis in Brazil. There he found
a tribe called the Xarayos. They were friendly. In
return for worthless gimcracks their king gave Ribera a
silver crown and a thick bar of gold. Ribera wanted
to know where they had come from. The King of the
Xarayos declared that they were the spoils of war taken
from a tribe of Amazons whose women had only one
breast and fought more fiercely than the men. This
was all that Ribera could learn. He returned, apparently without having accomplished the mission assigned
to him. When he reached Asunción, Cabeza de Vaca
arrested him and, according to Schmiedel, proposed to
hang him. The German does not tell us what offense
Ribera was accused of. Whatever it was, officers and
men alike rebelled against the Captain-General. Irala
took 200 armed soldiers and arrested Cabeza de Vaca
in his official residence. They sent him home and there
were rumors that two attempts to poison him were made
on the journey to Spain. (According to other accounts
the mutiny and his arrest took place at Los Reyes, not
Asunción.) Upon his arrival in Madrid he was thrown
into prison and his trial lasted three years. At the end
the Spanish courts found him guilty in 1551. So maybe
our German friend was not so far wrong.

After the departure of Cabeza de Vaca, Ulrich
Schmiedel continued in the service of Irala four years
more. The latter had once again been elected governor and commander-in-chief by acclamation. The

mutinous spirit that Irala had fostered against Cabeza de Vaca was turned, boomerang fashion, upon himself. There was a deadly fight between Don Francisco de Mendoza, a friend of Irala, and Don Diego de Abrego of Seville. Abrego cut off Mendoza's head, then defied Irala, fleeing into the jungle with fifty men. For two years a guerilla warfare was kept up. It was finally settled when Irala married his two daughters, born to him by Indian wives, to cousins of Abrego. The truce came none too soon. Seeing the Spaniards fighting amongst themselves, the Indians seized the opportunity to unite in another fierce attempt to wipe them out forever. But even with overwhelming numbers they could not stand up in pitched battle against the heavily armed Europeans. The Carios retired into their fortified town. Irala captured it by treachery and the slaughter was terrific. Schmiedel relates that in all this warfare the Spaniards took a total of 12,000 prisoners. "I had for my share about 50 men, women and children."

Irala then sent an expedition northwards. In this he achieved one valuable thing. He pushed through the country of the Mbaias, all the way to the borders of the then most important province of Peru. There he found a tribe that spoke a smattering of Spanish. It turned out that they were the subjects of Pero Anzures de Campo Redondo. He had been one of the officers on Pizarro's staff. Pizarro had sent him to conquer the Chuncho tribe. But at the time of Irala's advent, La Gasca was the governor of Peru. Irala sent four of his men to Lima. They went by way of Potosi and Cuzco. In this way Irala established the first overland communication from the Atlantic to the Pacific.

One day in 1552 re-enforcements arrived from Spain. They brought letters and among them was one for Ulrich Schmiedel. It was from Christoff Keyser, agent of the Fuggers in Seville. Ulrich's brother Thomas was dead. On his deathbed he had begged Sebastian Neidhart to write to Ulrich and tell him to come home. Schmiedel asked permission to depart, which was at first refused peremptorily. But the Bavarian pleaded and pointed out that he had completed almost twenty years of service in South America. He had suffered his share of wounds and privation and had almost died of the dropsy. In fact he was one of the few survivors of the original 2,650 who had sailed from Spain in 1534. So Irala not only relented, but entrusted the German with dispatches for the Emperor.

Schmiedel tells us that it took twenty Cario bearers to carry all his plunder. He started back on St. Stephen's Day, December 26, 1552, in two canoes. After four weeks' paddling they left the river and trekked overland. On the march the German was joined by a small band of Spanish deserters. Frequently they had to shoot their way through hostile natives; one such fight lasted four days and nights. They reached the River Uruguay, but that was only one stage.

Among the interesting encounters they had on the journey was that with Juan Ramallo, an exiled outlaw. For years this man had lived in the jungle out of reach of the authorities of his own land. He had carved out a small domain for himself, paying tribute to nobody, living like a patriarchal cacique surrounded by swarms of grandchildren.

The German soldier piously records the fact that it was on St. Anthony's Day, July 13, 1553, that he reached San Vicente. Though he was modest enough about it, he had accomplished an amazing and a valorous feat. He had led his tiny band over 467 miles of trackless forest and mountain. He had learned his lesson and earned the right to be considered a full-fledged conquistador. At San Vicente he found a ship belonging to Johann von Hulst of Lisbon, an agent of the Schetzen of Antwerp. She was loading with sugar, lumber and wool. He also met Peter Roessel at San Vicente. He was the local factor of Johann von Hulst. Roessel welcomed the returning compatriot with open arms and entertained him royally. The factor had built up quite a fortune for himself, owning sugar plantations, refineries and timber concessions.

Ten days later Schmiedel sailed in Von Hulst's ship for Spain. But his troubles and perils were not over. The first storm the vessel ran into lasted fourteen days and drove them into the harbor of Espiritu Santo. The voyage took four months to the Azores, two weeks

THE UNTOLD STORY OF EXPLORATION

thence to Lisbon. Ulrich set foot on European soil, after an absence of nineteen years, on St. Hieronymus's Day, September 30, 1553. He stayed in Lisbon fourteen days, where two of the Indian slaves he had brought with him died. He posted overland to Seville, and delivered Irala's dispatches to an officer of the Spanish crown.

Having done that he took passage from Cadiz in one of a fleet of twenty-five Dutch merchantmen bound for Antwerp. Again he had two narrow escapes. The skipper of the ship on which he was to sail got drunk and left him behind. That craft was wrecked and sank, with all hands aboard, off the English coast. Of the other twenty-four ships, eight more came to grief off the Isle of Wight. But Ulrich Schmiedel arrived safely at Antwerp on January 26, 1554. And he concludes his tale with the words:

"God be praised everlasting, He who so mercifully gave me such a prosperous voyage."

Ulrich Schmiedel returned to Straubing and lived to a ripe old age. He wrote or dictated his memoirs some years after his home-coming. We may be sure that the tales of his adventures furnished an excuse for many a convivial glass at his favorite tavern. Quite aside from that, his book, when it was published, was an invaluable contribution to the geography of South America and the history of its conquest, even though today few but professional geographers read it.

V

THE AMAZING PANDITS

V

THE AMAZING PANDITS

ONE day in the early sixties of the last century there was consternation in the office of Major J. T. Walker, superintendent of the Great Trigonometrical Survey of India. He had just received the following order from the palace of the Governor-General:

"Owing to disturbed political conditions north of the Himalayas, all travel permits in that direction are canceled. Until further orders no British officer or civilian, no European of any nationality, will be allowed to cross the northern frontiers of Her Majesty's dominions. You are also instructed to recall all surveying parties from the northwest provinces near the border."

It was a body blow to the enthusiasm of the gallant and devoted personnel of that superb service. As its name indicates, it was established for the mapping of Hindustan. But long before 1860 its highly trained officers had been risking their lives to explore the regions to the north of India. They had already laid the foundations of that vast body of geographical and other knowledge about Central Asia which today earns for the Great Trigonometrical Survey the admiration of the scientific world. Incidentally, in its matter-of-fact official records are buried enough stories of adventure for a dozen exciting books. The tale of the Pandits is only one of these.

In his distress over that order, Major Walker sent for his subordinate, Captain T. G. Montgomerie. The latter was already celebrated among Asiatic explorers for the difficult, dangerous and elaborate surveys he had achieved in Kashmir.

"Look at this, Montgomerie," exclaimed the super-intendent, showing the order. "Isn't it damnable? All our work knocked into a cocked hat. I suppose it's on account of that Tungan rebellion."

"I've rather been expecting it," replied Montgomerie. "All Chinese Turkestan is in an uproar. They hate us and all foreigners. I suspect the Russian agents have been stirring 'em up. His Excellency's Council have been in a blue funk ever since Adolphe de Schlagintweit was murdered on the expedition to Kashgar. All the tribes along the Indus bar us like poison. Hunga and Nagar are nothing but robber states. The Raj doesn't want to stir up any more trouble so soon after the Mutiny."

"Nevertheless, it's a hell of a situation for us," declared his chief. "Our transfrontier maps are practically a blank in spite of the travels of Bogle, Turner and the Stracheys." (Samuel Turner had visited the monastery of Terpaling in 1783 and had an interview with the Teshoo Lama.) "Heroic, and all that, but their descriptions are too vague. Of course most of those chaps went out without proper scientific equipment. Gilgit, Chitral and Chilas are absolutely unexplored. From the Black Mountain area in the west to Bunji in the north we know nothing about the Indus. Our only information about the Pamirs is what Wood brought back from his expedition to Lake Victoria in 1838."

As we eavesdrop on these officers and look at the maps of Asia today we can realize what an extraordinary task was ahead of them. Central Tibet was virtually unknown and unmapped. To be sure, the Lazarist monks, Huc and Gabet, had made their famous trip to Lhasa in 1845. But the story of the journey, written by Huc, though fascinating, was unreliable. The position of Lhasa was almost conjectural, shrouded in mystery. Only one part of Tsampo had been charted and that roughly. Western Tibet was also secluded and exclusive, despite the exploits of the De Schlagintweit brothers. Montgomerie said as much.

"What's more, sir, I'm sure the De Schlagintweits were at least 200 miles off about the position of Yarkand," remarked the captain. "And while they tell us Kashgar is in one spot, the Russians place it in a totally different one. No European has been to Khotan since the Jesuit Benedict Goes, and that was in 1604. That's a town we ought to know about, too."

"Yes, Montgomerie," agreed Major Walker, "we

ought to know about all those places, and as soon as possible. I have reports that there are gold mines, salt mines and other valuable deposits up north. But that order stumps our wicket."

"Couldn't some of us sneak across the border in disguise?" suggested the captain.

"Any man who tries it gets the hoof instanter, Montgomerie, make no mistake about that. Orders are orders," retorted his chief sharply. "Besides, it can't be done. Didn't you ever hear what happened to Moorcroft and Hearsey in 1812? They tried to disguise themselves as fakirs, under the names of Mayapuri and Hargiri. Slipped over to Hundes and Gartok. The Tibetans nabbed them about 80 miles northwest of Lake Manasarowar—place called Daba Dzong. They were rescued by a couple of natives from our side of the Himalayas who went bail for them, Devi Singh and Bir Singh. The Singhs had done some scouting work for us."

"I say, sir, that gives us an idea!" exclaimed Montgomerie. "Some of these Hindus from the hill country are deuced useful. Don't know what I'd have done without those I had helping me in Kashmir. Come to think of it, the De Schlagintweits employed Devi Singh's son—Mani Singh, his name was. He was with the Stracheys in Tibet, too. Clever chaps, some of 'em. Apt, don't y'know, could easily be taught to handle a prismatic compass or even a sextant. Plucky devils, too. Why not pick a handful of them and train 'em?"

"By Jove, Montgomerie, you may have hit it!" declared the superintendent. "Only thing is, might be costly if it doesn't come off. Can we trust the beggars?"

"With your life, sir!" replied the captain earnestly. "As for the cost, pay them only for results. Small wages, but a handsome reward if they come back with information."

"Damme if I don't take it up with the Burra Sahib at headquarters," said Major Walker. "If he says yes, it'll be your pidgin, Montgomerie. I mean, you'll have to pick your men and do the training."

"Thank you, sir," replied the captain. And that is how it came to pass that the gallant band of Indians known as the Pandits were sent out to add a brilliant chapter to the history of discovery.

For his first initiates, Montgomerie selected kinsmen of the same Singhs who had saved Moorcroft and Hearsey in 1812, who had later accompanied the De Schlagintweits and the Stracheys on their expeditions. The most distinguished of them were Nain Singh and his cousin Kishen Singh. They jumped at the opportunity and were sent to Dehra Dun for training. There they immediately displayed not only zeal but extraordinary aptitude and intelligence. They learned the use of compass and sextant. In remarkably short order they were even able to "shoot" the more important stars. They also received elementary instruction in the properties of European drugs. Frequently this stood them in good stead, enabling some of them to pass themselves off as physicians among the more ignorant in remote countries. Occasionally, by healing the wife or child of a local official, they became privileged characters among otherwise suspicious and xenophobe tribes.

As Montgomerie had suggested, they were paid a small stipend, from 16 to 20 rupees a month—roughly, $8 to $10. They were also given funds for expenses, food, drugs and, in case they masqueraded as traders, merchandise. Some disguise was essential. The Emperor of China, for example, had issued standing orders that not only "Feringhis" but Hindusthanis and even Pathans were forbidden to enter Tibet. The choice of disguise was left to their own sagacity.

It must be remembered that these Pandits, once they left headquarters, were absolutely "on their own." They set forth without passport, without credentials of any sort. Their mission was secret. On the government records they appear not by name but as symbols. Nain Singh, officially, was described simply as "the Pandit," Kishen Singh as "A-K" and so forth. When taken prisoner, as frequently happened, they had to escape as best they might. For them there was no protection from the great British Raj. No Foreign Office would intervene to save them, no troops march to avenge their murder. They went unarmed save with their wits and courage.

[112]

In 1864 Nain Singh went out on his first adventure. He tried to slip into Tibet by way of Kumaon, near his birthplace, a point in the valley of the Sutlej, not far from Lake Manasarowar. It was a complete failure. At every point on that part of the border he was turned back ignominiously. He returned to Dehra Dun, humiliated and abashed, wondering what Montgomerie Sahib would say. Would the *capitani* decide he was no good?

"If the Sahib will give me another chance?" he stammered humbly. His pale face was ashen. For Nain Singh was neither black, like those of Bengal, nor even copper-colored. He had a sallow complexion, with handsome, regular features of the Indo-European type. Small, dark, keen eyes were set far apart over a well-shaped, strong, broad nose, a long upper lip and a firm mouth. A good-looking, intelligent man in any country or continent. Montgomerie smiled sympathetically.

"Come, come, Nain Singh," he said boisterously. "Am I a child that I do not know it is difficult to sneak into Tibet? Buck up, man. Of course you shall have another chance. And another and another. Tell you what, Nain Singh. There's plenty of frontier. Try it further east and a bit south, through Nepal. Better wait until the rains are over, though."

"The Sahib is my father and my mother," said Nain Singh as he backed out, salaaming gratefully.

But again ill fortune beset the Pandit. He got into

Nepal, but there the first thing he did was to lose all his money. He had bribed a trader to take him with his caravan through the passes into Tibet. The trader, after the manner of his kind, tricked him. Nain Singh was left stranded, penniless. This time he was determined that he would not slink back to Dehra Dun again empty-handed. He kept a-going, begging his way, doing odd jobs, but all the while making observations and attending to his main job of surveying. He reached Tradom on the Tsampo. From Tradom he hiked laboriously to Ladakh, an important goal. There he contrived to get a job tending camels on a caravan bound for Lhasa. And at last, on the tenth of January, 1866, he arrived below the magnificent, towering structure of the Potala, the Vatican of the Holy City of Buddhism.

That was all very well. Montgomerie Sahib would be pleased with Nain Singh, if he but knew. But the problem now was: how to get back with his report. For months he could find no caravan willing to take a penniless wanderer back across the mountains. And penniless he was, literally. Remember, he could not have written to Dehra Dun for money, not even if there had been a mail service, of which there was none. He went to work in Lhasa. He gave lessons in arithmetic and accounting to the sons of ambitious merchants. To be sure, he earned no more than a pittance. But he kept himself alive. And he put in his spare time walking around the Holy City, counting his paces carefully,

taking observations whenever he could with safety.
Eventually he found his way back to Ladakh and thence
to Tradom. After that his luck improved. Instead of
returning to India as he had come, through Nepal, he
struck west and north towards Lake Manasarowar. He
had failed to sneak into Tibet via Kumaon, but he surveyed the route on his journey out.

One day late in 1866 he walked into Montgomerie's
office with a report that delighted the gallant captain.
Montgomerie was vindicated and he was justly proud
of his Number One pupil. His Pandit had traced the
course of the "Great River of Tibet" and his notes indicated that it was, actually, the upper reaches of the
Brahmaputra. (This theory was received with doubt at
the time but later confirmed beyond all dispute.) He
had definitely established the position of Lhasa and
brought back an authentic description of the Holy City
and the surrounding country which had hitherto been
veiled in romance, fable and fustian. He had made
an elaborate route survey, over 1,200 miles, of the whole
of the great Tibetan road from Lhasa to Gartok as well
as that from Katmandu to Tradom. He had acquired
definite knowledge about the gold fields near Lhasa and
Gartok. Into the bargain he carried news about places
and routes that previously were utterly unknown.

His achievement was hailed with delight, not only by
his own service but by the geographers of Europe. The
Pandit received a handsome reward from the Govern-

ment of India, also an engraved gold watch from no less a body than the Royal Geographical Society. (Sad to relate, it was stolen by one of his pupils.)

The success of Nain Singh gave a new impetus to this strange enterprise of the Government of India. The year after he returned he was sent out again, this time with two colleagues and kinsmen, Mani Singh and Kalian Singh. They were to explore the headwaters of the Sutlej and clear up several points hitherto doubtful. They were also to connect the map of this area with the regular survey of the easternmost parts of the region around Ladakh, which Montgomerie had completed in 1864. And it was hoped that they might bring back answers to a question about which there had been infinite controversy: Was there an eastern branch of the Indus? Furthermore they were to explore the gold-mining districts east and northeast of Gartok, concerning which Nain Singh had brought reports from Lhasa.

It seems to have been a rule that the expeditions of the Pandits should start on the wrong foot. The Singhs set out as Bashahri traders. That was a bad bet. During the preceding year some Bashahris had introduced smallpox into Tibet. Consequently and naturally, the authorities at Lhasa had prohibited the entrance of all Bashahris into the country. So Nain Singh and his mates began their journey into forbidden territory as objects of suspicion. Their adventure was almost a

NAIN SINGH KEPT A-GOING, BEGGING HIS WAY, BUT ALL THE WHILE
ATTENDING TO HIS JOB OF SURVEYING

failure before it had really begun.

Somehow or other they managed to stick to it. Among them they visited and surveyed the principal gold field at Thokjalung. They mapped the main branches of the Upper Indus. They reconnoitered and sketched 18,000 square miles of country, verifying their notes with latitude observations at no fewer than 75 key points. They also checked the position of Gartok.

The strain of these two expeditions had been considerable. Nain Singh, though full of courage and endurance, was not a robust fellow. Upon his return from Gartok, it became evident that he was sorely in need of a rest. So the heads of the Survey kept him out of the field for a considerable while. They made him an instructor and set him to training new explorers. Among the students sent to him, was Kishen Singh. It is not quite clear whether this heroic fellow, described in the records of the Survey, as A-K, was his cousin or his nephew. At any rate, Nain Singh did such a good job with Kishen Singh that eventually the pupil outdid the master. But that is running ahead of our story.

Another member of this distinguished family entered the picture at about the same time. Kalian Singh penetrated the hitherto exclusive and unknown districts of western Tibet. He made a route traverse from Spiti across the virgin territory of Chumarti, and Guge, in the valley of the Upper Sutlej. It had last been visited by the Jesuit Antonio Andrade in 1624. Then, crossing the Indus at Tashigong, he reached Rudok. This was a feat almost comparable to that of his cousin on his journey to Lhasa. Rudok was second only to Rosok among the holy places of Tibet.

After making complete observations at Rudok, Kalian Singh, in the guise of a Bashahri trader, tried to make a route survey from that place to Lhasa. That disguise was even more unlucky to him than it had been for Nain Singh. Kalian Singh was arrested at Shigatse. He suffered no harm, but was shipped back and released at Tradom. From there he went home by way of Nepal, a trip which enabled him to check up on the work of Nain Singh.

The latter remained at Dehra Dun, training young explorers, until 1873. In that year, Sir Douglas Forsyth was dispatched on a mission to Yakub Beg, who had just wrested Turkestan from the weakening grasp of China and was making overtures to the British. The main purpose of the mission was political, but the government improved the occasion by sending along Captain, later Sir Henry, Trotter, to survey the road to Yarkand and Kashgar. With him went Nain Singh, Kalian Singh, Kishen Singh, and several assistants. As the expedition had been invited by the Atalik Yakub Beg, the surveyors were able to do their work in the open and under the full protection of the Atalik's local officials. They made complete route traverses, corrected by theodolite and sextant observations. Thus they were able to make an elaborate map of the road from Leh across the Lingzithany plains to Yarkand and Kashgar. When they reached Yarkand, Nain Singh and Kalian Singh stayed there, making traverses of the surrounding country, while Kishen Singh and another Pandit, known as "The Munshi," accompanied Forsyth to Kashgar.

There the party was split up again. Under the command of Lieutenant T. E. Gordon, Kishen Singh and The Munshi made route traverses across the Pamirs and back. The Munshi, whose real name was Abdul Subhan, was sent on his own, to follow the course of the Oxus north to the totally unknown districts of Shigman and Roshan, to the place where the River Murghab flows into the Oxus. Unfortunately, however, the good Munshi disappeared. For a while it was thought that he had been killed. Actually, it seems that he had a change of heart about his job, for he was found later in the service of the Amir of Kabul.

At any rate, the Pandits all did invaluable work on this expedition. They established the positions of Kashgar and Yarkand. They came home with elaborate maps. What is more, they threw the light of geographical knowledge on the mysterious ranges of the Pamirs.

The experience evidently served to whet Nain Singh's ambition for further solitary work in the field. His chiefs did not want to let him go, not only because he was valuable as an instructor, but because his work in Tibet had earned him considerable notoriety on the frontier and made him an object of suspicion. However, the heads of the Survey felt an urgent need for more exact knowledge about the land of the Lamas. So when Nain Singh volunteered to take the field once more, they reluctantly gave him an assignment. This was destined to prove the most distinguished of all his exploits. Starting from Leh on July 15, 1874, he crossed the frontier disguised as a lama, with three servants. If you remember your *Kim*, you will already know that the garb of a lama is particularly useful for surveying work that has to be done in secret. The counting of the beads on a rosary is an ideal aid to making measurements. Furthermore, the Buddhist prayer wheel comes in handy for concealing compasses, notebooks, etc. On this journey, the task of mensuration of every observation that Nain Singh took had to be accomplished surreptitiously. He did his job with complete and incredible success. He went the whole length of Tibet to Lhasa by the great northern route. He traveled parallel to the Brahmaputra River as far as Tengri Nor and thence trekked south to the capital. There the danger of discovery became acute. He was afraid that if he were exposed, his notes might be confiscated. So he sent them home in the hands of his assistants by way of Ladakh. It would have been safer for him to have gone with them. But the urge to expand his work was too much for his sense of peril. Though liable to be unmasked at any moment and

imprisoned, if not beheaded, he undertook a new survey south. Going by way of the eastern confines of
Bhutan, he reached Assam.

All through the winter there had been great anxiety
about him at headquarters. He had arrived in Lhasa
November 18, 1874. For months nothing was heard of
him. He didn't turn up until March, 1875. But when he
did, he marched in with an achievement to his credit that
made him the admiration of the scientific world. His
work in Tibet was complete. He had lifted the veil
from that lama-ridden land of mystery. He had made
known the customs of its people and of the surrounding countries. On his last journey, though having to
work in secret as I've said, he had made a route traverse
of 1,319 miles over ground that previously was quite
unexplored. He had checked up his map by 276 sextant shots and 497 hypsometrical observations. He had
traced the great river of Tibet and identified it as the
northern reaches of the Brahmaputra. He had discovered a vast new range. He had added lakes of
enormous size to the map. In addition to this, he
had information about the history, politics, habits and
climates of all those semi-dependent Asiatic states.

For all this, the gallant Nain Singh had wrecked his
health. He was still less than fifty years old, but expo-
sure and hard work had undermined his constitution and
impaired his eyesight. The government was not ungrateful. The sahibs raised Nain Singh to the dignity

of a Commander of the Indian empire. What was still more to the purpose, they gave him an entire village with revenues amounting to a thousand rupees a year, which to him meant not alone comfort, but luxury. Not only all Asia, but the scientific circles of Europe rang with his exploits. The Geographical Society of Paris gave him a gold watch. He was awarded the rare honor of the Royal Geographical Society's medal as "a man who has added a greater amount of positive knowledge to the map of Asia than any individual of our time." The most noble the Marquess of Salisbury, celebrated as "the Master of Flouts and Jeers," wrote a glowing tribute of praise to the Pandit. And so we will leave Nain Singh, hoping that he had enough health left to get some enjoyment out of his rewards.

His cousin (or nephew) and pupil had already proved himself a credit to his master. Kishen Singh's first journey was made in 1869. He accomplished it with ease and dispatch—a route traverse up the Karnali from Kathai Gat by way of Khojarnath to Rakas Tal. These names perhaps don't mean much to us today. But they meant a great deal to the heads of the Great Trigonometrical Survey, to say nothing of the General Staff of the Indian Army. At Rakas Tal the explorer was not far from the home of the Singh family at Milam, near Kumaon. His trip apparently had been without any particular excitement or incident. But it was accomplished with such nerve and proficiency that Montgomerie marked down Kishen Singh as a man to be set aside for the most important jobs.

His first really tough assignment came in 1871. On this expedition he ran into excitement almost from the start. He left Kumaon accompanied by a young Tibetan and three other assistants. Ostensibly, they were traders; actually, they were all trained surveyors. They made a route survey all the way from Shigatse to the great lake known as Tengri-Nor, lying seventy miles north of Lhasa. Turning south, they ran into a band of sixty armed and well-mounted robbers. The bandits rode them down and overwhelmed the travelers with ease. But in the mêlée, Kishen Singh surreptitiously thrust his notes into the hands of his assistants, who concealed them under their robes. The assistants made a getaway and arrived safely home with the notes. Kishen Singh was captured and stripped of everything that he owned except his instruments, in which the bandits could see no value. They released him and he made his way to Lhasa. There he pawned his instruments for enough money to get him to Gartok. He returned home penniless, but his observations proved to be worth many times the cost of his equipment. Montgomerie wrote: "He has elucidated the geography of an area of about 12,000 square miles, thoroughly explored one northern tributary of the Upper Brahmaputra and given us some idea as to how far back the northern watershed of this great river lies."

When he accompanied Sir Douglas Forsyth to Yarkand in 1873, as we have observed, Kishen Singh was detailed with The Munshi to make a route traverse to the Pamirs. But his most valuable work in that year was done on the return voyage, which he made alone. Starting from Yarkand he accomplished a remarkable survey of the route to Karghalik, now known as Yehcheng. Then he went by way of Khotan (now Hotien) almost clear across the province that today is called Sinkiang to Polur. There he explored the headwaters of the Keriya (Yutien) River all the way to Tankse on the shores of the Pangkong Lake in the province of Ladakh.

This journey was interesting in several respects. In the first place, it added a huge area to the government's maps. But it also served to prove the accuracy of the traverse method invented and adopted by Montgomerie. The position of Khotan had at last been accurately plotted and all previous mistakes corrected. And it is significant that Sir Henry Trotter had such confidence in this Pandit that he accepted Kishen Singh's "traverse value" for the longitude of Yarkand rather than the one obtained by chronometric differences or lunar zenith distance. (In 1914 the eminent Sir Filippo de Filippi, equipped with the last word in modern instrumentation, checked up these observations that had been made forty years earlier. And he found the result given with the aid of radio varied from that of Kishen Singh by only nine seconds.)

On the 24th of April, 1878, Kishen Singh left Darjeeling on what has been described as "that long persevering adventure which set the seal on his labors and won him applause and honor throughout the geographical world." Montgomerie has left it on record that "as he might very possibly strike one of the great routes to China and be tempted to find his way to the coast, I particularly directed him to avoid China." He was instructed to cut through Tibet and find the best route to Mongolia. His equipment consisted of a nine-inch sextant, a Tibetan tea bowl to serve as a mercury trough, a prismatic compass, a pocket compass, a rosary, a Buddhist prayer wheel, an aneroid barometer and several boiling point thermometers to check up altitude observations. He also was provided with ample funds.

Going by way of Chumbi and Phari Jong, the route last traveled by Manning in 1811, he reached Lhasa in September, 1878. His rôle was that of a merchant. In Lhasa he used his funds to buy merchandise and tried to find a caravan northbound. He had no luck and was detained in the capital an entire year. He put in his time making a fresh and more complete survey of the Potala, the lamas' Vatican. Almost as interesting was his opportunity to see the New Year festivals held in mid-February, at which all the gods and goddesses are supposed to be present. He also improved the hours by studying Mongolian and the sacred books of Tibet.

It was not until September, 1879, that he was able to start north with a caravan of about 100 souls, mostly Mongolians with their wives. They were armed with spears, matchlocks and swords. We get an idea of the hazards of the trek from the fact that four guards were posted on sentry duty every night. From the beginning of this trip, moreover, Kishen Singh had a difficult problem to meet. Mongolians in one respect are like our own Western cowpunchers. They look down upon all people who walk. They see no reason why a man should trudge instead of riding ahorseback, unless he is a slave or a dub who can't stay in the saddle. So Kishen Singh was obliged to mount a pony to "save face." Of course, as we have seen, an explorer who has to do his surveying under cover prefers to walk because he needs to count his paces. Kishen Singh met the difficulty by training himself to count the steps of the near forefoot of his horse. And even today his accuracy is the admiration of all the modern surveyors who have followed him and checked his measurements.

Coming to the Chang-tang plain, he found the terrain changing from an agricultural to a pastoral region. There he saw the huge grazing grounds that nurtured the famous brood mares of the Dalai Lama. At the great monastery of Shiabdan the party took a brief rest. Crossing the Lani Lee Pass at an altitude of 15,750 feet, they found themselves in the territory of the Khirgiz nomads. Through the Dangla range the easiest pass they could find was no less than 16,400 feet high and Kishen Singh had cause to be grateful that he had been born near a hill country.

He then crossed the upper sources of the great Mekong River, which flows all the way through Central Asia to Cambodia and empties into the South China Sea near Saigon. Climbing the Angirtakshia range—a continuation of the K'un Lun—he descended into the vast salt plains of Tsaidam. Thinking there was nothing more to fear, the caravan dispersed, the Mongolians departing in a body to their own destination. Kishen Singh and the others rested a few days at a place called Thingkali, then continued in the direction of Sachow.

They had all calculated wrong. Near Chiamogolok they were attacked by a troop of 200 mounted robbers. There was a sharp, fierce, hand-to-hand scrap. The bandits were driven off, but not before they had a chance to seize most of the merchandise and the pack animals on which it was laden. Fortunately, however, Kishen Singh rescued his precious instruments and notes.

He pressed on to Lob Nor and the Gobi, reaching Hoiduthara in December, 1879. Here he and his companions were destitute but for a small amount of merchandise which they could not sell there profitably. So they took jobs with a Tibetan who had prospered in those regions. Kishen Singh hired out as a yak driver.

Now the yak is a slow-moving animal that wanders frequently from the path. Nevertheless the Pandit contrived to make his clandestine measurements so accurately that a later explorer, who checked up his maps with a measuring wheel, found few mistakes.

By the end of March, 1880, he had penetrated as far north as Yembi. There he stopped among the Mongolian nomads for three months, disposing of his remnants of merchandise. Taking stock of his possessions, he counted 200 rupees and a herd of mares and colts. But another calamity awaited him. His servant, learning that he proposed to proceed into the country of the Mohammedans, objected. He not only objected, he deserted, taking with him all the money and most of the horseflesh. It was a body blow. Kishen Singh and one companion were now left absolutely penniless. They went into service again, tending ponies and goats.

It was not until January, 1881, that Kishen Singh found a party of traders leaving Yembi for the south. He had now been away almost three years. But many more hardships and vicissitudes were ahead of him. On this leg of his journey he crossed the Altyn Tagh at a height of 14,000 feet, descending into the plains of Kansu at Tung Hwan Hsien. Here he was lucky enough to find another party of traders, but not lucky enough to stay with them. He had aroused the suspicion of the Chinese authorities that he and his sole remaining companion were spies. He was almost across

the border of the province when he was overtaken by
the police. They hauled him back, him and his assistant, and kept them prisoners for seven months.

There they might have died but for the intervention
of an influential lama whom Kishen Singh had met on
the road at Saithang. In August, 1881, this lama procured their release and took them on as servants. Unfortunately they were obliged to accompany the holy
man back across the K'un Lun to Hoiduthara. There
they received word that the servant who had stolen
all the money and horses was in the neighborhood. But
the information did them no good. The lama's travels
took them to the Thuden Gomba monastery in the
valley of the Dichu, a tributary of the Yangtze. And
they had to wait two months before they received the
pay for their labors from the reverend gentlemen.

Such bad luck couldn't last forever, though still more
was ahead. At the end of the two months' delay at the
monastery, Kishen Singh and his mate obtained employment with a merchant on his way to Darchendo. They
crossed the Ja-chu range at 10,500 feet to Kanzego,
where they saw one of the most famous monasteries in
Asia. They pressed on, finally reaching Ta-tsien-lu in
China.

It was a heroic achievement. Kishen Singh's feelings were comparable to those of a shipwrecked mariner
making a landfall after months of tossing about in an
open boat. For it so happened that he had a letter to

the Catholic Vicar Apostolic of that province. The distinguished prelate turned out to be not only sympathetic and hospitable, but trusting. He listened, fascinated, to the tale of the Pandit's wanderings. The fact that the man from Milam, near Kumaon, was not a Christian made not the slightest difference. His lordship entertained the travelers, fed them well, enabled them to get a good rest and sent them on their way with the loan of a small sum of money.

Meanwhile at home, Montgomerie and the other chiefs of the survey were worrying and grieving over the possible fate of their ace explorer, the best man in the service since the retirement of Nain Singh. For years now they had received no word from him. They had sent agents out to seek information. But only the most ominous rumors had come back. According to the worst of these, bandits had captured Kishen Singh and chopped off his legs. It was fortunate for him, at this juncture, that he did not know his only son had died in his absence.

He left Ta-tsien-lu and reached Batang in March, 1882. So doing, he added still more to the knowledge of the scientific world. He crossed a region of contiguous, parallel rivers in eastern Tibet, a region until then totally unexplored.

When he arrived at a place called Sama he had reason to believe that he was practically home, for he was only 30 miles from British territory. But all his hopes were dashed to the ground. He learned that that 30-mile strip to the British border was the most dangerous in Asia. Only a few months previously two French missionaries had been murdered there. So in May, 1882, he struck north again. His funds were again exhausted. So he marched from village to village. To support himself and his companion he recited passages from the sacred books of the Tibetans until he had accumulated the noble sum of 20 rupees. Once again he was arrested and held on suspicion. His familiarity with those sacred books eventually led to his release.

This time he decided that he had done enough exploring. He made his way to Lhasa and, checking up on the surveys he had made on the first leg of his journey, reached Darjeeling on November 12, 1882. He had been away four and a half years.

I'll wager we should all like to have been present when Kishen Singh and his one remaining faithful companion walked into the office of Montgomerie Sahib. We can imagine the joy of Montgomerie, the pride with which he presented the returned wanderer to his chief. It was about as triumphant a re-entry as heroes ever made.

And as well earned a triumph. When the authorities had time to study his reports they were as amazed as they were delighted. It turned out that Kishen Singh's traverse to the western confines of Kansu joined up, to a nicety of minutes and seconds, with the work of the

great Russian Colonel Prjevalsky and of Count Széche-
nyi. To quote J. N. L. Baker: "Not only was a vast
area of entirely unknown country crossed by the Pandit, but he found time to collect an amazingly complete
amount of general information, such as temperatures,
wind directions, population figures and details about
trade. In a single journey he linked areas where the
British were active to those reached by the Russians,
while his visit to Ta-tsien-lu connected up Indian and
Chinese route traverses, and he was able to accomplish
the task in which Gill and others had failed. It was a
magnificent end to the career of a great explorer."

His rewards, to our way of thinking, don't seem so
magnificent. But Kishen Singh appears to have been
satisfied. He was given the title of Rai Sahadur and a
village with annual revenues of 1,856 rupees. The
Geographical Society of Italy awarded him a first-class
medal, an honor which he shares with the Duke of the
Abruzzi and few others in history. Like Nain Singh,
he had accomplished his gallant and intelligent work at
the cost of his health. And he returned to his home to
find himself childless.

As you may have discerned, not all the Pandits were
Hindus and of the latter not all were Botias like the
Singhs. Some of them were Babus of the same type as
the one in Kipling's *Kim*. For instance, there was Hari
Ram, a Bengali as brave as any Sikh or Ghurka. This
picturesque fellow was the first man, colored or white,

to tackle Mt. Everest. As far back as 1868 he accepted the challenge of that forbidding peak. He penetrated the country north of the mountain as far as Tingri Maidan and there ran afoul of Tibetan religious beliefs, according to which any attempt to scale those heights is still sacrilege. (They look upon the recent earthquakes and the destruction of Quetta as a punishment sent by the gods against the British Raj for permitting the exploits of Noel, Somervell and, finally, Lord Clydesdale. I wonder whether the noble marquess thought of his humble Babu predecessor when he flew across that towering, snow-clad rock?) The Tibetan authorities intercepted Hari Ram and sent him back home with a flea in his ear and an invitation not to come back.

But that didn't feaze Hari Ram. He tried it again in 1871. This time he went from Darjeeling to Shigatse. Thence he traversed the Tingri Maidan once more and, eluding the authorities, crossed the axis of the great range 60 miles west of Everest by the Bhotia defile. From there he sneaked his way to Katmandu. But he wasn't content with that. He traced the course of the Sun Kosi for more than eighty miles. In type it doesn't look like much, but it was a back-breaking job. Having done it, he called it a day. He had been gone the better part of two years. He returned by way of Darjeeling and rested up for a while. But Mt. Everest was in his blood. He continued to devote his strength, health and life to that tantalizing range. He made several heroic and invaluable explorations, culminating in the discovery of a brand-new pass twenty miles west of Everest itself.

To appreciate what he achieved, let us see what the Sahibs had to say about this intrepid Babu. Major Kenneth Mason wrote: "This exploration was particularly valuable, for it gave a rough indication of the Indo-Tibetan watershed and proved that it lay north of the great peaks. A complete circuit of the Mt. Everest group was made and much information gained of the country from various sources. But the explorer was so hemmed in by mountains that he was never sure that he viewed the giant peak itself."

The Mohammedan Pandits never achieved as much celebrity among geographers as did their Hindu confreres. They did much noble work, as valuable, in the last analysis, as that of the others. It is less known because the districts they surveyed were not wrapped in so much mystery nor so interesting and difficult. We touched upon the story of The Munshi who disappeared from the party that accompanied Sir Douglas Forsyth. The Mirza, whom I have also mentioned, was for a while tutor to the sons of Shere Ali, Amir of Afghanistan. He perished on his last expedition, murdered in his sleep by his guides. The Mullah, whose name was Ata Mohammed, was a well-educated native of Peshawar. He was versed in Persian and Arabic, which helped him to do good work for the British Raj along the valley of the Indus. The Havildar distinguished himself principally by a route traverse from Kabul to Faizabad.

But the tale of these gallant native explorers ends on a note of real pathos. In 1880 the geographers still doubted that the Tsampo, the Great River of Tibet, was really the Upper Brahmaputra. The chiefs of the Survey didn't share those doubts, but they were determined to establish the identity of the rivers beyond armchair skepticism. So Captain Harmon, who had succeeded Montgomerie, now a Major, trained a Chinese lama in the art of the sextant and compass. The captain devised an ingenious plan for the lama to send back his information. He was to follow up the course of the river, to inscribe his information on logs and throw them into the stream which would carry them down to a point where servants of the Survey could pick them up. Obviously, if logs thrown into the Tsampo appeared on the surface of the Brahmaputra, there could be no more doubt of the identity of the two rivers. A humble fellow named Kinthup, a native of Sikkim, was assigned to accompany the lama.

The distinguished Sir Thomas Holdich observes: "If they had had my experience with lamas they never would have trusted one of them." For two years the agents of the Survey kept a watch on the Brahmaputra for those marked logs. Never a log showed up, no lama, no report whatsoever. This effort was given up as one of the unfortunate failures of the service. But one day, four years later, a worn, ragged Kinthup appeared at headquarters. He related an extraordinary tale.

The lama and Kinthup stuck to the job until they reached the point where the Brahmaputra changes its course abruptly from northeast to southeast. A few miles beyond that the reverend gentleman blandly informed poor Kinthup that he had been sold in slavery to a Tibetan official described as the Jongpen. This was on the 24th of May, 1881. In March, 1882, Kinthup escaped from his master and ran to a small monastery at Marpung. But the Jongpen was on his heels and appeared at the gate of the convent to claim his slave. The abbot bought Kinthup from his owner and the man from Sikkim worked for him faithfully. But evidently he never for an instant forgot the mission on which the Be-ritish Sahibs had sent him. After a few months, Kinthup asked leave to go on a pilgrimage to Lhasa. It was granted and Kinthup walked to the Holy City by way of Tsari. When he reached the Tsampo he started throwing logs into its current. Unfortunately, by this time Captain Harmon had died, the mission had been forgotten and the faithful Kinthup's logs floated down unnoticed.

It was in 1884 that a strange, travel-worn, ragged native appeared at the headquarters of the Survey. This happened two years after the death of Captain

Harmon, four years after he had sent that Chinese lama to identify the Tsampo River. At first nobody knew who the deuce the intruder was. He had difficulty in explaining. Finally they looked up the records and verified the fact that the late Captain Harmon had dispatched a lama on that secret mission with a native from Sikkim as his assistant. The stranger contrived to make the Sahibs understand that he was the man from Sikkim. In short, it was poor old Kinthup.

He told his story at length. Pathetically he related the long, painstaking labors he had undergone to send those logs down the Tsampo. Also he described in detail all the places he had passed down the great river to a point within sixty miles of the plains of India. The circumstantial evidence was conclusive that the Tsampo and the Brahmaputra were one. His story stood up under long hours of cross-examination. In the end the Survey chiefs accepted Kinthup as an amazingly faithful, honest and accurate fellow. They took care of him, gave him a chance to rest his tired bones and awarded him due credit. What was more, they published the results of his long travels.

The geographers of Europe, on the other hand, snorted. The men on the spot, the men who knew the terrain, the men best qualified to judge—they believed Kinthup. But the men who had never seen Asia said: "Buncombe! Just another lying native." It is a quaint and sometimes absurd condition that the fellow who has done the work, sweated, suffered, trudged and starved and climbed and shivered, can get no credit for what he has achieved until it is passed on by a lot of old boys in stuffed armchairs.

Thirty years elapse. Captain Moorshead and Captain Bailey are sent to survey the basin of the Dibang. They cross over and map the Tsampo for 380 miles. So doing they prove beyond all dispute that the Tsampo is the Brahmaputra. I trust old Kinthup was alive to hear the news.

VI

A VICTORIAN GENTLEWOMAN

VI

A VICTORIAN GENTLEWOMAN

LATE of an afternoon in 1868, Mr. George Kingsley wandered into the day nursery of his suburban home at Highgate. The distinguished traveler beamed fondly as he watched his lively six-year-old daughter playing a game of her own invention. But when he heard the obbligato of words that came through her innocent lips, his hair stood on end. Striding forward, he plucked her from the floor and, with his right arm around her little tummy, carried her, struggling, squealing, and—shades of Queen Victoria!—blaspheming down the stairs. He flung open the door of the drawing-room where Mrs. Kingsley sat demurely making lace and thundered with more indignation than grammar:

"Madam! Where does this child get its language from? Certainly not from me!"

In her amazement Mrs. Kingsley dropped her tatting. Then, recovering her composure, she retorted:

"I trust, Mr. Kingsley, you do not suggest she has it from me?"

The question remained unsolved. For that we have the word of the young lady herself in later years. The damsel whose speech so shocked her father—a man accustomed to hearing profanity in several languages and dialects—had been christened Mary Henrietta Kingsley. We can readily imagine the gossip she provoked among the good neighbors of Highgate. Pious Victorian matrons and spinsters would shake their heads as her treble voice was heard over the garden wall joyously shrieking forbidden words. "That child will come to no good end," they would prophesy.

As it happens, they were wrong. It is true that to the day of her death she never quite lost her predilection for racy, unconventional diction. But the hoyden who outraged delicate ears in Suburbia grew up to become one of the most distinguished and valuable of Her Majesty's subjects. You don't hear much about her now. But Mary Kingsley must unquestionably be numbered among the great Englishwomen. Her name belongs in the same noble category as that of Florence Nightingale and Gertrude Bell. Of all people, men or women, who have walked "the inviolate earth for newness' sake," none was more gallant, more unselfish, more modest than this daughter of George Kingsley. And she was a person of sparkling humor to boot, as well as an invincible fighter for justice and humane procedure, which her story will show.

As we have observed, she came of a celebrated family. Her uncle Charles was the author of *Hypatia*, *Hereward the Wake*, *Westward Ho!* and that saccharine monument of Victorian bromidity, *Water*

Babies. Her uncle Henry was also a novelist of distinction. (I must confess I have not read any of his works nor encountered anybody else who has. Nevertheless, he was considered seriously by such critics as George Saintsbury.) Her father, George, was a man of passionate curiosity, a trait she inherited. He was a traveler, scientist, writer, adventurer. It has been said that of the three Kingsley brothers, Charles was the most famous, Henry the most literary, George the most Kingsley. A small but square-shouldered fellow, he was pugnacious and of volcanic temper. Also a gentleman of infinite charm, dry humor, brilliant wit and a fascinating conversationalist. Eyes gleaming in a sunburnt, weather-beaten face, he could talk absorbingly about anything from philosophy to fishing. For years at a time his family would see nothing of him, for he was continually wandering about the earth, attached to this expedition or the other. He accompanied the Earl of Pembroke on an exploration of the South Seas, he walked and paddled over large stretches of Canada and other remote, untrammeled regions.

From the time she was able to listen and talk, Mary adored him. Most of her pranks were efforts to emulate him or suggested by conversation that she had overheard. One of his talks inspired her with an interest in military engineering. She got hold of his store of gunpowder and made a mine in the back garden. This was on a beautiful spring day and the family wash, including sheets and blankets, was hung out on the line to dry. Mary had ingeniously driven her main tunnel under a large butt of liquid manure. It must have been a powerful and well-devised mine because when she sprang it she blew that entire butt of manure twelve feet high all over the sheets, blankets and lacy Victorian undergarments.

At an age when normal little girls were playing with dolls or rabbits, Mary's favorite pets were fighting cocks. As she grew older her preferred reading was a periodical called *The English Mechanic*. She became the "handy man" around the house and could be depended upon for odd jobs of repairing and carpentering. For Uncle Charles's *Water Babies* she had no use whatever. The books she devoured in secret were such as Professor Norman Lockyear's *Solar Physics*, which she hid in her closet for weeks while her father was looking for it all over the house in order to lend the volume to a friend.

In 1884, when Mary was 22, her parents moved to Cambridge. There she eagerly seized the opportunity to study mathematics and other branches of the exact sciences. Remember, this was a day when such pursuits were considered most unwomanly. Spectacular undergraduate riots were provoked both at Cambridge and Oxford over the proposal to admit women to the universities. But Mary Kingsley's "unfeminine" devotion to science never weakened the devotion with which she nursed her mother through four successive years of illness. George Kingsley died in his sleep in 1892; his wife followed him six weeks later.

Thus at the age of thirty, Mary Kingsley was left alone in the world, bereft of the one person on whom her affections and admiration had been concentrated. She had no personal ambitions. Her scientific curiosity was keener than ever, but it had not as yet become directed towards the field in which she was destined to attain such authority and eminence. When she sailed for West Africa nothing was further from her mind than being an explorer and adding to the world's fund of geographical knowledge. And, as she put it herself, "it was no desire to get killed and eaten that made me go and associate with the tribes having the worst reputation for cannibalism and human sacrifice." Her motive was at once more simple and more complex. She wanted to gather more facts to complete her father's book. George Kingsley had collected all the necessary data on early religion and law except those about the African tribes. "All the authorities were agreed that in West Africa they were at their wildest and worst." So she sailed from Liverpool in August, 1893.

Her friends were most encouraging. "Oh, you can't possibly go there," they said. "That's where Sierra Leone is, the White Man's Grave, you know." And her medical acquaintances reassured her with the remark: "Deadliest spot on earth." The textbook of native dialects was just as heartening. The principal phrases in it were such as: "Help, I am drowning," or "Why has not this man been buried?" And she remarked with a Kingsley-like amusement the matter-of-fact manner in which the agents of the steamship company said: "We don't issue return tickets on the West African lines, Miss."

The warnings she received seemed only to whet Mary Kingsley's humor. On the voyage she observed that the principal topics of table talk were the various diseases prevalent in the region to which she was going. Airy chatter about kraw-kraw, Portuguese itch, guinea worm, ulcers, smallpox. Or else a trader would say to the captain: "Do you remember Jones? I brought him out from the bush when he died." However the conversation started, it would invariably wind up with the subject of death. "Have you brought any dress clothes? You'll need them for funerals." Or as another piece of polite advice: "You ought to get some introduction to the Wesleyans [Methodists]." "Why?" "Oh, they are the only people on the coast who have a hearse with feathers."

Next in order as a polite dinner topic came insects. "One of the worst things you can do in West Africa," she wrote home, "is to take any notice of an insect. If you see a thing that looks like a cross between a flying lobster and a figure of Abraxas, do not pay the least attention. Keep quiet and hope it will go away.

That's your best chance, for you have none in a stand-up fight with a good, thorough-going African insect. . . . It is best to leave insects alone. Of course, you can't ignore driver ants. But the same principle, reversed, is best for them—go away yourself."

It was characteristic of Mary Kingsley that she made the voyage by cargo boat rather than by a luxurious passenger liner. She did it deliberately and wisely. So doing, she learned a lot about the land of her destination, its customs and inhabitants before she even landed there. Moreover by the time she arrived she knew the entire literature of buccaneering and the history of the West Coast. She read the chronicles of Azurara, and the great figure of Prince Henry the Navigator became as familiar to her as though he were a contemporary acquaintance.

She made friends with officers, crew and with the traders who were her fellow passengers. Thus early in her career she acquired a profound respect and admiration for them, and a contempt for the people who used to run them down. For their part, these hard-bitten, hard-drinking, hard-working fellows did not quite know what to make of this pale, gaunt young woman in somber, dowdy clothing. She might have passed for a missionary, and at first they decided that she was collecting evidence for the Women's World Temperance Movement. Stephen Gwynn wrote: "When I went to Africa I was warned by brother officers never to be too friendly with the traders. Official and missionary alike looked askance at them. To show too much interest in them was to jeopardize one's career and lower one's caste." With this kind of prejudice Mary Kingsley had no patience. She did not care a whoop what missionaries or government bureaucrats thought. She became the trader's foremost champion. "The so-called palm-oil ruffian," she wrote, "is usually a man who goes to his death with a joke in his teeth. It is that type of man who has made and saved our West African possessions for England through a period when the government people were ready to abandon them." As a matter of actual fact, Downing Street had been about to evacuate the territory. A man-o'-war was sent out to take all British subjects away. But the traders refused to be taken. They hung on and preserved the Gold Coast for the Union Jack. They got no thanks for it until Mary Kingsley came to their defense. Ironically, it was left for a highly educated, highly respectable young spinster of the English upper middle classes to discern the pluck and guts behind the rough speech and hard cynicism of these "dusty foreloopers."

She genuinely liked them. She liked, not only their courage, but their honesty and keen, robust point of view. She learned from them and enjoyed it. In private intercourse her speech became interlarded with the argot of the West Coast, to the frequent horror of her stay-at-home friends.

"ON ONE OF MY PADDLINGS A 'MIGHTY SILURIAN' ENDEAVORED TO IMPROVE OUR ACQUAINTANCE"

She also made friends with the skipper, Captain Murray, and made a point of traveling on his ship each time she went to Africa. From him she learned seamanship and became proud of her ability as a pilot. She became so capable that eventually she piloted vessels across the formidable Forçados bar and up the creeks. "I would rather take a 200-ton vessel up a creek than write any book," she was wont to say.

By the time she arrived at Freetown Harbour on her first voyage, she wrote, "I knew the place so well that I might have known it all my life. I recognized as though I had been born there the mountains whose rumbling had caused Pedro do Ceuta to call it Sierra Leone when he discovered it in 1462."

Her first visit was a short one, from August to January. Starting from the Portuguese settlement of San Paul de Loanda, she went up through the Congo Free State into the Congo Français, finishing her journey in British territory at old Calabar.

Incidentally she made the acquaintance of Mary Slessor, the famous missionary of Calabar, "whose tact and courage had given her a unique position of authority among the inhabitants." Mary Slessor's intimate knowledge of native life and customs were of invaluable help to Mary Kingsley, as she acknowledged. "This very wonderful lady has been 18 years in Calabar, for the last six or seven years living entirely by herself, so far as white folks go, in a clearing in the forest. A rare

[149]

person, no wonder she stands alone."

From her first trip, Mary Kingsley brought back so many valuable specimens that the British Museum equipped her with an official collector's outfit for her next journey. On this occasion she visited Sierra Leone and the Gold Coast and spent several months on the Oil Rivers. But she passed most of her time in the French Congo where there had been less attempt to interfere with native institutions such as cannibalism and old religious customs. She settled down to a serious study of the Bubis. As she said: "No one but Dr. Baumann and myself has ever worked on them." She gathered a fund of new material about that interesting people which proved a revelation to scholars.

For a few weeks she stayed at Government House on the invitation of Sir Claude MacDonald, the same Sir Claude MacDonald who later was to organize the historic defense of Peking during the Boxer rebellion. Miss Kingsley did not care particularly for life in government circles: it could teach her nothing. But it produced one lively and characteristic anecdote. During the absence of the Governor upcountry, one of his assistants was reported seriously ill. "Send him up to Government House," said Lady MacDonald; "we'll nurse him." The man's illness puzzled the Governor's lady. Mary Kingsley studied him for a while, then said: "Do you know what's the matter with that young man? D.T.'s the matter, my girl." They nursed him through it just the same.

She put in her spare time "puddling about," as she called it, in a canoe through miles of rotting mud fringed by walls of mango swamp. That led to her first encounter with a crocodile. She went unarmed everywhere.

"On one of my puddlings a 'mighty Silurian' chose to get his front paws over the stern of my canoe and endeavored to improve our acquaintance. I had to retire to the bows to keep the balance right. (It is no use adding because I was frightened, for this miserably understates the case.) I fetched him a clip on the snout with the paddle, whereupon he withdrew. I quickly paddled into the very middle of the lagoon, hoping the water was too deep there for him or any of his friends to repeat the performance."

She had a revolver, but when she reached Gabun in May, 1895, she was informed that she would have to pay 15 francs for a license. So she left the weapon at the customs house, saying: "I never considered it lady-like to go about shooting things with a gun." By the same token she dressed for the bush pretty much as she had dressed in Cambridge: stout boots, skirts and everything. On one occasion, she relates, her skirts saved her from severe injury when, if she had been wearing the breeches of the modern woman, she would have broken her back. She fell into a pit that had been dug for a leopard trap. The skirt cushioned her fall and she emerged with only a few bruises.

Mary Kingsley "bore a charmed life," as the saying goes. Perhaps it was the utter sang-froid with which she went into the most dangerous, cannibal, and wild beast-infested jungles. One night in camp she was aroused by a terrific fight between a leopard and a couple of native dogs. The leopard was winning in a hurry. Mary fired a couple of native stools at the brute, which gave the dogs a chance to run. The leopard thereupon turned his attention to the lady. Having no more stools to throw, she hurled an earthenware water cooler at him. This caught him square in the head and burst, at which Mister Leopard spat, yowled and "went for bush one time."

That wasn't her only encounter with the Big Cats. One day her noon siesta was disturbed by the screeching of one that had been caught in a native trap. The animal was in misery and voiced its torture to the heavens. The blacks slumbered untroubled. Mary Kingsley couldn't stand it. She arose from her cot and, thinking she was unobserved, manipulated the bars of the trap and freed the brute. Instead of leaping off to enjoy his liberty, the leopard crawled out and took a good look at the strange, be-skirted, two-legged being who stood there. It was not quite sure whether or not to blame the Thing in skirts for its pain. It stalked up, paw by paw and sniffed at her clothes. Mary was trembling inwardly, knowing that to shriek for help would mean a quick, powerful leap of the great cat with its steely claws scratching the life out of her. She looked at it and, in the accents of Cambridge, exclaimed scornfully but quietly: "Go home, you fool!" The beast stopped in its tracks, turned tail and slunk off on silent pads.

Miss Kingsley thought she was unobserved, but she was wrong. She subsequently learned that a Fan, one of the wildest, deadliest cannibal tribes, had been watching the whole performance. (She was in the heart of the Fan country at the time, utterly without military escort, as always, and at the mercy of their anthropophagous humors.) But the spy was so impressed by what he had seen that he went back to his village and reported it with superstitious elaboration. "The White Woman speaks, and the jungle does her bidding." It was a great stroke of luck for her—luck and the fruits of her indomitable courage. From that time she became an object of veneration in those parts. The bloodthirsty Fans thereafter looked upon her as a goddess, and she could go weaponless alone through regions where a detachment of well-armed French soldiery might be massacred. Such was the mettle of this mid-Victorian spinster. But in her letters and narratives she related the episode as a funny story.

Mary Kingsley returned to England late in 1895 and began her literary career. She immediately demonstrated a rare gift for putting her vivid humanity on

[153]

paper. Added to her keen, original humor was a powerful capacity for descriptive writing. Her word pictures of scenes on the African rivers are still quotable as beautiful examples of prose painting unsurpassed if not unequaled by any other writers.

Her book, *Travels in West Africa*, was a huge success, despite the best efforts of her publisher to ruin it. Her style was absolutely unconventional, a reflection of her personality. For all the growing influence of Rudyard Kipling on English letters, London publishers were still under the obsolete thrall of Addison and Steele. So she was persuaded to allow her manuscript to be revised by a hack pundit. To this she had consented because she was not always sure of her grammar and punctuation. But she soon perceived that the hack editor was taking all the vitality out of her book, to the point of actually changing her meaning. He was turning her vivid, original phrases into dry, academic stuff. So she found herself continually at loggerheads with her literary advisers. They wanted her to be refined, she insisted upon being original. The learned littérateur toned her stuff down so far that at several points he made it positively inaccurate. That was too much for her. She kicked and won.

The success of her book rendered her in great demand as a speaker and contributor to magazines. She also wrote papers for the scientific journals and delivered lectures before geographical societies which won their instant respect. At the same time she began to be involved in a political squabble. West Africa was being parceled out among the nations of Europe. There were two causes nearest to Mary Kingsley's heart. One was frankly imperialistic. She wanted England to appreciate the opportunity in West Africa and to realize how valuable it could be to the Empire. She wanted her country to establish a British trade belt clear across Africa, from the Atlantic coast to the shore of the Indian Ocean. The other cause was justice for the natives. To govern Africa wisely, she claimed, you must understand the native mind. European rule must be based on justice. It is useless to attempt to transform negroes into black imitations of suburban Englishmen. It is not merely useless, but wrong, to attempt to prevent polygamy in Africa. In many cases such attempts are contrary to natural justice, and are always a disturbance of age-old customs. For one thing, African women insist upon polygamy for the simple reason that the more wives a man has the less work there is for each one!

With such arguments, naturally, Mary Kingsley ran afoul, not only of government officials who had never seen Africa, but of the missionaries. For the latter, as a class, she had no respect, though she had great admiration for certain individuals and was a close friend of a few, including one Wesleyan (Methodist). "Alas!" she wrote, "none of the missions save the Roman Catholic teach the thing most important for natives to learn —improved methods of agriculture and plantation." Again, she declared: "For reasons of my own I am unsympathetic with Christian missions." Few of them, she explained, either understood or tried to understand the native. They never could realize that, to an African, religion has nothing whatever to do with conduct. "They do not hold that devotion to religion constitutes virtue." They practice their religion—fetish—as a necessity, to propitiate evil spirits. But in their eyes the most virtuous person is he who is least mixed up in religious affairs. Such, said Mary Kingsley, are some of the facts that Europeans need to study and appreciate when they undertake to rule Africa.

The class among whom she found the most comfort in her polemics, strangely enough, was that of the business men. With the traders she was entirely in sympathy. Trade associations, exporters and importers, realized that here was one woman who spoke their language and knew what she was talking about. And when Joseph Chamberlain, himself a retired millionaire industrialist, came to rule over John Bull's colonial policies, she found an understanding listener right in the innermost circles of the government.

Like most travelers, Mary Kingsley found life at home excruciatingly tame. She enjoyed the success of her books and lectures principally because it provided her with the necessary funds for further travels. Also, it created an audience for the ideas in which she believed so passionately. For all the humor with which she described her encounters, she took politics tragically. Like most amateurs in that domain, she was impatient and wanted her reforms pushed through then and there.

She had another characteristic in common with the exploring fraternity—the hazards of life in civilized regions frightened her. She was terrified of hansom cabs and never rode in one, she who boasted of her ability to pilot a schooner over a dangerous bar. She detested bicycles and was timidly unhappy on top of a bus—this at a time when nobody dreamed of a motor bus. Furthermore, the amenities of polite society in Victorian England appalled her. Witness a letter she wrote to Stephen Gwynn, condoling with him on having had to pass an afternoon with relations at Clifton, a suburb of Bristol:

"There is something about Clifton which is inexpressibly awful. Nothing enables me to survive even an afternoon call there but a carouse in the back slums of Bristol in company with an ex-ship's carpenter and his wife and her sister, who plays divinely on the hair comb."

Among the interesting celebrities with whom she became friendly were Sir Henry and Lady Stanley. She was surprised to find herself liking him. She had been appalled by what she had seen in the Belgian

Congo—the country so unforgettably described in Joseph Conrad's *Heart of Darkness*. She was inclined to censure Stanley because some of the really extraordinary work of exploration he had done in those regions was financed by the unscrupulous King Leopold. So she held her fellow explorer partly to blame for the infamous, cruel exploitation of the natives in the Congo Free State.

A picture taken of Mary Kingsley at this time shows her all harnessed up in the quaint, stiff, stuffy panoply of a Victorian lady of the upper middle class. One of those funny little beflowered bonnets sits back on her head to show hair parted in the middle and rigidly slicked down. Her dress is of dotted black material that looks about as comfortable as a suit of armor, with huge, puffed sleeves. The laughing glint in her eyes and an ill-restrained grin appear to register: "I feel as funny as you think I look." Actually a handsome, charming face, poorly disguised by the awful fashions of the day. People who knew her say she really was beautiful, "like a Dürer Madonna, angular, yet full of grace. Her head was nobly poised on a long neck. In body she was tall, with limbs noble and dignified in line."

To her own astonishment, she found herself presently fighting side by side with the Rev. Dennis Kemp, a Wesleyan, for the reform of British government in West Africa. With him she organized a service of trained nurses for the hospitals on the coast, among other things. "It is a strange end to the drama," she wrote, "to have a missionary and me arranging for the government of Africa and peacefully agreeing. I do not think Chamberlain himself can resist so touching a spectacle."

It would appear that Mary Kingsley made her third journey to West Africa in 1889. At this juncture let me add that there is some confusion about dates in the history of this gallant lady. Her principal biographer, who has written charmingly about her, had at the same time a habit of skipping backwards and forwards in her career so that it is not quite clear whether her most memorable expedition was made on her second or her last visit. Fortunately this point of chronology is not of paramount importance. If I am inaccurate in relating her most unusual adventure in this part of the narrative, the professors will have to forgive me.

Her main object in braving the perils of the Ogowe River was—it sounds ludicrous to the layman—to collect fish. She wanted specimens from a river north of the Congo to prove a point in her father's book. For that, as she expressed it herself, she went for months "walking along a narrow line of security with gulfs of murder looming on each side. For the African is a very fine fellow in his way. Being an ethnologist, I know within a little what the West African is likely to do. But the gifted man who compiles Old Moore's

Prophetic Almanac could not know exactly when the West African will be likely to do it. Herein comes the limit of danger."

Everybody tried to dissuade Mary Kingsley from her purpose. The Ogowe lies almost bang on the equator and for 500 miles of the journey she would be at the mercy of the rapids. Then she proposed to strike off through the heart of the cannibal Fan country to the Rembwe. This would take her into the Ouronogu land, the densest forest belt in West Africa. Here she would be far from any French station, far from the protection of the French flag. But dissuading Mary Kingsley from a dangerous job on which she had set her heart was mere waste of time.

On her way upriver she had another of those experiences that delighted her sense of humor. She stayed for a few days with two English traders on an island in the Ogowe. They were most considerate, as usual, gave up their quarters to her and religiously respected her privacy. One night they received word that the lone French official in those parts was feeling sad. His aunt had died, or something, so of course they had to console him. At 12.30 that night Mary Kingsley was awakened by a terrific crash. Briggs, apparently quite sober, knocked at her door, saying: "Smith is upside down in the water butt and I can't get him out. I've tried and I've tried—I wonder if you could help." The lady dressed hurriedly and found poor Smith's legs

waving madly from out of the top of the water butt.
Fortunately the thing was almost empty, or poor Smith
must have drowned long since. It required Miss Kingsley's mirth-ridden common sense to suggest the simple
solution of pulling out the bricks on which the water
butt rested and thus toppling it over. In that fashion
they got Smith out. But the dregs in the water butt
were swarming with insects and his unhappy face was
a sight to behold.

She started up the Ogowe in a canoe with four Igal-
was, men of a riverine tribe. She could not induce any
of the Talagouga Fans to accompany her because they
were certain they would be eaten by the wilder Fans
upriver. Her description of paddling up the rapids has
been called the best word picture of wild water in the
English language. With the canoe scrunching and
creaking as it squeezed through the boulders, she was
in constant peril from "that lurking, submerged needle
or knife edge of a pinnacle rock which was to rip our
canoe from stem to stern, neat and clean, into two
pieces." Again she writes of "playing a knockabout
farce before King Death in his amphitheater in the
Sierra del Cristal." While exploring in the bush she was
twice stalked by native hunters and almost shot.

Leaving the banks of the Ogowe, she struck off into
the Ouronogu country. She was now in territory that
had never been traversed by any white person. Here
the West African native was at his most unadulterated

stage of wildness. Even the Mohammedans had never penetrated there. She traveled as a trader, her usual custom, because in that fashion she was able to achieve the most intimate and natural approach to the natives. What was more, she had made herself quite adept in trading, in order to avoid being swindled too much. Her escort was armed with muzzle loaders. But she neither fired a shot herself nor ever caused a single shot to be fired or hand to be raised against a native. "I was too frightened of the Fan and too nervous and uncertain of the stuff my men were made of to dare show the white feather at anything that turned up." The Fan had a complete suspicion and hatred, not only of whites, but of any blacks with whom he was not acquainted. Each village had to be approached with complete uncertainty.

Encamped one night in a Fan village, she was aroused by noises as of a hurricane and a runaway express train. Huts were being crushed into splinters, men, women and children rushing around aimlessly in terrified helplessness. A hippopotamus was running amuck. Mary compared the spectable to "a furniture van in hysterics." That wasn't her only encounter with a hippo. Upon another occasion she found herself alone with one on a small island. That big antediluvian was making no overtures, friendly or hostile. But she was, candidly, anticipating in terror the moment when it would decide that it wanted complete solitude on that tiny strip of land. What did she do? She walked up behind the brute and scratched him behind the ear with her parasol. He beamed as only a hippopotamus could beam, moved his enormous head from side to side in gratitude and, after a few minutes, waddled peaceably into the waters and swam off.

Among the fierce man-eaters of the wildest Ba-Fan country Mary Kingsley acquired renown, not only as a trader, but as an accomplished jurist in criminal law. Many times she won their friendship by adjudicating tribal quarrels. Once, for instance, she was startled by a shot fired across the bow of her canoe. The shooter was a Fan whose wife had been stolen by one of a rival tribe. His tribe was comparatively weak, but the clan whose member had stolen his woman possessed guns of the most deadly power. So, according to custom, it was up to him to enlist allies. It is a part of West African institutions that an attack upon strangers in such circumstances makes it incumbent upon such strangers to take your side. Thus Mary was obligated to join in a tribal war. She went ashore and to the village whither the stolen bride had been taken. Instead of fighting, she undertook to adjudicate the affair. She did it so tactfully that everybody was satisfied, with a good profit in trade goods all around.

At another stage of her wanderings she found a village that was being annoyed by crocodiles. Three wives of the chief, Mohumba, had been bitten by the saurians within a week. She taught them how to catch the brutes by hooks fashioned out of wood and for days after there were rejoicing and feastings on crocodile meat.

At the time when Mary Kingsley was exploring West Africa the armchair geographers were avidly attacking the reputation of Paul du Chaillu, particularly his descriptions of the gorillas. She confirmed practically everything that Du Chaillu had reported. She saw gorillas in action, likewise the remains of a man who had been killed by one of the big apes. His shoulder blades had been literally torn from his body.

For her most dangerous trek of all, the expedition to the country of the Ba-Fan, she joined a party of three Ajumba ivory hunters. She stopped at the principal village, while the Ajumbas went ahead. It was a particularly ticklish situation for her. The Fans were peaceable enough so long as she had goods to sell. But her stock was low. She was forced to keep on selling so long as the Fans wanted to buy. The moment there was nothing more for them to get from her, they were certain to rush upon her small escort and within a couple of hours they would all be in the stewpot. She sold and she sold until all her trade goods were gone. Then she started disposing of her stockings. In her terror she still had humor enough to admire the use to which the cannibals put her hosiery. They wore them as headgear. Presently she had to sell even more intimate garments. Frilled underthings soon adorned the naked torsos of huge man-eaters. The last thing to which she clung was a toothbrush. Finally even that had to go. It was a desperate moment. Just as the Fans became most threatening, the ivory hunters returned. But alas! they too had sold everything they had. Everybody took time out for supper. While the cannibals were gorging, Miss Kingsley and the Ajumbas sneaked off to their canoes and quietly started downstream.

It was a horrendous voyage. They had to do all their traveling at night and, being without trade goods, did not dare to touch at any villages. The smell of the raw ivory almost overpowered the Englishwoman's senses.

"Two of us kept the canoe on her course by steering," she wrote, "one from each end with a paddle, where the current was strong. Where the current was slack we had to paddle cautiously under water so as to make no noise. This went on all night, broken only by catastrophes such as running full tilt into floating trees or great pinnacles of rock—things that seemed to be the kernels of all the extra dark places. And the worst of it was, we were obliged to keep our feelings to ourselves for fear of being heard by local natives.

"But I would go back to that canoe again tonight, for the beauty of the scene was beyond description. The river here was narrow though very deep and ran

[165]

between great, heavily forested walls of the range of the Sierra del Cristal, and their noble summits stood out clear and black against the star-lit, purple sky. The air around us was be-gemmed with fireflies and so heavy with the scent of flowers that we smelled them above the stench even of our own ivory. Every now and again we dropped down past a native village, seeing the natives dancing by the light of their fires and hearing the thump, thump, thump of their drums and the long-drawn, melancholy cadence of their song. It is in regions such as these that the charm of West Africa seizes on you, a charm that, once you fall under its sway, you never escape from."

No matter what the year in which these brave things happened, Mary Kingsley richly earned the respect of the geographical world. She discovered Lake Ncovi, which previously had not been on any map. She visited and reported on the island of Corisco and the famous "singing sands" of Okanda. She climbed Mungo Mah Lobeh in the Cameroons, another pioneer achievement. And she covered hundreds of miles in the most savage and unknown part of all Africa. She justly felt herself to be of the school of Du Chaillu, of Dr. Barth, Joseph Thomson, Dr. Livingstone, and of De Brazza, whom she describes as "the greatest of all West African explorers." Captain Rattray, who became celebrated as an authority on Ashanti, declared that "Miss Kingsley was the greatest white woman who ever went to West Africa."

When she returned to England for the third time it was to engage in more polemics. The preface to her second book contains "a free description of life on a West Coast cargo boat, with some observations on the natural history of mariners never before published." The course of politics in Africa was not to her liking, though some of her wishes were achieved after her death. The French historians maintain that Chamberlain accomplished most of the policies that Mary Kingsley had outlined as possible. But her dream of a British trade belt clear across Central Africa remains to this day unrealized.

In 1900, while the Empire was still struggling to subdue the indomitable Boers, Miss Kingsley went to South Africa "to collect fresh-water fishes." Once she arrived in Capetown, she volunteered for service. At the request of the government, she tried to establish orderly conditions at Simon's Town, where numbers of the Boer prisoners were being held. Their plight was quite shocking. Just as she was making headway, she died of heart failure. On a trip to Ireland a few months previously she had caught influenza from which she had never entirely recovered.

They gave this magnificent woman just the burial she would have wanted. Her body was taken to sea in Torpedo Boat No. 29 and committed to the deep.

Two institutions exist today which were most appropriately established to preserve her memory. One is the Mary Kingsley Hospital for the study and treatment of tropical diseases. The other is the Mary Kingsley Society of West Africa for the systematic study of native customs and laws. As Sir Percy Sykes observes: "Wilberforce and Buxton had abolished slavery, Livingstone on land and the British Navy at sea had carried this abolition into effect, while Mary Kingsley showed the world how to govern the negro with justice based on understanding and mercy."

A nobly phrased epitaph, General, befitting a noble lady.

VII

THE GREATEST LIVING EXPLORER

VII

THE GREATEST LIVING EXPLORER

THERE was unusual excitement in the port of Muscat one day late in 1924. The flat-topped houses shone dazzlingly white under the hot Arabian sun as a British gunboat entered the harbor from the green waters of the Gulf of Oman. She steamed slowly past the old Jalali fort, built by the Portuguese in the sixteenth century.

His Majesty's gunboat was bringing a personage upon whose character and disposition, tact or blundering, wisdom or stupidity, depended a large measure of the peace and comfort of Muscat for the next few years. He was a representative of the British Raj, appointed by the Government of India to be Financial Adviser to the Sultan. So it is obvious why His Highness's bearded Council of Ministers and all the Elder Statesmen of Muscat and Oman were worried. What sort of an Unbeliever had the British Raj sent them?

They gasped with dismay as a young, blond and blue-eyed Englishman stepped ashore.

"Wah! Does this stripling come to advise us?" muttered one veteran graybeard.

"By Allah! Has the British Raj no men that it sends

beardless boys to teach us our business?" replied another.

The comment was hardly accurate, for the representative of Britain's empire stood six foot two in his socks and weighed a good two hundred pounds. And his florid complexion had been well burned by eight years of Mesopotamia's suns. However, he was unquestionably young, hardly turned thirty. He looked younger to a race of men who frequently are grandfathers at his age.

The distress of his Elder Statesmen was conveyed to the Sultan. But that wily sovereign had observed that the Englishman, for one thing, spoke fluent Arabic, the idiomatic Arabic of a man who not only can talk but think in the language. He spoke with the firm voice of accustomed authority but also with the voice of immemorial Oriental courtesy.

So the Sultan, who had a sense of humor, advised his advisers to hold their horses and watch the young Englishman. They watched and he watched. He learned that the "stripling" had had six years' experience as a Political Officer in Mesopotamia and Transjordania. He had administered wide districts, the only Englishman in thousands of square miles governing wild Arab tribes with none but native police—whom he had recruited and trained himself—to uphold his authority. Muscat discovered further that the young Financial Adviser was a man with a keen sympathy and admiration for the

Arabs, a student avid of learning.

Now His Highness, Sir Saiyid Taimur bin Faisal bin Turki bin Sa'id, K.C.I.E., C.S.I., Sultan of Muscat and Oman, is an educated and cultivated Mohammedan. Also, he has never been fond of work. He has always preferred to pass most of his time enjoying life at his palace in India. So, with a philosophy not untinged with cynicism, he appointed the beardless stripling Finance Minister and, finally, head of his Council of Ministers and Wazir. Thereupon he boarded his yacht and set sail for India to have a good time, leaving the new Wazir to hold the bag.

Thus Captain Bertram Thomas, who ten years before had been a research student at Trinity College, Cambridge, became not only secretary of the Treasury and Prime Minister but *de facto* ruler of an independent Oriental state. It was the first time in history that such a thing had happened. What was more amazing, he got away with it. The state of Muscat and Oman prospered. Peace and order were maintained as never before.

"How the deuce did you do it?" I asked him.

"Oh, one gets along," he replied in his ultra-English accents. "One picks the wisest and most knowledgeable chaps for the important jobs and relies upon them."

Bertram Thomas belongs to that peculiar type of British soldiers and proconsuls who are also scientists, great humanists and distinguished men of letters. In this same category comes Sir Percy Sykes, a Brigadier-General in the British army; the diplomat who negotiated the historic Sykes-Picot agreement with France, concerning Syria and Mesopotamia; a traveler over ten thousand miles of the most difficult territory in Asia; author of a definitive *History of Persia* and other works, as well as his recently published *History of Exploration*. Then there is Sir Hugh Clifford, who put in the greater part of his life as an administrator and magistrate in Malaysia. He used his spare time to contribute invaluable papers on Malay customs to scientific societies and wrote, besides, two volumes of sketches on Malay life that are literary gems and models of sympathy and understanding. Again, consider Sir Harry Johnston, who administered some of the most troublesome regions of Africa with the utmost tact, wrote invaluable scientific monographs and is, in addition, author of such delightful and sophisticated novels as *The Gay-Dombeys* and *Mrs. Warren's Daughter*.

But perhaps the archetype of the species of which Bertram Thomas has become such an illustrious example was the famous Sir Richard Burton. There is no need to recount his accomplishments. He was soldier, political agent, explorer, anthropologist. Supremely a man of action, he was also of scientific trend and an artist in words.

Perhaps I should add here that there are salient differences between Bertram Thomas and Burton. Thomas has nothing of Burton's truculence and capacity for quarreling with superior officers. Burton was always getting into trouble with his chiefs and reaping the reward in the shape of assignments to uninteresting posts. Thomas has always compelled the affection as well as admiration of his bosses.

Again, Thomas has none of Burton's occasional tendency to ribaldry. He never has written and probably never will write anything remotely resembling the extraordinary *Terminal Essay* in Burton's translation of the *Thousand Nights and A Night.*

On the other hand, the man who conquered the Rub' al Khali has all of Burton's humanity and understanding of such people as the Arabs, people whom the average European and American treats with contempt and naturally antagonizes.

But enough of comparisons. Personally this great explorer is a quiet, reticent but cheerful and eupeptic fellow of abundant vitality and energy. When I saw him in New York, after he had finished delivering the Lowell lectures in Boston—a distinction reserved for only the top-notchers in their respective domains—he was considerably stouter than when he came out of the Great Arabian Desert, where he had lived for weeks on nothing but camel's milk! He also sported an extra chin which he never had when exploring those arid sands.

I have known Bertram Thomas now some four years.

Our meetings have been spasmodic and I have always found it excessively difficult to blast out of him any information about himself. He will describe his experiences for you, he will discourse freely about Arabs, he will give generously of his vast fund of knowledge about Mesopotamia, Transjordania and Arabia Felix. Ask him about his own antecedents, thoughts, habits and he will dodge your question with the polite adroitness and self-effacement that comes only, in my experience, to a man of his background. On the reticence of an English country gentleman, schooled at Cambridge, he has been obliged to superimpose the suave, agile caginess essential to a British Political Officer *in partibus infidelium*. Than such, believe you me, there is no cagier. But we are getting ahead of our biography.

Bertram Thomas is of a good Somersetshire family, good but not too snooty for sane human intercourse. He went to Cambridge, as we have observed. I don't know any men who were "up" with him, by which I mean his classmates, but he seems to prefer to give out the impression that his University career was undistinguished and without any particular aim. He was at Trinity College, Cambridge, the overwhelmingly largest of that university. He left there to go to Flanders as a subaltern in the Somerset Yeomanry, one of the first 70,000 "Contemptibles." He went through all the devastating campaigns of Mons, of First, Second and Third

"Wipers." He came through unwounded until 1915, when he was invalided home. Upon his recovery he was detailed with the Somerset Light Infantry to the Mesopotamian push, under General Maude, who retrieved the Townshend disaster at Kut-el-Amara. He was in Mesopotamia for the rest of the war, attaining the rank of captain. His spare time he put in learning Arabic, which he now speaks fluently, as well as several of the dialects of Transjordania and southeastern Arabia.

On his own confession, he began the study of Arabic "for the sake of the extra pay" that British officers get who master the language. But once he had started, he found himself interested in the study for its own sake. He also developed a latent passion for archaeology. He was stationed, from time to time, in country that is known as the archaeologists' paradise and Thomas soon caught the fever for digging among the ruins.

After the war he gravitated from the army into the political service. There was a paradoxical condition in Mesopotamia. Though officially there was peace following the Armistice, no treaty was signed with Turkey until 1926. Consequently, according to international law, the British held Mesopotamia as "enemy-occupied territory!" It took eight years to settle the question of the oil fields in northern Mesopotamia. Meanwhile the British set up an administration to govern the country until such time as peace was formally declared and they did it largely with officers who had served in Maude's army. One of these was young Captain Bertram Thomas. His chief was the argute Sir Arnold Wilson, K.C.I.E., C.M.G., C.S.I., D.S.O. The best idea of the relations between them may be gathered from the dedication of Thomas's second book, *Arabia Felix*, which reads: "To Sir Arnold Wilson, etc., etc., tenacious in counsel, swift in action, to whose advice and encouragement in the years 1918-1931 my journeyings in Arabia owe their inspiration."

One can readily imagine what a problem it must be for a young Englishman in his quite early twenties to be thrust into a position where he has to serve as ruler and judge over a people so different from the peasantry of the peaceful, law-abiding countryside of Somerset as the Arabs of southern Mesopotamia. Thomas was stationed first in what is known as the Muntafiq, in the heart of the country between the Tigris and the Euphrates. Three Turkish governors had been assassinated there. In fact, for ten years prior to the war, the Sublime Porte had given up all pretense of ruling the unruly tribesmen of the marshes. As late as 1926, while Sir Alan Cobham was passing over this country on his historic flight to Australia, he was shot at from the ground and his mechanic killed at his side.

It was among such chatty folk as these that young Bertram Thomas served his apprenticeship as Political Officer. Troops? Not a troop, not even a file of

[178]

British Tommies. There was strong feeling in England against the holding of Mesopotamia. Consequently Sir Arnold had scant funds at his disposal and his entire military establishment consisted of a battalion of infantry, two squadrons of cavalry, one field battery and six rickety airplanes. With these he had to maintain peace from the Syrian border to the Persian Gulf.

Bertram Thomas observed in his first book, *Alarms and Excursions in Arabia*, that: "I was the only Englishman in a district of, perhaps, one hundred and thirty thousand souls. . . . For force one depended upon native *askaris*, of which I had thirty. The *Shabana*, as we called him, was one of God's own. A tribesman whom we ourselves recruited locally, he brought his own rifle and horse with him and was put into uniform and cloaked with authority. . . . Brave and bold, he was altogether a great fellow, though one learned to avoid using him in his own district where, in the nature of things, he had old scores to settle."

I wondered what equipment a young Briton, 24 years old, could have to administer justice with in that wild Muntafiq marsh country.

"No, I had never read any law," he replied to a question. "It wouldn't have done me any good if I had. You can't apply the English law to those people. They wouldn't understand it. Even the Ottoman penal code, founded on the Code Napoleon, was most unsuitable to the tribesmen of the Muntafiq."

Here's an excellent illustration of his sagacity. A certain community was being overrun by thieves. Bertram Thomas tried every means of bringing them to book, a tough proposition in a country where you can buy a murder alibi for the price of a drink. So he took the principal thief, whom he couldn't convict, and made him chief of police. There was no more crime in that town! Surely there's a touch worthy of Balzac.

But another problem had him baffled for a while.

A seventeen-year-old lad came before Thomas charged with the murder of his mother. He made no bones about it. On the contrary, he declared he had done the only possible thing compatible with his honor. And, according to the tenets of his tribe, so he had. His father had been dead several years and his mother was about to have another baby.

"I loved my mother, Sahib," he said, "but what else could I do? My face was blackened."

With his name so tarnished, his friends would ostracize him. He could not sit around in the local *madhif* (café) and drink coffee with his equals. So, dearly as he loved his mother, he stabbed her in the breast while she was asleep.

Political Officer Thomas listened with the sympathy he had acquired for these so strange people. Then his English training asserted itself.

"But look here!" he exclaimed. "We can't have this! It's murder!"

SOME OF THE WATER HOLES WERE FIVE OR EVEN EIGHT DAYS APART

The local shaikhs assured him that if he had the boy executed according to the law of the Unbelievers, or even imprisoned, his court would be boycotted. He consulted his nearest senior who said to him flatly:

"Don't be a bloody fool. You aren't a J.P. in Somerset now. If you apply the letter of the law, your usefulness in this land is at an end."

At the same time the boyish English magistrate had to save his own face. He cut the knot by sentencing the seventeen-year-old matricide to six months' "political arrest" which confined the prisoner to a small area within the town. The lad turned out to be an excellent gardener and served out his six months growing flowers around the Official Residence.

In such fashion Thomas learned his business.

Nineteen twenty was the year of the big insurrection in Mesopotamia. British troops had been withdrawn from Syria and the French had driven the late Amir Faisal and his Arabs out of their mandate at the point of the sword. All over Mesopotamia tribesmen were refusing to pay taxes and using the money to buy rifles.

At this period Bertram Thomas was at G.H.Q. in Baghdad. It was a pleasant, interesting life, he relates, especially the famous "Pleasant Sunday Afternoons" at the house of the distinguished traveler and Orientalist, Gertrude Bell. There he met constantly men who were unrivaled in their knowledge of Asia. But he hated desk work.

One morning Sir Arnold Wilson sent for him. A report had come from the Assistant Political Officer in charge at Shatrah, a danger spot. The situation was so black that the A.P.O. wanted to resign.

"What do you make of it?" asked Sir Arnold.

"I'd very much like to be posted there, Sir," replied Captain Bertram Thomas.

"Posted there you are, my lad," said the Chief.

For six months the young Britisher from Cambridge and Somerset held the fort alone in the middle of a district teeming with disaffection. It is significant that he placed his chief reliance on a rich and powerful shaikh of the Muntafiq confederation who, a year before, had been the most determined enemy the British had in those parts.

To the left of him and to the right of him his colleagues were being evacuated by airplane, but Thomas held on. In one district an A.P.O. was murdered. Finally the place became untenable. Communications had been cut, district after district was being evacuated by the tiny British army. So G.H.Q. sent a couple of planes to bring Thomas away, delegating his authority to the once hostile shaikh. Of course, it was not long before a division was on the march with Bertram Thomas as Intelligence Officer. Order was restored and six months later he made a triumphant re-entry into the district where he had won the respect and friendship of all the solid shaikhs. When finally he was trans-

[182]

ferred from Shatrah to Transjordania they gave him a sword, the sword that had led them into their most victorious battle, which is today among his prized possessions, "recalling old and unforgettable loyalties."

So when, in 1924, it became necessary for the Government of India to send a man as British representative to the capital of His Highness, the Sultan of Muscat and Oman, Bertram Thomas, then barely thirty years old, was the man. Now this is one of the oldest independent states in Asia. Its independence, incidentally, is guaranteed not only by the British, but by the Dutch, the French and your Uncle Sam. The Sultan is a cousin of the Sultan of Zanzibar, in fact at one time the Sultan of Muscat was also Sultan of Zanzibar.

Throughout Muscat and Oman, Bertram Thomas won the increasing respect of Elder Statesmen, of well-to-do merchants, of bearded shaikhs and of the poorest tribesmen. His Highness the Sultan reveled in the leisure he was able to enjoy by passing the buck to his "infidel" Wazir. He sympathized with the young Englishman's passion for knowledge. He soon learned that his Prime Minister was bitten with the ambition that had seized every English officer who had served in those parts, from Sir Richard Burton down. That was the crossing of the Rub' al Khali, the arid, perilous, sandy waste, covering thousands of square miles in Southern Arabia, the last remaining stretch of unexplored land on the globe. One day, while on a hunting expedition with the Sultan, Thomas was being twitted because he was unmarried.

"*Insha'allah* (God willing), I will help to marry you one of these days to that which is near to your heart—Rub' al Khali. A virgin indeed," remarked His Highness.

Bertram Thomas took six years preparing himself for his great achievement. Already fluent in Arabic, he learned four local dialects well enough to write a grammar of the languages later. Instead of going to India for his vacations he used the time for exploration. His first important contribution was a camel trek of six hundred miles through the drear, sandy southern borderlands from the toe of Arabia nearest India all the way to Dhufar. This *was* virgin territory. Thomas had great difficulty in obtaining permission of the Amir Muhammad bin Nasir, shaikh of the fighting Bani bu Ali and the actual overlord of the wild tribes in that hinterland. The latter explained that not even any one of his tribesmen had made the entire journey that Thomas was beginning. Obstacle after obstacle was put in the Englishman's way. But he finally made those six hundred miles of South Arabian desert previously untrodden by white men. (He has told the story graphically in that first book, *Alarms and Excursions in Arabia*.)

All this time, of course, he had to attend to the job of running the state. This included the putting down of a rebellion in the peninsula of Musandam, the land of the Shihuh. He suppressed that insurrection without the loss of a single life on either side, took the leading shaikh captive and let him off with eighteen months' imprisonment. Incidentally, he established the theory that Oman was the scene of the action that took place in the Book of Job, Bildad the Shuhite, one of Job's comforters, being of the tribe that today are called the Shihuh. This theory has been accepted by most geographers and antiquarians.

By the autumn of 1930 Bertram Thomas felt himself ready for the biggest and most dangerous journey of all. During the preceding winter he had explored the steppe north of Dhufar, the biblical Ophir, on the southern coast of Arabia, to the edge of the sands. It was from Dhufar that he intended to trek northeast across the formidable but alluring Rub' al Khali.

Now you might suppose that, having the sympathy of the Sultan, all the Prime Minister needed to do was to use the resources of the state, organize a military expedition and cross that desert with comparative ease. But if you look at the map of Arabia you will perceive that the sultanate of Muscat and Oman consists of a thin trip of territory along hundreds of miles of coast line. Beyond that strip a safe-conduct from the Sultan would be of no more use than a New York police reporter's card. In fact, as Thomas has said, the Sultan himself could get his throat cut as easily as anybody else, if he ventured into that desert.

So one morning in October, 1930, Bertram Thomas slipped quietly and unannounced out of Muscat. He had not asked for official permission from the Government of India because he knew it must be automatically refused. He went by sea to Dhufar. He was dressed as an Arab and had grown a beard, because in the desert nobody is considered a man without one. An Arab swears by his beard. Thomas's food and talk, as well as his dress and beard, had to be the same as those of his companions. Also, like them, he abstained from alcohol and tobacco. However he did not, like Burton on his pilgrimage to Mecca, disguise himself as a Mohammedan. (Philby, who made a later expedition into the Rub' al Khali, had actually and sincerely become converted to the religion of the Prophet. He is today a devout and puritanical Muslim.)

When Thomas arrived in Dhufar his first disappointment awaited him. The Rashidi Shaikh who had promised to meet him and guide him over the first leg of his journey was not there. Instead, he found news of a war between the Rashidi and the Sa'ar tribes of the northern Hadramaut. But the young Englishman had learned not only the languages of the country. He had also acquired the prodigious Oriental patience. He put in six weeks exploring the Quara range of mountains. And, soon after his return thence, there appeared in Dhufar forty "dainty riding camels and as many ragged

Badawi (Bedouins)."

So that historic trek began December 1, 1930. Now, Thomas's purpose was not merely to cross that horrendous desert, but to collect complete scientific data— geological, astronomical, geographical, etc. But he did not dare to use his scientific instruments in the presence of the Badawi. If he were to be seen using a camera or shooting the sun at noon he would be suspected of magic or worse. All that had to be done surreptitiously, his instruments carefully concealed. He obtained his longitudes by shooting the stars at night. When he took photographs the camera was tucked under the folds of his robe.

The journey had to be made from water hole to water hole. Some of these were five or even eight days apart. Extreme care had to be used when approaching them, scouts sent in advance to make sure the place was not occupied by enemy. In those parts pitched battles occasionally are fought for the possession of the water holes.

At several points Thomas had long waits for other shaikhs who alone knew the way across that arid hell. No one shaikh can guide you clear across the Rub' al Khali, every district being the stamping ground of different and mutually hostile tribes. Then, too, it was necessary to wait for re-mounts of camels.

They reached every water hole with empty skins. On the way Thomas discovered the now famous Sing-

ing Sands. He obtained geological and zoological specimens, bugs, butterflies, moths, locusts, grasshoppers.
He made chemical analyses of the sands and waters.
Above all, he was in constant danger, not only of starvation or death from thirst, but from hostile, fanatical
Badus. For weeks on end he lived on nothing but
camel's milk, which is so poor in fat content that you
can make neither butter nor cheese out of it.

Not until February 5, 1931, was Thomas able to say,
like Xenophon's famous Ten Thousand: "The sea, the
sea at last." As he reached the top of the final undula-
tion of the sand dunes in the peninsula of Quatar, he
saw the towers of Doha silhouetted against the blue
waters of the Persian Gulf. Thus, as he puts it in
Arabia Felix, his fascinating account of the journey:
"The Rub' al Khali had been crossed!" The most difficult expanse of unexplored territory had been conquered.

Every time I reconsider this feat of Bertram Thomas's
I have to admire it more. As T. E. Shaw (Colonel
Lawrence) has observed, "he might have flown an
aeroplane, sat in a car, or rolled over in a tank. Thomas
did his journey in the antique way, by pain of his
camel's legs, single-handed, at his own time and cost."
And, to quote General Sir Percy Sykes, himself a veteran explorer, "unless he had displayed qualities that
the Arabs themselves admired, they would in all proba-
bility have murdered him, all the more so as he never

concealed the fact that he was a Christian."

So there, Sirs, we perceive why Captain Bertram Thomas, O.B.E. is called by his peers "the greatest living explorer.

In addition to the two books mentioned, Thomas has written a grammar of the dialects of southeastern Arabia. He has written a work on the ethnography of those regions which the Cambridge University Press is about to publish. He holds gold medals from the Geographical Societies of England, Scotland, America and Antwerp and is President of the Cambridge University Anthropological Society.

I mention all these things because it is always a surprise to find a man who is both a doer and a thinker, a man of action who is also a man of science and a man of letters.

We shall hear more of this amazing fellow. He is proud of his honors, but fed up with lecturing. The nostalgia for Asia has got him, so there he has returned.

VIII

THE FIRST ADVENTURERS IN THE ARCTIC

VIII

THE FIRST ADVENTURERS IN THE ARCTIC

If you go to old Marseilles—actually the oldest city in Western Europe—one of the first places you visit will be the *Vieux Port*, the Ancient Harbor, once known as the Lacydon.   One Spring day more than twenty-two centuries ago there was great excitement around the Lacydon.   Crowds jostled along the now famous Cannebière, so called because at that time it was a rope walk. It was a big day in the history of Massalia, as the city was then known.

A young man named Pytheas had scraped together all his savings and obtained backing from some of the rich tin and amber merchants for an expedition which many Massalians considered foolhardy.   He was going to try something that no Greek sailor had ever dared before.   Hitherto even the Ionians, hardiest of Hellenic navigators, had never sailed past the Pillars of Hercules. The Carthaginians had dominated the straits and, like the British of later years, they looked upon the Atlantic as their ocean and their trade rivals were notified to jolly well keep out of it.

But by the time Pytheas was ready for his great adventure, the power of the Carthaginians had begun to

wane. The sensational news of the Battle of the Grani-
chos had spread all over the Mediterranean. Alexander the Great had not only smashed the might of
Persia, he had raised the prestige of Greeks everywhere.
Also, his triumphant progress through Asia had made
the Greeks realize the world was much larger than they
thought it was.

So our friend Pytheas was weighing anchor on this
Spring morning shortly before 300 B.C., to slip past the
Carthaginian watch on the straits of Gibraltar. He proposed to sail out into the dreaded Atlantic to find the
Cassiterides, the Islands of Tin that lay somewhere off
the shores of Gaul. He hoped also to discover the still
more legendary coasts where people picked up the amber that came from the mysterious North and was
brought into the teeming markets of Massalia by trading
vessels down the Rhone.

To have a proper picture of Pytheas and the wealthy
merchants who backed his expedition it might be well
to take a look at their background. Pytheas was part
Greek, part Gaul. The place of his birth had been
founded by settlers from Phocaea around 600 B.C. Of
all the Ionian Greeks, the people of Phocaea were the
most enterprising and independent. They were so independent that when their citadel was about to be
stormed by a general of King Cyrus in 554 B.C., they
obtained a twenty-four-hour truce, embarked the entire population, men, women and children, aboard their

fleet and sailed to the colonies they had established in the western Mediterranean.

The flourishing and cultured Ionian civilization in Asia Minor began about 1060 B.C. The great astronomer Thales, who first fixed the length of the year at 365 days, was an Ionian. Of all the Greeks, the Ionians were not only the most daring navigators but the best colonizers.

There is a legend with a romantic flavor connected with the founding of Massalia. An expedition of Phocaeans, led by Euxenios, set foot on the southern shore. They were hospitably received by Nannus, chief of the Segobrigians, a tribe of Gauls that lived in the South of France. His daughter, Petta, fell in love with the handsome adventurer from Asia Minor. Evidently the path of romance was smooth, for Nannus not only gave Euxenios his daughter's hand in marriage, but as a dowry he threw in all the land now occupied by the historic city of Marseilles.

The Greeks were not *conquistadores*, robber-conquerors of the Cortez-Pizarro type, destroying and pillaging. They were adventuring traders, making friends wherever they went, but fighting like blazes whenever they had to defend themselves. And in Massalia they had a princely gift. It was admirably situated for commerce. On the one hand they had the fruits of the water-borne traffic that came down the Rhone from the interior of France, the tin that crossed the channel from

Cornwall, the amber that trickled down from Germany, to say nothing of the corn, wine and wool. On the other hand they had access to the profitable trade with the coasts of Spain and Italy.

But they had trouble aplenty protecting themselves. They were interlopers, and two formidable enemies did their utmost to drive the Greeks back East. Of these the Phoenicians were the most powerful.

For centuries that Semitic race, the people of Tyre and Sidon, had led the western world in navigation. In a period when the Greeks were mere coasters, the mariners of Tyre and Sidon ventured far out of sight of land, steering by the stars. Six hundred years before the founding of Massalia they had reached the straits of Gibraltar, and in 1100 B.C. they established a colony at Gades (Cadiz). At the time when Euxenios was marrying Petta and founding Marseilles, a squadron of Phoenician sailors financed by Pharaoh Necho of Egypt was putting over the gallant feat of sailing from the Red Sea around the Cape, up the west coast of Africa, doubling the Pillars of Hercules and making a final landfall at the mouth of the Nile.

The Phoenicians founded Carthage around 840 B.C., a century before there was any such place as Rome. So it is not difficult to understand why, like the English of a much later date, they tried to put a "Keep Out: This Means You" sign to the rest of the world.

So there was the principal enemy the Phocaean colo-

PYTHEAS PROPOSED TO SAIL OUT INTO THE DREADED ATLANTIC

nists had to fight in those western waters. Meanwhile, on their left they also had the constant menace of the piratical Etruscans.

History went on remorselessly. In 554 B.C. the home town of the Phocaeans was conquered by the famous King Croesus of Lydia. During the following year they sent out another expedition and established a colony in the island of Corsica which they called Alalia, now Ajaccio. Nine years later the generals of King Cyrus overthrew the short-lived empire of Lydia and clamped a still harder yoke on the Greek republics of Asia Minor. The other eleven Ionian cities surrendered, but the Phocaeans, as we observed, took bag and baggage and emigrated, sooner than became Persian subjects. They went to Corsica and Marseilles.

The conquests of Cyrus had another effect. He also captured Tyre. From that day Carthage, previously known as Tzor, became the center of Phoenician civilization. A king, or leader, named Maleus arose in that African colony. He started up a vigorous policy of commercial expansion and of throttling all the competitors of the Carthaginians. He played the game with ferocity, particularly against the Phocaeans, who had by then become the most formidable rivals of Carthage. He contracted an alliance with the Etruscans and ganged up on the Greeks. An allied fleet of sixty Etruscan and Carthaginian men-o'-war fell upon the Phocaeans off the island of Sardinia and, to the astonishment of Maleus, was annihilated. But it was what the Greeks used to call a Cadmean victory. The winners lost forty ships and their others were crippled. That left them practically without a navy, whereas the losers had plenty in reserve. As a result, the Etruscans grabbed Corsica, and the expelled Greeks took refuge either in Massalia or in Velia, near Naples.

When Maleus died, an even more aggressive fellow named Magon took up the reins in Carthage. All he wanted was everything, in that part of the Mediterranean. In his treaties with other peoples he said: "Here you may trade, and there, but nowhere else."

Meanwhile, however, the Phocaeans at Massalia kept up a policy of "peaceful penetration." Originally colonists themselves, they established branches all up and down the coast of Spain and as far down Italy as the Etruscans would let them. There were raids from time to time, and disasters. But they were all in the day's work, if you count a century as a day.

In the fifth century B.C. the long arm of Asiatic politics again stuck a hand into the West. The great Xerxes determined to include Greece in his huge dominions, once and for all. This seemed to the greedy merchant princes of Carthage to be the Big Moment. In 483 B.C. they tied up with Xerxes, hoping that all the Greek colonies in the western Mediterranean, including Sicily, would be their share of the loot. That was a tough time for Massalia, rich and powerful as she had become. She had to stand off, not only the Carthaginians and the Etruscans, but the Ligurians as well. In pitched naval battles the Greeks always won, but not decisively enough to protect their rich colonies on the west coast of Spain from enemy raids.

Avaricious Carthage appeared to have made a sound bet. In her own waters she had the Phocaean colonists on the run. Gelon, Tyrant of Syracuse, had offered them help. But the Massalians were republicans and suspicious of tyrants. In the motherland the generals of Xerxes were having a walk-over. However, his admirals weren't so good. They were hopelessly defeated at the great battle of Salamis in 480 B.C., which is not merely a tiresome date to annoy schoolboys, but a victory that affected the course of everybody's life, especially the descendants of the Massalian Euxenios and his mates. The Persian boa constrictor had to withdraw into its hole, leaving Carthage in a tough spot. Gelon of Syracuse routed the Carthaginian forces at Himera and four years later crushed the naval power of Etruria forever at the battle of Cumae, 476 B.C. From that day the Etruscans gradually ceased to exist as a nation. And Carthage was too exhausted to pick on Massalia any longer.

So, by the time our hero Pytheas was born, his home town was a rich and highly interesting center of civilization. His family was not rich, but it must have been sufficiently well off to give him the best scientific education available. He studied under the mathematician, Eudoxos of Cnidos. Pytheas was the first—and for many years the last—of the scientific explorers. He was an astronomer of an exceedingly high order. He prepared himself for his big adventure by establishing the exact latitude of Massalia within a few minutes of the correct figure, and this by laborious methods and calculation.

For all that he was a scientist, this Pytheas was shrewd. It is a peculiarly Greek combination. We know that he was not rich. But he wanted to go places and find out. So he sold some rich Massalians the idea of breaking the monopoly of the Atlantic trade which the Carthaginians still held.

Pytheas believed that the Phoenicians already had had their day. It had been an illustrious day. We have considered the sturdy mariners who sailed around Africa in the seventh century B.C. One century later an admiral named Hanno set sail from Carthage with a huge flotilla carrying 30,000 colonists, and navigated down the west coast of Africa as far as Sierra Leone, establishing cities as he went.

Hanno had sixty ships of fifty-oar-power each. If we consider what it meant to organize, equip and provision such a fleet, we have a fair idea what a rich city Carthage must have been.

In that same period another Carthaginian commander attempted an exploration of the Atlantic, north of the

Pillars of Hercules. This Himilco never got further north than the coast of Brittany. But he achieved part of his objective by establishing communication with Cornwall in the southwest corner of England, so that in the future Carthage was able to get her tin direct and monopolize the Atlantic trade.

However, from 310 to 306 B.C. the Carthaginians again were too busy defending themselves against the powerful Syracusans to keep a strict watch on the straits. This was the opportunity for the Massalians, who had had their eye on the tin traffic for years. So they sent Euthymenes south, where Hanno had gone two centuries earlier, and Pytheas to follow the route of Himilco. We don't know much about Euthymenes; apparently he did not accomplish much.

Now Pytheas was far better equipped as an explorer than Himilco. As we have observed, he was the first of the scientific travelers. Before he ever set sail, he had been a pioneer. He had been the first astronomer to realize that the celestial pole was not a fixed star.

We don't know how many ships were under the command of Pytheas. But we do know that they had a tonnage of from 400 to 500 tons and were from 150 to 170 feet long, much larger than the *Santa Maria* in which Columbus discovered Watling Island. The Greek vessels were strongly built, with a draught of from 10 to 12 feet, one quarter as wide in the beam as they were long. Two oar-shaped parallel rudders, worked by ropes from amidships, were the steering gear. The mainmast was amidships, big enough to carry yards for square sails, a mainsail, maintopsail, topgallant and sometimes a triangular royal. Fore and aft were two smaller masts for lateen sails. (So says Sir Clements Markham, though other authorities declare the Greek biremes had only one mast and could not sail into the wind.)

It is interesting to conjure up a vision of those Greek adventurers, without compass or sextant, steering for the Sacred Promontory (Cape St. Vincent), having first saluted as they passed the beautiful temple of Artemis that the Phocaeans had erected to crown the heights of what is now Cape St. Martin. Luck was with them as they slipped through the straits. Once out in the ocean, Pytheas began to make the scientific observations which revolutionized the knowledge of his day. In a fascinating book called *The Ancient Explorers*, by Cary and Warmington, we read that his journey was "more fruitful in scientific discovery than any others until the age of Prince Henry the Navigator," more than seventeen centuries later! From his voyage Pytheas came back with the first correct information about the rise and fall of the tides, astonishing both geographers and astronomers with the proof that they were connected with the waning and waxing of the moon.

Past Gades (Cadiz) he sailed and around Cape Ortegal. After several weeks at sea—we don't know how many—he made his first geographical discovery, the island of Ushant off the coast of France, which the Ancients called Ouxisamia. Thence he navigated direct to Land's End and visited the Cornish tin mines. He found the natives of Britain (England) "unusually hospitable and, thanks to their intercourse with foreign traders, gentle in manner." He also noticed that they lived a primitive life and that they used chariots in their infrequent wars. "They are simple in their habits and far removed from the cunning and knavishness of modern man," observed Pytheas, three hundred years before Christ. Among other things he brought back to Southern Europe the first information of the brewing of beer and mead.

After Cornwall he sailed east and discovered Cantion (Kent). He made extensive explorations in Britain (England) on foot. Some of his measurements were none too accurate, but it must be remembered that the Greeks had no instruments for even approximately accurate surveying. However, the observations of Pytheas were extraordinarily good, considering. As he went north he gathered data about the length of the longest days. This enabled astronomers to check up on him. In the Orkneys he found land where the longest day is nineteen hours. He told of seeing waves in those waters more than eighty cubits high. That led the arm-chair geographers of a later day to brand him a liar. Such waves were never seen in the Mediterranean, so it could not be true! Actually, as Cary points out, big storms in Pentland Firth frequently produce waves more than sixty feet high, the spray flung hundreds of feet higher.

But Pytheas went even further north. Some people think he reached Iceland, but that is doubtful. He did find a place called Thule, which means "the limit." Cary, following the Frenchman Clerc and the German savants, concludes from the traveler's descriptions that Thule must have been the coast of Norway, a trifle beyond 64 degrees north. On the strength of this, the German writers have acclaimed Pytheas as the first of all Arctic travelers.

He accomplished more than this, however. He followed the coast of the European continent "beyond the Rhine to Scythia and as far as the River Tanais," probably the river we know as the Elbe. At the mouth of a broad estuary he discovered an island on which amber was cast up by the tides. Some people believe this means that he actually penetrated into the Baltic. But the more conservative have decided that the island must have been what we call Heligoland. We do not know whether Pytheas did this on his first or on a subsequent voyage. At any rate, he was the first to give names to the large tribes of Northern Europe, the Ostioni, the Guthones and the Teutons.

When he returned to Marseilles he wrote two books, an account of his travels and a volume of scientific data on the Atlantic Ocean. He added many thousand square miles to the geographical knowledge of his time. It enabled the map-makers of his generation to enlarge their maps one quarter, it enabled the geographer Eratosthenes, for instance, to place Ireland correctly with relation to England and Scotland.

It has been one of the misfortunes of the learned world and of Pytheas's reputation that those two books, every copy of them, were lost within the next two and a half centuries. Owing to this calamity, he was, for some two thousand years, branded as the Great Liar. About one hundred years after that epochal voyage the Greek historian Polybius, himself an explorer of strictly minor importance, wrote a savage abuse of Pytheas. Polybius was an officer on the staff of the Roman General Scipio and traveled a bit in Africa, Spain and the Alps. He never came within shouting distance of the exploits of the man he was holding up to scorn. But he rendered us this service: in his diatribe he included several quotations from Pytheas's books.

Curiously enough, the volume in which Polybius poured out his ridicule was itself lost, but not before the geographer or rather the geographical writer, Strabo, had an opportunity to read it. Strabo followed Polybius's line and immortalized Pytheas for nineteen centuries as the first of the Great Fakers. Strabo himself traveled extensively, but never beyond the network of Roman post roads and military stations. He was the first to unify the world's available geographical knowledge in a well-organized book. But he stubbed his toe hopelessly when he attacked Pytheas. In doing so he made such glaring mistakes of his own as to locate Ireland to the north of Britain!

Thus it is from the quotations of Strabo from a lost book of Polybius containing quotations from the lost books of Pytheas that we today have our knowledge of the Greek explorer from Marseilles! And it is from the criticisms of his detractors that modern geographers established the fact that it was Pytheas—and not his critics—who was telling the truth! Not until late in the nineteenth century did modern scholars, by examining those quotations carefully and comparing them with known facts, vindicate the man who had been stigmatized as the Dr. Frederick Cook of Antiquity.

The moderns observed that neither Polybius nor Strabo was an astronomer. So they pointed out that the real astronomers of the day, men of scientific approach, such as Eratosthenes and Hipparchus, recognized the scientific mind in Pytheas, checked up on his observations and found that they must be true. For nearly twenty centuries he was called a liar on the testimony of unscientific men!

Not only his books, but the economic as well as the scientific values of Pytheas's heroic adventure were soon lost to the world. For more than one hundred and fifty years nobody followed him through the straits of

Gibraltar. The entire western Mediterranean was thrown into a turmoil by the Punic Wars between Rome and Carthage, so his discoveries were forgotten.

It is a misfortune—our misfortune—that we know so little about this gallant, intelligent predecessor of Peary and other great Arctic travelers. We don't even know how the citizens of Marseilles rewarded his big achievement. So his shade, resting in the Elysian Fields, will have to be content with the declaration of Professor Rhys that "Pytheas was one of the most intrepid explorers the world has ever seen."

IX

A CORSAIR OF PARTS

IX

A CORSAIR OF PARTS

THIS story begins with misbehavior and mystery. Upon a certain day late in 1523 there was a great scandal and disturbance in the establishment of a noble lady of Lisbon. We don't know what it was all about, but the affair was so serious that a young page or esquire of the lady's household had to run for his life. By his own account he was not much more than fourteen years old at the time. The disgrace drove him, practically an outlaw, into a career of traveling, adventure and roguery that lasted for the better part of thirty-five years. His name was Ferdinand Mendes Pinto.

It is curious that the escapade which preceded his flight should be to this day still a mystery. It leaves us free to make the most lurid conjectures. In his story about his voyages he relates one rascality after another with the utmost candor and naïveté, but leaves us in the dark about what happened in that noble household. The easiest explanation is that he felt perfectly safe in admitting outrages committed beyond the seas, but decided to take no chances over his malfeasances so close home.

Ferdinand Mendes Pinto was born in the city of

Montemayor or, as it was then called, Monte-mor Ouelho. His family was poor but apparently of good origin. At any rate his uncle had sufficient influence to place him with that noble lady of Lisbon, which he did not only to improve his condition but to remove the lad from the "caresses and cockerings of my mother." Pinto himself seems to date his adventurings from 1537, when he actually sailed for the East Indies. But as a matter of fact he was plunged into melodrama almost from the day that he barely escaped with his life from Lisbon. Hardly knowing where he was running, he found himself on a pier in a near-by port. There a small caravel was about to sail for Setuval, whither King John III had removed the Portuguese court to escape the plague which was then raging. Young Ferdinand slipped aboard among the retinue and horses of a nobleman.

"But alas! a little after we had set sail, having gotten to a place named Cezmibra, we were set upon by a French pirate who, having boarded us, caused fifteen or sixteen of his men to leap into our vessel. They, finding no resistance, made themselves masters of her." In short, the French corsairs pillaged the caravel, sank her and took the seventeen survivors with the intention of selling them as slaves to the Moors at La Rache in Barbary whither they were bound with a consignment of firearms. (The incident is interesting because it gives such a picture of the Christian brotherly love that prevailed among peoples of Christendom while the Turk was hammering at the gate of Vienna.) For thirteen days Pinto and his luckless comrades were held in the hold of the French corsair, their principal diet being lashes from the whips. But at sunset of the thirteenth day they overtook another and much richer Portuguese galley. The Frenchmen boarded and captured her and took so much rich booty that they decided to return to Bordeaux. On the way they marooned several of the less able-bodied captives ashore, including Pinto. These were landed at St. Jago de Caten, "our bodies covered with nothing but with the stripes of the lashes which we had received."

In such fashion the young Ferdinand eventually made his way to Setuval. The next few years of his life were without interesting incident. He passed them in the retinues of a couple of noblemen. The pay was small and the perquisites nil. Pinto may have been a ne'er-do-well, but he was not minded to be a starveling and a servant all his life. He was ambitious. Two terms of such services were enough for him, so on the 11th of March, 1537, he sailed with an expedition of five ships bound for the Indies and thus started the most important phase of his long and nefarious career. For twenty-one years thereafter he wandered all over Asia and part of Africa.

The voyage around the Cape of Good Hope seems to have been without incident. The squadron put in at Mozambique to refit and there received orders to proceed to Diu, "On His Majesty's Service." That flourishing Portuguese colony and fortress had just withstood a terrific attack by a combined Turkish and Egyptian fleet. Upon his arrival at Diu, Pinto encountered a friend, the master of a vessel under orders to sail for the Straits of Mecca on a scouting voyage A still more ferocious assault by the Mohammedan fleets was expected, hence the reconnoitering. Pinto's ship and her consort ran into stormy weather and barely made landfall at the island of Socotra, "where Don Francisco d'Almeyda caused a fortress to be built in the year 1507 when he came from Portugal as the first Viceroy that ever was in the Indies. In the said place we took in fresh water and some provisions of victuals that we bought of the Christians of the country which are the descendants of those whom the Apostle St. Thomas converted in those parts." Thereafter they sailed through the straits and into the Red Sea. Off Massua they encountered a vessel captained by a man from Judaea. They captured, looted and sank her. Then, discovering that her captain was a renegade Christian who had become a Mohammedan for love of his beautiful Greek wife, "our captains gently persuaded him to quit this abominable belief. . . . Whereunto the wicket caytiff made answer with a brutish obstinacy. . . . The captains, perceiving there was no hope of recalling him from his damnable error, caused him to be bound hand and foot and so with a great stone tyed about his neck to be cast alive into the sea." In such fashion was the Kingdom of God maintained upon earth.

After this glorious victory Pinto and several other Portuguese were landed at Massua (Massowa). From there they were to go inland and take a letter from Antonio de Sylvera to the Portuguese agent at the court of the Negus of Ethiopia. At every place they visited in the kingdom of Prester John they were welcomed. Indeed, they found that the Princess, "the Emperour's mother," employed a bodyguard of forty Portuguese. Under her auspices they traversed the country, reaching the coast again at Ercoco. The Queen Regent had provided them with an escort, made them a handsome present of money and also "sent a rich present of divers jewels of gold and stones unto the Governour of the Indies." An Abyssinian bishop, bound for the court of Portugal and thence on a pilgrimage to Rome and Jerusalem, also accompanied them.

They had hardly weighed anchor again when they sighted three vessels, which they took for harmless traders. The Portuguese gave chase and caught the harmless traders, but they turned out to be Turkish galleys. The Christians put up a good fight but were outnumbered. Moreover, at this time few European forces were a match for the Turks even with numbers equal. Pinto and eight other survivors were taken prisoner and landed in chains at Mocha. They were beaten, tortured and thrown into prison. In short, they received just as much mercy as Mohammedans might expect when captured by Christians. While the captives were being auctioned off in the market place an insurrection broke out against the governor of the town, a person of overbearing manners. The émeute terrified the prisoners so much that to save their lives they ran back to the prison of their own accord, imploring the gaoler to take them in. On the following day, the outbreak quelled, Pinto was sold to a Greek "renegado." Judging him by the standards of the average Greek to be encountered today in the Levant, our Portuguese was as much out of luck as he said he was. The Greek starved, abused and beat him. "I was seven or eight times upon the point to have poysoned myself." Release came when he was bought by a Jewish merchant from a place within a league and a half distant from Mt. Sinai. The Jew was about to leave with a caravan bound for the Persian Gulf. So Pinto had the experience of seeing Babylon and a place which he calls Cayxem. Thence the caravan went to Ormuz, where the Jew sold Pinto to the Portuguese governor.

(It should be remarked here that a great many of the place names in Pinto's "Peregrinations" are so corrupt as to be beyond identification. But it should also be remembered that the same is true of many of the passages of Marco Polo's great narrative and of all European travelers of that period. Many important place names in Asia have changed in the last five centuries and to transliterate the originals was particularly difficult for strangers of limited education.)

Now the wanderer's fortunes changed for a while. We may assume that he was well worth the ransom that Don Pedro Fernandez paid for him. He brought important information concerning the Arab establishments in Asia Minor. And probably the news he had obtained in the Red Sea concerning the plans of the Pasha of Cairo, though a few months old, was still of value. After seventeen days at Ormuz, he embarked on a vessel carrying horses to Goa. On the way down the coast they narrowly escaped capture by a squadron of Turkish galleys, but arrived safely at Goa. There Pinto was assigned to an expedition under Gonzalo vas Coutinho against the Queen of Onor. Such as it was, the foray was successful and ended in a treaty favorable to the Portuguese. But in the fighting Pinto sustained a couple of wounds.

By this time he had already acquired a reputation in those parts as at least a tough and experienced fighter. He had been through several engagements and survived where many another had perished. So when he offered his services to Don Pedro de Faria the new Captain-General of Malacca, Don Pedro not only took him on but promised him promotion. And he soon

[217]

gave Pinto an important assignment. He sent him on a mission to the King of Batas, who was at war with the Tyrant of Achin. "Don Pedro prayed me carefully to observe whatsoever should pass there, and especially to learn whether the Isle of Gold, so much talked of, was in those parts." He took with him a consignment of trade goods of which he disposed profitably (to Don Pedro) in Sumatra. Pinto acquitted himself with credit and returned to Malacca with much useful information. Among other things he reported that Sumatra was not as rich as it had been reported to be in Malacca.

De Faria next sent him on a mission to the king of Aaru, in fact, he kept Pinto employed in this fashion for several months among the petty rajahs of the Malayan peninsula and archipelago. Time after time he barely escaped with his life. He was shipwrecked off the northeast coast of Sumatra, rescued by pirates, beaten and tortured to make him tell them where he had hidden the gold that he never had, and finally sold into slavery again. In Malacca he had been given up for dead, as nothing had been heard of him for months. But he contrived to persuade one of the Arab traders into whose hands he passed that he would fetch a good ransom at Malacca. Don Pedro received him with astonishment as a long-lost son. It took the hapless adventurer a month to recover from the effects of the hardships and beatings he had undergone. Incidentally he had learned a great deal about Malay customs. He had also made himself useful to his superior officers by the knowledge he had acquired of archipelagic politics.

He had now been adventuring several years. Twice he had been taken prisoner and as a slave he had known five masters. And still he was, to all intents and purposes, penniless. On his next mission he was entrusted with ten thousand ducats and sent north to redeem some Portuguese captives. He also borrowed a small sum for himself in the hope of turning over a profit in trade. At Patana, four hundred miles from Malacca on the east coast of the Malayan peninsula, he ran into Antonio de Faria, a kinsman of Don Pedro's. They found several points of sympathy between them. Both were dissatisfied with the fruits of all the adventures they had gone through in the Indies. Neither of them had anything to show for two years of wandering and fighting. The upshot of their conversations was that Mendes Pinto decided to throw in his lot with that of Don Antonio. The latter had borrowed 12,000 *crusados* in Malacca and invested them in trade goods. Mendes Pinto added his few borrowed ducats to the partnership funds and they chartered a foist, a light galley propelled both by oars and sail, to take them to Lugor, a rich port in Siam some three hundred miles to the north. Pinto went along in charge of the cargo. He arrived safely within a few miles of Lugor. He anchored in the mouth of the river, intending to remain in that spot overnight. Just as the crew were sitting down to mess there was a powerful crash. They had been rammed by a large junk. Aboard the foist were only sixteen Portuguese and some thirty-six native sailors and rowers. Aboard the junk were at least eighty Arabs and Malays. Ensued barely five minutes of hand-to-hand fighting at the end of which twelve of the Portuguese lay dead upon the deck and practically all the natives.

Pinto and three others jumped into the river, one of whom promptly drowned. The other three took refuge in the bush. They waded through marsh, they swam creeks, all the time having to keep out of sight of the natives. One of Pinto's companions died. For seven days the two survivors wandered along the bank of the river. Finally they espied a huge barge laden with salt. Pinto and his comrade fell on their knees and shouted, begging to be taken off, but the men on the barge paid no attention. An aged woman, hearing their lamentations and prayers, compelled the crew of the barge to rescue the stranded fugitives. She turned out to be a Christian, widow of the "Xabandar of Prebedim," a woman of considerable means and influence at Lugor. She not only saved the lives of Pinto and his companion, but took care of them and sent them back to Patana with a merchant who was a kinsman of hers.

So Ferdinand Mendes Pinto returned to Don An-

DE FARIA ENTICED THE CREW OF ONE JUNK ABOARD HIS OWN SHIP

tonio de Faria bearing him the glad tidings that the cargo, in which he had invested not only his own fortune but his credit and that of his friends, was lost beyond hope. For half an hour poor Don Antonio was speechless. Nor were his feelings lightened by the entrance, one by one, of other Portuguese in Patana who had also invested their money to enrich the pirates. Some seventy thousand ducats of good cash had gone south.

"Well," said Faria finally, "there's nothing to be done about it. Frankly, my friend," he admitted to Pinto, "I haven't the courage to go back to Malacca and face my creditors. I've the courage to go after those pirates with my bare hands, if I can find them. But I haven't the courage to tell my friends in Malacca that I've lost what they entrusted to me."

He managed to scrape together enough funds to fit out a small cruiser. He set sail in May, 1640, with fifty-five Portuguese soldiers of fortune, including our friend Pinto, ostensibly to look for the robber junk. Actually he was determined to recoup his shattered estate in any fashion that offered itself. To all intents and purposes he was sailing "on the account." In one encounter he attacked and captured three junks at the same time. From this little engagement the loot was considerable. Among the prisoners he took were pirates who had committed outrages upon Portuguese friends of De Faria's. Pinto relates with unctuous satisfaction the vengeance that was taken upon them. A cord was tied around their foreheads and twisted until their eyes popped out of their sockets. Between the cruelty of the Orientals and the "righteous punishments" meted out by the Christian invaders there was precious little to choose.

Don Antonio de Faria soon had not merely a light cruiser but a squadron of three junks and a couple of light auxiliary vessels, called lancharas, under his command. Moreover his original force of fifty-five Portuguese fighting men swelled as he captured Malay and Arab praus and set their captives free. Practically, he was the equivalent of a buccaneer and some of his freebooting amounted to piracy. But with all this, one fact emerges clearly from Pinto's narrative: none of the buccaneers of the Spanish Main was more cruel, more merciless or, to be fair, more brave and capable than this De Faria. He was as redoubtable a ruffian as L'Olonois, John Davis or Sir Henry Morgan himself. A fierce and intrepid fighter, he also had the faculty of rousing his men to irresistible attacks upon overwhelming numbers of an enemy renowned for courage and ferocity. Moreover, he acquired an extraordinary capacity for the tactics of buccaneering.

His band included not only Portuguese, but Malays, Dyaks, Siamese, Arabs and Chinese. The Asiatics, of course, served principally as sailors and rowers, though they took a share in the fighting too and of course in the loot. In Siamese waters, De Faria in Chinese guise would approach a vessel he had marked down for attack. All the Portuguese were kept carefully out of sight and only Chinese were visible on deck. When the victims were completely off their guard, the corsair would abandon his disguise, riddle his prey with a broadside and then swarm aboard leading his armored Portuguese desperadoes. In Chinese waters he masqueraded as Siamese.

In this fashion he went as far as the coast of Cochin-China, raiding, sinking and pillaging but never forgetting his principal object. That was to take vengeance on Coja Acem, the pirate who had highjacked his first precious cargo near Lugor. He found the island of Ainan, the Coja Acem's lair and a fair amount of booty. But no Coja Acem.

A couple of episodes illustrate the quality of Ferdinand Mendes Pinto, his captain and associates. They came to the Bay of Camoy, then the principal center of the pearl-fishing industry in those parts. The fishing fleet was there in large numbers. Don Antonio took counsel of his captains whether they should sneak in, attack and capture outright or go in as merchants and trade for the pearls. It was decided that fighting wasn't necessary, that they had so much trade goods among their booty that they could make ample profit out of a simple business transaction. At this point, however, a Chinese quartermaster offered a valuable bit of information. It was not advisable to approach those pearl-fishing grounds in any capacity or disguise whatsoever as they were the personal property of the Emperor of China. That wouldn't have stopped the Portuguese but for the additional information that the Mandarin in charge had a strong naval force at his disposal.

So they continued their search for Coja Acem. In the mouth of the river of "Tanauquir," where they had gone for the purpose of selling the less portable volume of stuff they had stolen, they were attacked by a couple of large pirate junks "chaining themselves together for the more strength. The first salutation we had from them was a peal of six and twenty pieces of ordnance, whereof nine were faulconets and fieldpieces. Antonio de Faria, as a man verst in such affairs, perceived their drift and therefore made as though he fled, as well to win time to prepare himself as to make them to believe that we were no Christians." The ruse was a complete success. The pirates cast loose from each other, De Faria led them on until they had exhausted their ammunition, and then enticed the crew of one junk aboard his own ship, "so that there began a most bloody fight, wherein it pleased God within an hour to give us the upper hand." In the end, De Faria captured both pirate junks with the loss of one Portuguese, five boys and nine mariners killed and several wounded. An inventory showed the booty to be worth forty thousand taels besides seventeen pieces of brass ordnance.

Another episode shows our corsairs in still a different light. They came upon a small flotilla of four lancharas, light craft "like unto foists." It was a joyous convoy carrying a pretty young bride to her wedding. The Portuguese were at first afraid they might be decoys, so De Faria anchored and kept all his men below decks except his Chinese sailors. He captured the craft and set everybody ashore except the bride and her two little brothers. She was the daughter of the Governor of Colem and betrothed to the young son of the captain of "Pandurea." "He had written unto her that he would attend her in this place with three or four junks of his father's who was very rich. But alas! we shamefully cozened him. . . . The bridegroom arrived seeking for his bride, with five sail full of flags, streamers and banners. Passing by us he saluted us with great store of musick and shews of gladness, ignorant of his misfortune and that we carried away his wife."

A scoundrel, this Don Antonio, but a doughty one. Before long his name inspired such terror in those waters that the Chinese merchants conceived the idea of paying him for a safe-conduct for their vessels. On top of that the Chinese viceroy offered him the position of admiral, with a salary of ten thousand taels a year, to protect the mercantile marine of the Celestial kingdom! At the end of three years he was to be advanced to high mandarin rank with a salary of one hundred thousand a year. Whether De Faria suspected a trap or whether he considered such exalted rank too dangerous we don't know, but he gratefully declined the offer. He continued to accept tribute from Chinese merchants and municipalities.

He was not without intelligent curiosity concerning the places and countries he visited. Wherever he went he asked questions about the geography and resources of the region, he learned about the great rivers and lakes of Siam and Cochin-China and that "in this land were many mynes of copper, tin, saltpeter, sulphur." But, like the buccaneer captains, he had his troubles with his men. "After we had been seven months and an half in this country . . . the souldiers weary of so long and tedious travel assembled together and desired Antonio de Faria to make a partition of that which had been gotten." He yielded for the time being and agreed to shape a course for Siam where the goods might be sold and the proceeds divided. He dropped anchor off the Island of Thieves to wait for a favorable wind. A hurricane blew up, and the entire squadron was wrecked. Four hundred and eighty souls perished. Only twenty-three Portuguese were saved and thirty Asiatics, slaves and mariners. As the tempest died down, the shore of the island was literally littered with corpses. And now again we see the mettle of this doughty corsair. "Antonio de Faria . . . concealing the grief which we could not dissemble, came to where we were, having on a scarlet coat that he had taken from one of the dead. He made a short speech unto us . . . he firmly believed that though we now had lost five hundred thousand crowns, we should ere it were long get six hundred thousand for them."

He put heart into them, these woebegone fellows who had been transformed overnight from rich men into penniless naked castaways. And his luck returned. He espied a sail and hid his crew in the woods. It was a small craft carrying some thirty Chinese. They landed and tied her up while they prepared a meal and set about washing their linen. De Faria seized his opportunity, also seized the ship and, the first thing those cleanly Chinese knew, their vessel was running for the open sea and they were marooned. Within a couple of days he and his cutthroats had stolen themselves a Chinese junk. So, just a few days after their shipwreck, they were in possession of two vessels, though not large ones. Moreover, they joined forces with a friendly Chinese pirate who had thirty Portuguese fighting men in his crew as well as an abundance of cannon, small-arms and ammunition. Presently they overtook a small fishing boat with eight wounded Portuguese aboard and at last Pinto and De Faria got definite information concerning their hated enemy, Coja Acem. For their eight wounded countrymen had just escaped with nothing but their lives from a terrific fight with him. They were part of a convoy sailing from Liampoo (Ningpo) to Malacca when they were attacked by the same Coja Acem commanding three large junks, four lancharas and fifteen hundred men. He had captured the convoy, but his own squadron had been severely damaged in the battle. De Faria leaped for joy. His men had their doubts about picking on such overwhelming odds, but their captain was determined. It was the big opportunity—they had been waiting months for it. Now they knew for the first time exactly where Coja Acem could be found. Furthermore, he had been through a tough, bloody engagement, whereas they were fresh and could take him by surprise. But first—and this shows what a good general Antonio de Faria was—he put into port for a complete overhauling of his little squadron and bought a supply of powder, lead, bullets, victuals, cordage, timber, planks, masts, sails, sail yards, pulleys, anchors and fresh water. Not until he had thus equipped himself did he sail for the place where Coja Acem was licking his wounds. And even then De Faria took the precaution of sending spies, masquerading as fishermen, ahead of him to get his information complete.

The battle that ensued was as stirring and exciting as if it had been fought in a good cause and as if both parties to it had not been thorough scoundrels. De Faria's plans were executed without a hitch. With his two junks he attacked the three large vessels of Coja Acem. When the latter's smaller craft hastened from shore to take the Portuguese in the flank they were met with stink pots and artificial fire. The hand-to-hand fighting was desperate. Shouts of "La illah illah-la, Mahmoud resoul illah" were met with De Faria's "Courage, valiant Christians, trust in our Lord Jesus Christ nailed on the Cross for us!" Thereupon he jumped towards Coja Acem, who had on a coat of mail lined with crimson satin that he had taken from a dead Portuguese. De Faria jumped at him and "discharged so great a blow on his head with a two-handed sword that, cutting through his cap of mail he laid him at his feet, then redoubling with another reverse stroke he lamed him of both his legs. . . . In half a quarter of an hour forty-eight of our enemies lay slaughtered on the dead body of Coja Acem and but fourteen of ours, whereof there were not above five Portugals."

The victory was complete and the booty enormous. The dead Malay had been continuously successful, and his junks were crammed with treasure. By way of celebrating, the Portuguese went ashore where they found ninety-six wounded Malays and Arabs whom they burned alive for the glory of God. After three weeks' rest he set sail for Liampoo, but a terrific northwesterly storm blew up as they were abreast of Cape "Micuy." One of the junks was wrecked, the one carrying De Faria and most of the treasure. However, he transferred his flag to another junk and undertook a land raid by way of a change. He assaulted a town that Pinto calls Nouday and took it by storm, plundered it from cellar to garret, and then set fire to it. The loot was beyond counting. Even the native sailors carried away huge chests of it for their own. "Only it was a great pity to behold a number of handsome maids led away, tyed four and four, weeping and desolate whilest our people did nothing but laugh and sing."

So Pinto and De Faria had achieved the first main objects of their cruise. They were even with Coja Acem and they had recouped their fortunes. The squadron now sailed for Liampoo, where the Portuguese colony received these bloody-minded ruffians as though they had been Crusaders. They attended Mass at the church and listened to a sermon in praise of De Faria, "but that in words so ill-placed and so far from the text that our Captain was much ashamed at it." The festivities ended with a bull fight.

At Liampoo they rested five months, spending their ducats and *crusados* after the immemorial and unchangeable fashion. It had been the plan to return West and make a raid on the mines of "Quoaniaparu." But the friendly Chinese pirate died, the ally who had been with them in the attacks upon Coja Acem and the city of Nouday. Moreover, word came of wars between the *Prechau Muan* and the King of Chamay and Champaa (Cambodia?), which made that country unsafe for raiders. So De Faria decided to act upon information from another Chinese pirate and sail to the island of Calempluy in the Gulf of Nanking for the noble purpose of rifling the tombs of seventeen ancient Chinese kings. There has been a good deal of argument concerning the latitude and longtitude of that island. Some authorities place it in the Gulf of Peking, others up the Yangtze, while one geographer believes it might have been part of Korea, which was once called Kalo. A tradition exists there of a race of heroes that sprang from golden eggs; moreover there was considerable junk traffic between Chusan and Quelpaert during the Sun dynasty. Wherever it was, the grave robbers got there after a terrifying voyage and started on their ghoulish purpose. They were interrupted by a man of noble appearance and speech "that seemed to be an hundred years old, apparalled in a long, violet-coloured damask gown, who said 'Whoever thou art, know that I perceive but too well thy damnable intention.'" De Faria was so impressed by the venerable gentleman's remarks that he ordered his men to desist for that day. When they returned to their sacrilegious thievery on the morrow they found the guardians of the holy places had given the alarm and summoned the troops. The Portuguese had to flee for their lives, only to be shipwrecked in the Gulf of Nanking. There Don Antonio de Faria perished and our friend Ferdinand Mendes Pinto found himself without his indomitable captain. For he, with thirteen others, was saved to lead a pretty miserable existence for the next year or so.

He and his companions made their way to the mainland of China. For weeks they begged their bread from place to place. Finally they were arrested on suspicion of being thieves and sent to Nanking for trial. They were convicted and sentenced to the loss of their thumbs. Pinto evidently had acquired a smattering of the language of the country during his association with Chinese pirates. Through the intervention of a sympathetic woman and friendly officers the Portuguese were permitted to appeal to Peking. There the appeal was allowed, the sentence reversed and their accusers were condemned to pay them damages. However they were sent north to the town of Quansi on the frontier where they were obliged to do forced labor on the Great Wall. This lasted eight months, and they might have been there yet but for the invasion of the Mongol, Altan Khan, chief of the Tumeds, a grandson of Dayan Khan. He fell upon Peking with an army of 1,800,000 men, according to Pinto's exaggerated account. At any rate the Portuguese were brought back from Quansi and led into the presence of the Mongol conqueror, a man "about forty years of age, full stature, somewhat lean, of good aspect; his beard was very short, his mustaches after the Turkish manner, his eyes like to the Chinese and his countenance severe and majestical." Despite his huge force he failed to capture Peking and retired, taking the Portuguese corsairs with him. Thus Pinto's enforced travels brought him into Tartaria. He crossed the Great Wall in the train of Altan Khan, took ship on the Hoang-ho and, passing by Lancama, arrived at Tuymican where Altan Khan kept his court. In later years Ferdinand wrote as though he had been taken to Samarkand, but that is doubtful. At any rate, he and his mates saw plenty to remember. To Altan Khan came the ambassadors from six mighty monarchs, Shah Tamasp, the Sophy of Persia, the Emperor of the Yueos (Yue Chi?) the Calaminham, the Great Moghul, the King of Siam and the Emperor of Caran. Some of these are not so easy to identify.

After a few months Altan Khan allowed the Portuguese to leave in the suite of an ambassador whom he sent to the King of Cochin China. It was an illuminating journey for Pinto. He passed through the country of the Tumed Mongols, thence south through the lands on the frontier between China and Tibet to the Gulf of Tonking. Thus he became the first of all Europeans to travel that route. He traversed the headwaters of one of the great rivers which rise in the eastern plateau of Tibet, probably the Mekong. Descending the course of the river for several hundred miles, he was then taken across the mountains to the valley of the Songkoi, the Red River of Tonking. On the way the ambassadorial party visited a "very fair town" which Pinto calls Quanginau (Shiabdan?) where there was a large monastery. There they heard a sermon by the

[233]

"Talapicor of Lechuna," whom Pinto describes as the Pope of that country. It seems likely that the prelate they heard was either the Dalai Lama or the Teshoo Lama. In those days the Dalai Lamas did occasionally leave Lhasa and even Tibet itself on visits to China. After "Quanginau," the expedition reached Lechuna, "the chiefest city of the religion of these Gentiles and such it may be as Rome is amongst us." Soon thereafter they came to Lake "Singapamor, an admirable masterpiece which Nature hath opened in the heart of this country. From it flow four very deep and large rivers." In this our good Ferdinand's observations were not so accurate. But, as Sir Henry Yule has remarked, it is a mistake common to several travelers, including at least one of a much later date.

At any rate, the ambassador and the Portuguese arrived safely in the capital of Cochin China. His Excellency procured them safe-conduct and passage to the island of Sanchian, whence they hoped to find their way back to Malacca. They reached Sanchian just five days after a Portuguese convoy had left, so they went on to the island of Lampacau. This had already become a resort for merchants, rovers, rogues and pirates. Not long afterwards the Portuguese town of Macao was built there which is still notorious as a resort of thieves and a place of iniquity. However, though the wanderers now were among compatriots, they were penniless and jobless. At this crisis in their fortunes a Chinese pirate sailed into the harbor. He had just been through a desperate engagement with the Chinese Imperial fleet off Chincheo, a large city half-way between Canton and Liampoo. His two remaining ships were sorely battered, and most of their crews wounded. The Portuguese castaways could not afford to be fussy. Five of them took service aboard one of the Chinese pirate craft and lost their lives soon after. Pinto, with Diego Zeimoto and Christopher Borello, embarked on the other corsair junk. They ran for the Loochoo Islands, where the captain had hopes of intercepting some defenseless merchant vessels. But the wind shifted against them and after beating about for twenty-three days, they anchored in seventy fathoms of water off an island of considerable size. It turned out to be the island of "Tanixumaa" (Tanegashima) and part of the empire of Japan. "The Nautaquin, lord of that island, would willingly permit us to trade, if we would pay the duties customarily paid in Japan which, said he, is that great island which you see there over against us." Consequently the ship was piloted into a good harbor outside a considerable town.

Ferdinand Mendes Pinto thus became in 1545 the first articulate European to set foot on Nipponese soil, although three years previously his countrymen, Antonio de Moto, Francisco Zimoro and Antonio Perota, had been blown there in a junk while trying to make

Liampoo. They did not remain long, apparently, and it is certain that they brought back no information of value.

Soon after the Chinese vessel was anchored in the harbor it was visited by the Nautaquin, accompanied by his retinue and several merchants carrying chests of silver. The first persons aboard to attract the governor's attention were Pinto and his companions. Perceiving how different they were in complexion and features he asked who they were. The Chinese corsair explained, whereupon his lordship turned to his gentlemen and exclaimed: "May I die if these be not the Chenchicogis, of whom it is written in our ancient books that, flying on top of the waves, they will subdue all the lands about them until they become masters of all the countries in which God has placed the riches of the world. We should esteem it a great piece of good fortune that they come to us with offers of friendship and good will." The governor called in a woman of Loochoo as an interpreter and poured a stream of eager questions upon the Portuguese. Pinto did the talking for all of them. Upon his own admission he did not hesitate to draw the long bow and emit enough boasting about his country to impress the Japanese. He told the gullible "Nautaquin" that Portugal was larger and richer than China, that his king had conquered the greater part of the world, that he had two thousand houses full of silver and gold, that—well, he told what the governor seemed to want to hear. The upshot was that he made a hit, and the Portuguese became the guests of a rich merchant near his lordship's own house. The Chinese were assigned warehouses which enabled the captain to trade off his cargo at a profit of some 1,200 percent. "Meanwhile we three Portuguese enjoyed our time in fishing, hunting and visiting the temples, where the priests or bonzes, as they are called, gave us a very good reception, the Japanese being naturally well disposed and very conversable. Diego Zeimoto went often forth to shoot with an espingarda [a large musket], which he had brought from Tartary and in the use of which he was very dexterous. One day, at a lake where there were many kinds of birds, he killed at various shots six and twenty ducks. Some Japanese, observing this new method of shooting which they had never seen before, reported it to the prince. Zeimoto, being called, came into his presence with the gun on his shoulder and two Chinamen loaded with the game . . . as the Japanese knew nothing of the secret of the powder, they ascribed it all to enchantment, which Zeimoto increased by shooting on the spot a kite and two doves." The Portuguese shrewdly presented the weapon to the prince who responded with a gift of a thousand taels of silver. "The prince caused other guns to be made like it so that when we left, which was in five months and a half, there were more than six hundred; and when I visited Japan in 1556 as

[237]

ambassador from the Portuguese viceroy to the Daimyo of Bungo, the Japanese told me that in the city of Fucheo, the capital of that kingdom, there were more than thirty thousand guns."

Returning to the year 1545, while the Portuguese were at Tanixuma, a messenger arrived from the daimyo of Bungo. He had heard of the presence of the three "Chenchicogins" and was curious. He wanted to see one of them, so the Nautaquin sent Pinto. He was taken in an official galley and, stopping at various places, presently reached Osqui (Osaka?). Thence he was escorted to Fucheo, the capital of the province. He was sumptuously entertained and made such a good impression upon the daimyo and his gentlemen that the Japanese exclaimed: "This cannot be a merchant, engaged in the low occupation of buying and selling! He must be a learned bonze or at least a corsair." And, though he was no doctor and did not pretend to be, he had the good fortune to cure the daimyo of his gout with an herb he had brought from China, probably ginseng.

The Portuguese had brought a gun with him to Bungo which excited just as much curiosity as it had at Tanixuma. The second son of the daimyo, a lad about eighteen, begged to be allowed to use it, which Pinto cautiously refused. However the boy contrived to get hold of it while his guest was asleep. He overloaded it so that it burst, wounding his hand and almost shooting off one of his thumbs. While the young prince lay on the ground unconscious the courtiers, who rushed in, accused the foreigner of having murdered the daimyo's son. Fortunately the lad came to in time and took all the blame upon himself. Pinto, following the methods he had seen used by surgeons in India and elsewhere, cured the young man in three weeks, whereupon his credit at court was higher than ever. Soon after that he and his companions sailed for Liampoo.

The news they brought created tremendous excitement in the Portuguese colony. There was a scramble among the traders to fit out ships to grab a share in this rich traffic. Most of them sailed ill-found and sank, with cargoes to the value of 300,000 *crusados*. Pinto was aboard another which was blown off its course. Once again he was shipwrecked, but escaped drowning and was washed ashore on one of the Loochoo islands. He was arrested on suspicion of piracy and taken to the governor of the islands. While he was trying to prove his innocence a Chinese corsair, who had the governor as a silent partner, dropped anchor in the harbor. As luck would have it, he was an enemy of the Portuguese and recognized Pinto. The natural consequence was a sentence of death for poor Ferdinand. But as usual in his worst extremities, a woman came to the rescue. She was a Portuguese and fortunately a close friend of the governor's daughter. She worked upon

[239]

the feelings of the governor's daughter to the end that a petition was conveyed to the mother of the viceroy. (It was not the first time that Pinto had escaped death through feminine intervention.)   After a long wait and much intriguing, the sentence of death was commuted. Pinto and his companions were released and sent back to Liampoo.   Thence he made his way without further misadventure to Malacca.

Pedro de Faria was still captain-general at the post and astonished to see his former ambassador once more. We may well believe that many cups of sack were consumed while De Faria heard the Homeric tales of his dead kinsman's exploits.   In the next few months he employed Pinto on several missions to Asiatic rulers, including the King of Burma.   He visited Pegu, Siam again and Java.   In 1547 he set sail once more for Japan in a ship commanded by George Alvarez.   He was warmly welcomed at the court of Bungo but, shortly after his arrival, an insurrection broke out and his friend the daimyo was murdered.   In the course of the civil war the city of Fucheo was left practically in ruins. Alvarez and Pinto steered their vessel ninety leagues south to Hyamonyoo on the bay of Cangoxima.   There, unfortunately, they found such an enormous fleet of Chinese trading junks that the market was flooded. After they had waited around for two and a half months, "by the special providence of the Most High," a terrible storm occurred in which almost all the foreign traders were destroyed—almost two thousand vessels, said Pinto. But he and Alvarez escaped and were able to dispose of their cargo at a handsome profit. When they left Japan they took with them two Japanese, evidently fugitives from the vengeance of some angry lord —one of them, named Angiro, "an instrument selected by the Lord, for his praise and the exaltation of the holy faith." What he means is that they took Angiro to Malacca where they introduced him to St. Francis Xavier who converted the Japanese and was by this means persuaded to his historic mission in the land of the Mikado. Angiro, who took the name of Paul when he was baptized, taught St. Francis his language. The great Jesuit took a Spaniard, Juan Fernandez, and in August, 1549, landed at Miako in the easternmost part of Japan. He was amazingly successful here as elsewhere. Thus began a new and eventually a troublesome era in the history of that empire.

Pinto made a third visit to Fucheo in 1551. The young daimyo whom he had cured of his wounds in 1545 was now firmly established as ruler of the province of Bungo. The journey appears to have been profitable; at any rate, there is no record of an addition to the numerous disasters in his life. He renewed his acquaintance with St. Francis, and apparently the encounter worked on his conscience. The faith and magnetism of the light, spare, blue-eyed saint melted even the tough, hardened sensibilities of the cutthroat corsair. For soon after that we find him making a general confession to Father Nuñes Barreto, vice-provincial of the Jesuits at Goa. What a confession that must have been! One would like to know the feelings of the Very Reverend Nuñes Barreto, S.J., as he listened to that catalogue of outrages. Indeed, Pinto got religion so acutely that he was on the point of taking orders and joining the Jesuit mission in Japan. He even talked of offering his entire fortune—for he had prospered since his voyage with George Alvarez—to the founding of a seminary at Amanguchi. But the wise Jesuits knew better than to take a so suddenly repenting sinner at his word. They made him serve a term in the hospitals at Malacca, they put him through the entire regimen of a novice. So his new found zeal began to evaporate. In 1556 he was appointed ambassador from the viceroy at Goa to the daimyo of Bungo. It was arranged that he should not take his final vows until he had completed his diplomatic mission.

When he returned for the fourth time to Japan the zeal of Ferdinand Mendes Pinto declined speedily. It has been suggested that he was alarmed at the emaciated appearance of Father Cosmo de Torres, whom he had last seen as a plump, well-fed, cheery gentleman. The sharp-eyed Jesuits were not slow to perceive the fading of Pinto's fervor. So, as they had no use for faint-hearted members, they quietly and politely absolved him from his preliminary vows. Having accomplished his mission in Bungo, he returned to Goa and soon after sailed for Malacca and Lisbon.

He arrived home on the 22nd September, 1558, with a highly commendatory letter from the Viceroy to the Queen Regent, Madame Catherine. She listened, fascinated, to the tale of his adventures, which doubtless was carefully expurgated. But when it came to taking advantage of his experience by giving him office in the government, she turned him over to her minister. That potentate evidently did not want a man around who knew too much, or else he feared that anybody who had been so long in the Indies might have his own axes to grind. At any rate Pinto was kept hanging around for four or five years without any appointment, at the end of which time he gave it up as a bad job and retired to a country estate which he was able to buy. He claimed to be poor and probably his fortune was exaggerated. But he must at least have had a competence.

Ferdinand Mendes Pinto, in his twenty-one years of absence in the Indies, was taken prisoner thirteen times and sold as a slave seventeen times. His travels, as we have seen, were prodigious. He wrote his *Peregrinations* in 1580 for the amusement of his grandchildren, but the book was not published until after his death. On the one hand it achieved an enormous success as a contribution to literature. The *Peregrinations* were proclaimed the finest achievement in Portuguese prose and the book went to four editions. It was translated into French for two editions and also, in an absurdly abridged version, into English. The religious prejudice or the fears of the English publisher caused, among other things, the elimination of all references to St. Francis Xavier. Many more interesting passages were cut out. Fortunately, the French version is complete.

Scholars and armchair geographers pounced upon the *Peregrinations* as the work of a liar, and re-christened the author Ferdinand Mendax Pinto. It was the same treatment that was first accorded by the Venetians to Marco Polo. Pinto was inaccurate in several respects, but it has been definitely established from other contemporary sources that he did visit many of the places that he said he visited. He exaggerated many details and lied about others. Nevertheless his story stands out as one of the most absorbing tales of travel and adventure that ever came off a printing press.

X

THE ROMANCE OF MASTER WILL ADAMS

X

THE ROMANCE OF MASTER WILL ADAMS

One day in the spring of 1598, Mistress Adams is busy at her housework. We can picture her preparing some of the roast beef of Old England, or maybe a boiled sheep's head, as Captain Adams bursts breathless into their cottage in Limehouse.

"Pack my sea chest, wife," he cries. "And where be my compass? And my maps? Where did you put those charts of the South Sea I got from Tom Candish (Captain Thomas Cavendish) after he returned from the Spanish Main?"

"Angels and ministers of grace defend us, what ails the man?" exclaims his wife. "Can a body not cook the dinner in peace?"

"My love, I have great haste," he explains. "A hoy is in the river all ready to sail for Rotterdam. She drops down river with the tide, and I must be aboard her or lose an enterprise of great moment. I have much to do, woman."

"Ill fares the woman that weds a sea-faring man," complains the captain's lady. "Will Adams, you did promise you would go to work again for Master Nicholas Diggins, in his shipyard, and settle down for a few months with your wife and family. That should be enterprise sufficient for an husband and father."

"Softly, sweetheart," urges the captain as he begins to gather his instruments and haul out his sea chest. "You know how long I did wish for to be employed on the Indish traffick." (He means that he has craved to sail to the East Indies.) "Now there be a company of Rotterdam merchants who do furnish and equip five ships for the Indish traffick. They yet lack a pilot. Master Diggins at his shipyard got news of this. The Hollanders did seek out John Davis, who is but newly come back from those Indish waters with Cornelius Houtman. But Davis will not go, he will rest a while. If, by God's grace, I can persuade the Hollanders, I will go and make a little experience of the small knowledge which God has given me."

At this, we may be sure, Mistress Adams still more loudly bemoans her lot as a sailor's wife. She has every reason to realize that, even with the best of luck, it will be at least two years before she sees her Will again. The great John Davis, who has just returned from his voyage as pilot-major with Cornelius Houtman—the first successful expedition sent out by the Dutch—was gone two years and four months. As a matter of fact, though she does not know it, she will never again set eyes upon her husband.

Nevertheless, Will Adams kisses his wife and children good-by and goes to Rotterdam. The five ships that are being outfitted are to sail under the command of a merchant named Jacques Maihore, more commonly known as Mahu. This "generall," as the leader of such expeditions was then called, is no seaman. So when he leaves Rotterdam in July, 1598, he takes with him, as his chief navigating officer, Captain William Adams.

For this Englishman it is the realization of a dream he had cherished for thirty-two years, perhaps even more. As a small boy he lived practically within sight of good Queen Bess's ships in the navy yard at Chatham. He was born at Gillingham in Kent, just a mile away, in 1554. The first tales his young mind fed upon were of far Cathay, of wonderful Cipangu, as Marco Polo had called the islands of Japan and the Isles of Spice. His parents evidently compromised between the lad's craving to go to sea and their desire to keep him at home. They apprenticed him to Master Nicholas Diggins, the shipwright at Limehouse. But there his ambitions were still further inflamed by the stories of the men who came to the Diggins shipyards to have their vessels repaired. In his spare time he must have picked up a sound knowledge of navigation and a smattering of mathematics. (In afterlife we find him giving instructions in geometry to the ruler of Japan. But that is getting ahead of our story.)

Will Adams worked twelve years for Nicholas Diggins. Many a day he must have chafed at the restraint. During those twelve years the news constantly came to

[249]

England of more achievements by the Spaniards. They planted their first colony on the Philippine Islands. Andres de Urdaneta achieved the feat of sailing across the Pacific from west to east. Alvaro de Mandana discovered the Ellice group, the Solomons and the Marshall archipelago. And at last the English were beginning to go after their place in the sun. Richard Chancellor, looking for the Northeast Passage, had failed. But he had discovered the White Sea, traveled thence by dog-sled to Moscow and met the Tsar, Ivan the Terrible. To Chancellor, Ivan had not been at all terrible. On the contrary, he made his eyes pop with the sumptuousness of his court and the magnificence of the entertainment he provided for the first Englishmen in Russia. Thereupon the Tsar bestowed upon Chancellor and his companions exclusive trading privileges for the Muscovy Company. The Chief Factors of that corporation began a series of explorations in Central Asia which are amazing to contemplate today. Anthony Jenkinson, who had been with Chancellor on his visit to Moscow, was the first of these. As Chief Factor of the Muscovy Company, envoy of Queen Elizabeth and of Ivan the Terrible as well, he sailed the Caspian Sea, visited Khiva and Bokhara. Later he went to the court of "The Great Sophie" at Khazvin and brought back information that was a revelation to English geographers.

Meanwhile good Queen Bess's men had started their

adventurings on the other side of the globe, too. Frobisher and Davis had begun the centuries-long search for the Northwest Passage to the Indies. Queen Elizabeth had publicly ridiculed the Papal Bull that, she declared, made a present of the western hemisphere to Spain and Portugal. The intrepid Frankie Drake dashed to the mouth of the Tagus and burned all the shipping in the harbor "to singe the beard of the King of Spaine." And just as the articles of apprenticeship for young William Adams were about to expire, Drake started from Plymouth on his famous raid around the world in the *Golden Hind*, to be followed soon after by John Fenton and Thomas Cavendish.

Adams left the shipyard at Limehouse to go to sea. With the knowledge he had picked up on the side, he made rapid progress. He soon became a pilot and finally a ship's master. In the naval campaign against the Armada he was in command of a 120-ton pinnace, carrying supplies to Sir Francis Drake. Doubtless he did his share of fighting, too. For the next ten years he led what must have been a somewhat humdrum existence, considering his dreams. He was a master in the employ of the "Worshippfulle Companie of Barbarie Marchants." In other words, he was trading between Morocco and England. Probably that service had its moments of excitement, but he never mentioned it in his letters. At any rate his big opportunity, as we have observed, came in 1598.

Jacques Mahu, the "generall" of the expedition, was neither a seaman nor a very good "generall." His preparations and equipment were inadequate. Supplies ran low and scurvy appeared among the crews before they reached the coast of Guinea. At the island of San Thome they had to fight and defeat the Portuguese garrison before they could land and obtain fresh water. Jacques Mahu died and was buried at sea. So many of the men were ill that they were obliged to establish a hospital on one of the islands off Guinea. Mahu was succeeded in command by Sebald de Weert. At the island of Annabon they had another fight with the Portuguese. They raided the place and obtained a fair supply of fresh meat and fruits. Already the original force of almost 500 men that had sailed from Rotterdam was sorely diminished.

It was not until January, 1599, that De Weert was able to make a definite attempt at crossing the Atlantic. Off the coast of South America he met with more misfortune, illness and death among the crews. It was a depleted expedition that reached the Strait of Magellan, almost a year out from home. That ill-omened strip of water lived up to its evil reputation. Hail, gales, snow, blizzards and more gales kept the Hollanders anchored off the bleak coast of Patagonia. They lost a hundred men. Adams wanted to drive through. He pointed out that nothing could be worse than the sufferings they were undergoing, that they would find relief once they got out into the Pacific. But "Generall" de Weert had one quality worse than recklessness: he was timid and he would not listen to his pilot. He kept them hanging around in misery six full months, subject to frequent raids by the Patagonian natives. When he finally weighed anchor and reached the Pacific he ran into just seven days of fair weather. Thereupon came two gales in rapid succession. The second dispersed the entire squadron. De Weert in his flagship was driven back into the Strait of Magellan. One vessel called the *Liefde* (Charity), with Will Adams aboard, had better luck, though she was separated from all her consorts. The others were scattered in all directions.

As this is the story of Will Adams we will not attempt to follow all those unhappy ships in detail. De Weert made his way back the way he had come and in July, 1600, reached Rotterdam with thirty-six men left of his crew and all of them ill. He had to report a total failure to Pieter van der Hay and Hans van der Veek, the two rich merchants who had financed the expedition. Another vessel, after her captain and twenty-seven men were slaughtered on an island, foundered with all on board, somewhere in the Pacific Ocean. The crew of still another raided a couple of Spanish islands, got away with some loot and were finally captured, most of them slain, by the Portuguese. Six of them escaped, after many years, to Holland. A fourth ship of this hapless squadron, with only nine men left aboard strong enough to hoist sail, limped into the harbor of Valparaiso. The crew, such as survived, were impressed into the Spanish navy.

That accounts for them all except the *Liefde*. She dropped anchor off the island of Mocha. Promptly she was surrounded by canoes, filled with apparently friendly natives. The captain and twenty-three of her men, starving for the lack of fresh food, went ashore. They were ambushed and slaughtered to a man. Among the dead was Thomas Adams, brother of the pilot. A Dutchman named Jacobus Quaeckernaeck was elected official captain. Actually the officer to whom the survivors looked for leadership was William Adams. The fact that they decided to make for Japan is significant. You will remember that to see "Cipangu" had always been one of the English pilot's foremost dreams. Europeans at that date probably had less information about the island empire than about any other part of Asia. Marco Polo had described it with an accuracy extraordinary, considering that he did so from hearsay. The country had defied the attempts of even Kublai Khan to conquer it.

The first Europeans in Japan, as we have observed, were those three Portuguese adventurers, Antonio de Moto, Francisco Zimoro and Antonio Perota, who discovered it by accident, in 1542. Owing to this accident and the subsequent adventures of Ferdinand Mendes Pinto, the Portuguese had obtained a foothold in the Empire. They were the pioneers among traders in Japan and enjoyed preference and privilege.

But the twenty-eight survivors of the crippled and unseaworthy *Liefde* were now making for a country to them utterly unknown. Adams had learned something from the first mate of one of the expedition's other vessels. This man, Dirck Gerritsz, had been to Japan once aboard a Portuguese ship. He had told Adams that the expedition would find there a ready market for its cargo of woolens. But Dirck Gerritsz was aboard the fourth vessel of the squadron that we mentioned above. That was the one which was blown into the harbor of Valparaiso and whose crew were impressed into the Spanish navy. So it was entirely due to Adams's skill as a navigator that this battered band of Dutchmen made their Japanese landfall, "having no more but nine or tenne able men to go or creepe upon their knees." Twenty-two months out from Rotterdam they dropped anchor near Bungo on the island of Kyushu.

Their arrival was instantly reported to the feudal lord of the place. The presence of Europeans was no novelty to the daimyo of Bungo. The Jesuits had a mission there, the Portuguese had been trading in and out of the place for several years. The daimyo made the Hollanders welcome, gave them a safe anchorage for the sea-worn *Liefde* and placed a house at their disposal, as well as abundant victuals. The weary, sick adventurers seemed to have found a safe haven after all their sufferings. But a new danger sprang up.

The Portuguese immediately lodged a protest with the daimyo of Bungo. They perceived that the arrival of the Hollanders meant the end of the precious trade monopoly which the Portuguese enjoyed. And the Jesuits abhorred them as heretics. Their Japanese converts, as they admitted, were still "tender in the Catholic faith." If Protestants were admitted their "perverse doctrines" might infect those converts and damage the influence of the Catholic missionaries. The Portuguese not only protested to the daimyo—they told him that Dutch sailors were all pirates and thieves. There was just one punishment that the Japanese employed for pirates: they crucified them. However, the daimyo did not take the word of the Portuguese. He sent couriers to the Shogun at Osaka. In his report he must have mentioned that the Englishman, Will Adams, appeared to be the most intelligent of the lot. The Shogun sent an imperial junk to Bungo and it was Adams whom its commander was ordered to bring back to Osaka.

For all the danger hanging over his head, it was a thrilling trip for the Englishman. He was taken through the inland sea, past Shikoku, past numerous smaller islands. By day he could see villages and towns on the coast, such scenery as he never had beheld before. He admired the fleets of fishing sampans with their colored sails as they made way for the imperial galley. Adams's letters prove that he was no proverbially insular Briton. He liked what he saw. He had hardly landed in Osaka before he realized that he was in a happy, flourishing country. Its inhabitants might be mostly heathens, but it was a region, as he said, as civilized as England. There is not a land, he wrote, "better governed in the world by civil policie." Its people were courteous, honest and brave.

When he entered the presence of the Shogun he found himself in a palace as beautiful as it was richly adorned. Though "guilded with gold in abundance," it was in the best of taste. By comparison, Hampton Court would have seemed crude and primitive. The manners of the ruler and his courtiers were exquisite. Such was the scene of Adams's first audience with the Master of Japan. It was an ordeal, for all its extreme politeness. A Portuguese served as interpreter. We may well imagine that his interpretation was none too scrupulous. The Shogun questioned the pilot exhaustively. The sovereign of his country was a woman? Well, well. Eyebrows were raised over courteous, slanting eyes. A powerful woman? How great was her country? Was she rich? What god did these "Ingrish" worship? Aha! A different god from the one to whom the Spanish and Portuguese bowed. The Shogun nodded his head. He began to understand why the Portuguese held these newcomers in such abhorrence.

[257]

But the English pilot had more than words with which to explain himself. He had brought with him a map of the world, as known to European geographers. This was something new to the Shogun's eyes. Adams pointed out on the map the course of the long voyage that he and his companions had taken to reach that court. He told the Shogun that the Dutch and English desired no conquests. All they wanted was peaceful relations, to exchange the wares of Europe for the things that Japan had to sell. He talked straight out from the shoulder, by his own account, honestly and without fear. He talked so interestingly that the Shogun kept him at it until the middle of the night. Then he dismissed the Englishman courteously, leading him to believe that he had made a favorable impression.

One wonders how well his words had been translated by that "Portingall" interpreter. For when Adams left the presence he found himself a prisoner. After three days' incarceration he was brought back for another audience. This time he was questioned still more minutely, not only about England, but about all the other countries of Europe. Again the Shogun inquired into his religious beliefs. When that ordeal was finished the Englishman was transferred to better quarters. But still he was a prisoner. And so he was kept on tenterhooks for six weeks, anxious about not only his own fate but that of his Dutch shipmates, languishing in captivity at Bungo. He had reason to worry. The Portuguese and

Spaniards were bringing all their influence and eloquence to bear on the Shogun. The Franciscans joined with the Jesuits in demanding the expulsion, if not the execution, of the heretic interlopers.

But there was one great piece of good luck for Adams. The Shogun who ruled Japan in the year 1600 was Iyeyasu, the third of the brilliant Tokugawa family. In the previous century the sacred line of the Mikados, the Sons of Heaven, had become hopelessly effeminate and feeble. As had happened in Europe, great feudal nobles had fought among themselves for the supreme power and devastated the country with their feuds. The Tokugawas, like the "mayors of the palace" in the European feudal times, had restored order. They did not dethrone the Mikado, but kept him as a sacred, invisible personage, a nominal fountain of authority "behind the veil" but without real power. The Tokugawa Shoguns were the actual emperors and Iyeyasu was the greatest of them all. In fact, even at this date, he appears as the greatest Japanese that ever lived. He had made his people happy and prosperous. He was strong and an able fighter when he had to be. But with it all he was peaceful, wise, humane, generous, broad-minded. In short, from our perspective, he seems to have been a far finer person than any European ruler of his time.

One cannot help believing that the vehemence of the Franciscans and Jesuits against Will Adams and the Dutchmen helped to turn the scales in their favor.

Iyeyasu took his time. But meanwhile the English navigator and his shipmates endured no physical sufferings. The Shogun's decision was a polite but definite rebuke for the Portuguese and Spaniards. All the prisoners to be released, though Adams was courteously but firmly "invited" to remain at court. The Dutchmen to be compensated for the goods which had disappeared from the *Liefde* while they were comfortable prisoners ashore at Bungo. They were allowed to settle anywhere they liked in Japan, but not to leave without permission.

It was a blow to the Iberians, a blow from which they never recovered. For it soon became manifest that the Englishman they opposed was becoming the Shogun's chief adviser for Foreign Affairs. Foreigners who came to Japan had to approach the ruler through Will Adams. For instance, the next time a Dutch ship dropped anchor off Japan, it was Adams who procured trading privileges for its supercargo. What was more, he persuaded the Shogun to allow the survivors of the *Liefde* to return home. It appears from the records that the over-zealous Catholic missionaries hurt their own cause.

Between the Spanish Franciscans and the Portuguese Jesuits they had some 300,000 converts at this time. Not content with that, they tried to use force to increase their numbers. They egged on the Japanese Christians to attack the shrines and temples of the Buddhist and Shinto creeds. Naturally, it annoyed the government. This sort of conduct inevitably made Adams

SUCH WAS THE SCENE OF ADAMS'S FIRST AUDIENCE WITH THE MASTER
OF JAPAN

all the more powerful at the Japanese court. One of
the first things that had amazed him was the religious
tolerance of the people of Cipangu, rulers and populace
alike. To a traveler from Europe, torn by the bitter
hatred between Catholic and Protestant, it was bewil-
dering. However, his simplicity and honesty helped to
steer him through the storms. He was quite as zealous
a Protestant as his adversaries were Catholics. But he
played fair. To be sure, he used his influence against
the Jesuit and Franciscan missionaries but he also used
it in behalf of the European traders, Catholics or Protestant. The Spanish and Portuguese merchants soon
found, to their astonishment, that the man they had
hated and feared was their staunch, impartial advocate
at court. He realized that it was to the advantage of
the Japanese to do business with the Iberian traders.
And he so advised the Shogun.

On the other hand, he threw all his weight against
the missionaries. He told Iyeyasu that the activities of
Catholic priests were usually followed by the invasion
of conquering troops. He painted a highly colored picture of what Hernán Cortes had done to the rulers of
Mexico and Pizarro to the Incas of Peru. He had the
ear of the Shogun, his arguments were plausible and the
actions of the Jesuits weighed on his side. They not
only incited their converts to the defiling of native
shrines, they tried to foment active rebellion. Iyeyasu
found that provincial daimyos who tried to defy his

power had a large number of Christian proselytes among their followers. All of which strengthened the position of the former apprentice of Master Nicholas Diggins.

The Catholics tried to solve their problem by converting the heretic pilot. A Franciscan friar undertook to prove to Adams that the days of miracles were not over. The Englishman made him a sporting proposition.

"If you can work a miracle," he offered, "if you can walk upon the water as did St. Peter, then I will join your Romish order."

The good friar, in all sincerity, took him up on it. A day was appointed for the performance at Uraga, on the seashore. A huge crowd assembled. Not only Adams and the Dutchmen, but thousands of Japanese, including officials of the court, Buddhist and Shinto priests, came to see the exhibition. The Franciscan arrived in his flowing brown robes and carrying a heavy wooden cross. Intoning an *Ave Maria* he stepped boldly into deep water. Of course he promptly sank. Encumbered by his robes the drowning miracle-worker lost his grip on the cross which might have kept him afloat. The Englishman smiled grimly, the Dutchman chuckled, the Japanese roared with laughter. The Japanese would have let the unfortunate friar drown as a good joke. It was one of the Dutchmen, Melchior van Santvoort, who sprang into a sampan and rescued the would-be saint. Perhaps he would have preferred to drown. His failure was a serious misfortune in Asia. He "lost face"—not only his own, but also that of his entire order and of the Catholic cause. The word was carried to Manila, the arch-diocese. The Provincial of the Franciscans recalled the ambitious miracle-worker, rebuked him bitterly and awarded a severe penance.

Naturally, that episode served to glorify the prestige of Will Adams. The former shipwright's apprentice became more influential at the Japanese court than many a noble daimyo. And we learn, not from English, but from Japanese sources, that he was also extremely popular among the people at large. He was known as Anjin Samma—"Honorable Pilot," or, more strictly, "Lord Director of the Wandering Needle," meaning the compass. That helps us to understand why within a few years he was living as a Japanese nobleman. Iyeyasu presented him with a handsome estate at Hemi-Mura, eight miles from Uraga, now known as Yokusuka. His pleasant, luxurious manor house was on the wooded heights overlooking the Bay of Yedo, now Tokyo. It was a "living like unto a lordship in England, with eighty or ninety husbandmen that be as my slaves or servants." Actually they were nothing like slaves. In Roman law they would be called "adstricti glebae." In other words, they belonged to the land, not to its owner. In practice, they looked up to the owner of the land as a benevolent father. This was noticed in later years when Adams brought some of his own traveling countrymen to Hemi-Mura on a visit. For this enviable property the ex-shipwright's apprentice paid tribute to the Shogun in the shape of one "tai," —a sea bream, just one fish—a day. (His descendants continued to send that tribute to Yedo seven times a week, until Commodore Perry and a squadron of Uncle Sam's ships made their historic entry into the Bay of Yedo.)

Such was the condition, seven or eight years after he had left Rotterdam, of Master Will Adams, born in Gillingham, Kent. When the Shogun did not demand his presence at court, he lived in state at Hemi-Mura, with ninety retainers. He had been raised to the rank of a two-sword Samurai, a peer of the realm. More important still, he was the confidant and personal friend of the greatest of the Tokugawas. Adams taught the Shogun all he himself had picked up of Occidental geometry and other mathematics. They passed long hours together, the Englishman explaining the mazes of European politics to the intuitive ruler of Japan. We can easily believe that Iyeyasu confided many secrets to the Kentish pilot that he never would have entrusted to any Japanese, even of his own kin.

From this distance, it is an interesting and touching picture to contemplate. Imagine the wise, weary ruler of Cipangu, bedeviled by the intrigues and jealousies of the powerful daimyos who were looking for the slightest loophole in his armor, the first chance to pull him out of the seat of power. Threatened, too, by a new danger—the suave, crafty, pious men from the other side of the world, with fair words in their mouths that their actions belied. We can almost hear him saying, after a hard day's arguing with all those troublesome people: "Where is Anjin Samma? Send for the Lord Director of the Wandering Needle. I would hear a few honest, simple words after all these lies and bickerings." And we can see the English Daimyo of Hemi-Mura bringing in his astronomical tables for an hour of quiet study with his patron so that the lord of all Japan might get the taste of courtiers' intrigues out of his mouth.

There was just one thing that Iyeyasu would not do for his favorite. He would not let him go home. "In the end of five yeares I made supplication to the king to goe out of this land, desiring to see my poore wife and children according to conscience and nature. With the which request the Emperor was not well pleased," wrote Adams. Later on he had an opportunity to go. To that we shall come in due time. Meanwhile he contrived to send sums of money to Mistress Adams, whether she was now living in Limehouse or in his native Gillingham.

Iyeyasu, as we have observed, was a wise man. He needed this blunt, plain-spoken confidant from overseas. He realized that his English favorite had qualms of conscience and probably a bit of homesickness from time to time. But he also knew, as the proverb says: "A woman's hair is strong enough to bind even the foot of an elephant." At least, those are the words put into his mouth by the Japanese playwright who preserved the legend of the romance of Will Adams in a drama. For it is interesting to observe that the tradition of the first Englishman in Cipangu is more alive in Japan this very day than it is in England.

Not far from Hemi-Mura lived a small landholder named Magone Kageyu. In the play he is called Giheigi. He had a charming young daughter, Otsu. Adams had watched her from time to time, had plenty of opportunity to note that she was a lovely child. She was not only beautiful, she had the exquisite manner, poise and anxiety to be pleasant that you can perceive in Japanese ladies even today. But the Lord Pilot was still an austere Protestant. His conscience bothered him about Mistress Adams, "in a manner a widdow and my two children fatherlesse" in England. So he smiled upon Otsu whenever he saw her, but never considered her seriously.

There were men in that part of the country who had other ideas about Otsu. Their intentions were not honorable, but they were serious. Foremost among them was the Ronin, Iwai. A Ronin was a rebellious noble, turned highwayman. You might compare him to a robber baron of the same period in Europe. Or to Major Quantrell of Missouri and his like, who declined to be "reconstructed" after the war between the States in America.

At any rate, Iwai San wanted the lovely little Otsu and took her in the only fashion compatible with the honor and prestige of a Ronin. He swooped down upon her father's homestead, tied up the parents and servants and carried the girl off. The court and the head of police authority were some distance away. The nearest powerful noble was the Anjin Samma. As soon as the maiden's father got loose from his bonds he ran to the manor house at Hemi-Mura. The English Samurai collected a troop of his tenants and hurried off in pursuit of the Ronin. There was a short, sharp fight. Adams got the girl out of the clutches of Iwai and brought her in safety to his own house. But in the mêlée the Ronin escaped. Iwai scoured the country and got together a company of other Ronin. They descended upon Hemi-Mura, overcame the Lord Pilot's bodyguard. Not only did they recapture Otsu, but they took her English champion prisoner as well, and carried both their captives off into the hills.

A travel-worn fellow then dragged his weary body into the presence of the mighty Shogun. It was Otsu's father, Magone Kageyu. At first the court attendants would not admit him. Iyeyasu heard the tumult in the antechamber and had the intruder brought in. Magone

Kageyu fell to his knees with his forehead making the kotow.

"Great Lord—my daughter—the Anjin Samma—" he muttered.

"Your daughter is your own business," replied the Shogun. "But what of the Anjin Samma?"

The bereaved father stammered out his story. When Iyeyasu learned that his English favorite was a prisoner in the hands of the Ronin, he fumed.

"Call out the guard!" he cried. "My armor, quick! Samurai, we have work to do."

When the Ronin Iwai started his amorous enterprise he expected no more than the usual difficulties with the imperial police. Like the Highland chieftains in Scotland, the Ronin had their clans and followers. Living in hideaways, they were difficult to catch. And for the most part their raids were not important enough for the central authority to bother with them. But when it came to the kidnaping of a prominent court official, even though he was a foreigner, Iwai had bitten off more than he could chew. He had hardly got the girl and the English pilot to his fastness before he found the entire military forces of the empire on his heels. Iyeyasu, himself, led the disciplinary expedition. They slew the Ronin with all his band and brought Otsu and Adams back, safe and sound.

This is a tale that might have been told with proper decorations by the author of *Under the Red Robe*. It can be left to your imagination to conceive how the Kentish pilot fell in love with the dainty little Japanese girl with whom he had experienced such an adventure. The wise Iyeyasu perceived that accident had given him a chain as strong as it was delicate to keep his English councilor by his side. He gave Otsu to Adams for a bride. In the Japan of today such a marriage would bring nothing but trouble and humiliation on both sides. But for the obscure landholder, Magone Kageyu, it was an honor to become the father-in-law of the Anjin Samma, the privy councilor of the great Shogun.

However you look at it, theirs was a happy marriage. Otsu may have been dainty and fragile to look at, but she soon proved herself equal to the position of mistress of the household of a two-sword Samurai with an estate of eighty or ninety tenants. We find records that, in the absence of her lord, she transacted his business with authority and responsibility. No lady of the manor in Elizabethan England could have displayed more capacity.

Presently the Shogun demanded more from Adams than advice and instruction in mathematics. From time to time he had entertained visiting Spaniards and made them flowery Japanese compliments on the comparative excellence of Spanish sea-craft. The Dons had responded with promises to send some of their best ships to Japan as a present to the Shogun. The moment they departed they had gaily forgotten their promises.

[269]

This was another factor that made Iyeyasu dislike the Iberians. He determined to show them that he did not have to depend upon them. He asked Adams to build him a couple of ships. Master Will protested. He said he did not possess the necessary skill. To be sure, he had been an apprentice in the yards of Master Nicholas Diggins at Limehouse for twelve years, but most of that time his real ambition had been more for seafaring and navigation than the craft of the shipwright. The Shogun insisted, so Adams set to work. He had to teach Japanese carpenters how to build ships after the English manner. Laboriously he had to flog his memory for the principles of the art. After all, nearly forty years had passed since he left the shipyards at Limehouse. But he accomplished the job. He managed to build a couple of ships for the Shogun that were at least seaworthy and could be navigated. And they were a vast improvement upon the Japanese junks.

We now come to a critical point in the career of the Lord Director of the Wandering Needle. To make it quite clear we have to go into a phase of commercial history. The great Empire of Portugal was becoming effete. The magnificent achievements of the explorers and adventurers inspired by Prince Henry the Navigator seemed to have exhausted the virility of the Portuguese. "Their kingdom was divided"—and the Dutch were the first to pick up the pieces. The English got wise when the merchants of Amsterdam raised the price of pepper to eight shillings a pound. (In present-day values that would mean about eight dollars.) At first hearing, this may sound strange in our ears. Pepper? Why should pepper be so important? We have pepper on our tables every day, with plenty of other spices in the pantry. Almost anybody can afford to buy them. But before somebody invented refrigerators, pepper was enormously important for helping to preserve food. For instance, when Alaric descended upon Rome in 408 A.D., part of the ransom that the Gothic conqueror demanded was the city's supply of pepper, three thousand pounds. That may help us to realize why the spice trade led to men's risking their lives, waging epoch-making wars and discovering new continents.

At any rate, the merchant princes of London became alarmed when the city of Amsterdam so raised the price of pepper and other spices. "High time that Englishmen took their part in this traffick," they said. Accordingly, in 1600, Queen Elizabeth granted a charter to the East India Company, "John Company," as it was later called popularly. (Far-sighted as good Queen Bess was, she probably little dreamed that the charter she handed out in 1600 was destined to add the empire of India, Burma, Ceylon and part of Borneo to the dominions of the English crown.) John Company throve from the start. The great corporation was headed by no less a dignitary than the Earl of Cumberland. Among the stockholders were two hundred and fifteen knights. Its first expedition was sent out in February, 1601, under the command of Captain James Lancaster, a typical adventurer of Elizabethan times. He was partly a legitimate trader, partly no better than a pirate. One of his exploits had been a raid upon the Portuguese colony of Pernambuco, in Brazil. He had captured the town and brought back seven shiploads of loot to London town. So we can see that old John Company had picked a good man to head its first enterprise. The ruthless Lancaster not only brought back all his four ships, safe and sound, loaded to capacity with rich cargoes, he had made friends with the Sultan of Achin at the northwest end of Sumatra and obtained permission to establish an English "factory" there. (That does not mean a plant where they manufactured things, but a trading post.) And he set up another at Bantam, in Java.

All this happened soon after the arrival of Will Adams in Japan. When he had made himself solid at the court of the Shogun he got into correspondence with his countrymen at Bantam. Through them, he sent letters to England, including the remittances to his wife. Not all of his letters reached their destinations. They had to be conveyed by the courtesy of Dutch trading captains. And the Hollanders were not any too keen to let the English pilot bring a flock of competitors from London into Japanese waters. However, in one way and another, the directors of John Company got news of that strange countryman of theirs who in some mysterious fashion had acquired influence with the ruler of Japan. Accordingly, when they sent Captain John Saris out to the East Indies in 1613, they instructed him, among other things, to get into contact with Will Adams. Saris was also furnished with a letter from King James I to the "Emperor" of Japan. He landed at Hirado, north of what is now Nagasaki, where the Dutch had established their factory.

The arrival of the East Indiaman was a critical event in the life of the Anjin Samma. For the first time in thirteen years, since the death of his brother, he was to set eyes upon his own countrymen. Naturally, he was their advocate in all negotiations between John Company and Iyeyasu. If he could conduct the business to satisfy both the Shogun and the English captain he could achieve what he thought he had wanted so long —a return to home. Iyeyasu would give him the permission and the company should be only too glad to give him free passage and pay him for his services. So it is particularly interesting to observe what happened.

When the court received the news from Hirado, the Shogun said kindly: "Go, my friend, welcome your countrymen and bring their head man back with you. We shall be glad to see your honorable friend." We can imagine the exile's excitement and anticipation as he hurried off on his mission. Adams went with the retinue and circumstance befitting the rank of a two-sword Samurai. The Englishmen, instead of being amused and delighted, were abashed and disgruntled. The lord of Hemi-Mura, on the other hand, was sadly disillusioned by the men of his own blood. After thirteen years among the Japanese, the manners of the Britons seemed crude and rude. Furthermore, their captain was a cad, a snob, a bully. As we read about John Saris we are reminded of the British officers in Palestine who looked down upon T. E. Lawrence because he associated with Arabs and went around in the costume of a shereef. Captain Saris was one of those insular individuals who think an Englishman can best prove his superiority to other peoples by being overbearing and contemptuous. When Adams said to him: "I have found these Japanese an admirable and most courteous folk," Saris snorted.

"This fellow gives so admirable and affectionated commendations of the country that it is generally thought amongst us that he is a naturalized Japanner," he reported to the home office. In other words, only a renegade Englishman could possibly approve of any other people than his own.

Saris considered it his duty to keep Adams in his place, as a person of low origin. What if the pilot had lived among the "Japanners" for thirteen years? Captain John Saris was an English gentleman, therefore he must know more about everything than a person who had once served as an apprentice.

Nevertheless, Adams swallowed the captain's supercilious manners and did his best to get along with John Company's man. And he used his most powerful persuasions with the Shogun to procure privileges for the English. Iyeyasu received Saris with all the ceremony of Japanese etiquette but also with exceptional favor. He sent the English to the court of Hitetada, his son and heir apparent, at Yedo. And then, at the special request of the Anjin Samma, the Shogun granted the East India Company a charter, awarding it full trading rights throughout the empire, with such privileges as previous comers had not even dreamed of. As we would express it today, John Company was sitting pretty, thanks to the ex-shipwright's apprentice whom Saris despised. England had suddenly become "tops" in the Japanese export and import trade. But then the pompous captain showed his genius for doing the wrong thing. Adams urged him to establish the company's factory near the court at Yedo. Even from this distance it seems such obviously sound advice that one cannot understand why it was not accepted. What was more, the mighty Shogun himself backed up the suggestion politely but emphatically. A sane man, you might think, would have taken the hint. But John Saris knew better than even the country's ruler. He located the East India Company's factory at Hirado, near the Dutch. Adams was chagrined, while the Shogun shrugged his shoulders and what he thought may be

left to the imagination. Nevertheless, out of consideration for the Lord Director of the Needle, Iyeyasu let
the charter stand.

He also yielded to the pilot's repeated prayer for
leave to return home. Saris, under instructions from
his directors, offered Will Adams passage to England.
And at the eleventh hour, Adams declined. One can
hardly blame him. Even a short voyage under that
arrogant captain would have been unpleasant and the
journey might, with unfavoring winds, have lasted nine
months or a year. Furthermore, his encounters with
Saris had given the lord of Hemi-Mura a shrewd in-
sight into what he might expect back in Kent or Limehouse. On the soil where he was born he would be no
peer of the realm with ninety husbandmen as tenants.
He would be plain Bill Adams, possibly an object of
suspicion because of his sympathy and liking for "fur-
riners." He had become accustomed to the gentle manners of the Japanese. The men who came with Saris
evidently considered politeness a symptom of weakness.

So Will Adams remained in Japan. Iyeyasu must
have chuckled. What was more, for the next few years
English ships visited Japan frequently. But the Anjin
Samma sailed on none of them.

However, he did enter the employ of the East
India Company. Here again, John Saris showed his
mettle. A reasonable agent would have valued the services of a man who knew the country so well, a court

favorite to boot, as worth a considerable salary. Saris held him down to a hundred pounds a year. As the pilot observed, he had earned almost twice as much from Pieter van der Hay and Hans van der Veek of Rotterdam, as pilot major. But Saris declared that he was "only fitting to be master of a junke and to be used as linguist at court." Well, we do not need to consider Captain Saris any more. The only remarkable fact about him is that such a stupid fellow should have left behind him an interesting contribution to the history and geography of his times. His description of his voyage is still an exceedingly important document.

Adams accepted the insulting pittance from the East India Company because he had a bee in his bonnet. If he did not return to England, he thought, at least he could further satisfy his original ambition to see more of the world. Life in Japan was luxurious and pleasant, but tame. The lust for adventure was still in him. He hoped to persuade John Company to send him on an expedition to find the Northeast Passage from the Pacific side. It was a gallant idea. Iyeyasu was in full sympathy with it. Indeed, he himself furnished his pilot the means for a journey to Yezo, then the northernmost of the islands of Japan. There Adams obtained enough information to convince him that the search for the Northeast Passage from that quarter of the world was feasible. But to accomplish it he needed certain supplies not available in Asia. Also he needed "fifteen or twenty English seamen or less, it is no matter." He implored the directors in London to send him what he wanted. He cut down his requisitions to the bone. But John Company was blind of that eye. It remembered that Sir Hugh Willoughby and two ships' crews had perished off the North Cape in 1553; it forgot that Richard Chancellor had returned from that disaster with a charter from Ivan the Terrible for the Muscovy Company. The best the directors would do for Adams was to let him make voyages to Siam and Indo-China, establishing trade relations. On one of these trips he visited the King of Siam and his court in Ayuthia and obtained trading concessions.

In 1615 a rebellion broke out against the rule of the Tokugawas. It was so serious that the stronghold of Osaka was besieged. The records do not say what part the Anjin Samma took in the conflict. Possibly he was on a voyage to Cochin China while it occurred. Some time previously Iyeyasu had officially retired, leaving the details of government in the hands of Hitetada. Nevertheless, his influence was paramount so long as he lived and it was his presence and prestige that subdued the rebels in 1615. But one year later he died, leaving his son the sole ruler. That was an anxious moment for Will Adams. And, for a fact, his position in the empire never was the same thereafter. He was no longer the actual Foreign Minister. Hitetada liked and respected Adams well enough. He consulted the English pilot, but did not take his advice as Iyeyasu had. The reason was that the Japanese ruling classes were becoming exasperated with the persistent intrigues and trouble-making of the Spaniards and Portuguese. The Catholics were not content with the privileges they had. They wanted to convert the whole empire and quickly, by force if necessary. Catholic converts were numerous among the rebels in the uprising of 1615. This began to exhaust the patience of the government. Hitetada, consequently, tended to lump all foreigners together and set them down as a nuisance that it was not necessary to endure. The English and the Dutch suffered from this, along with the Catholics. Their concessions were restricted. Hitetada ruled the Jesuits out altogether, as European rulers had already begun to do. The Portuguese, Dutch and English were confined to Hirado and Nagasaki. It did not damage Adams personally, though he felt disappointed and defeated. The result was to drive him more exclusively to the society of his Japanese relations and friends. He made a few more voyages, but gave most of his time to his estate at Hemi-Mura.

He died in 1620. Three years later the East India Company withdrew from Japan entirely. Another twenty years and Japan decided that it was not only possible but desirable to get along without any intercourse with Europeans at all. It had brought the empire too much trouble, incessant squabbling. The people of Dai Nippon had been most hospitable. But they had the sense to perceive, after trying it out for a hundred years, that they were ill rewarded for it. So they kicked all the foreigners out except for a few Dutchmen, who were restricted to a tiny factory on the island of Deshima. They were not allowed to set foot on the larger islands. And any Japanese who left his country was punished with death if he returned. So the sacrifice and inspiration of the great Christian St. Francis Xavier, the honesty and steadfastness of the English pilot, had alike gone for nothing.

However, the memory of the Anjin Samma has been kept alive in Japan throughout the centuries. In Tokyo there is a street named after him, the "Anjin Cho." A small celebration is held on that street every year in honor of the English pilot. And there is a monument to him near the Nihon-Bashi. In the country of his birth there is none.

In all history you will find few more curious friendships than that between the greatest of Japanese rulers and a former shipwright's apprentice from Limehouse.

XI

THE BUCCANEER WHO BECAME A GREAT EXPLORER

THE BUCCANEER WHO BECAME A GREAT EXPLORER

ON the afternoon of the sixth of August, 1698, several of the most distinguished men about London were dining at the house of the famous Mr. Pepys—Samuel Pepys. English "People of Quality" knew him as Secretary of the Admiralty.

Among the People of Quality present were such as Charles Montague, President of the Royal Society, Sir Hans Sloane, founder of the British Museum, and John Evelyn, whose diary was destined to make him almost as famous as Pepys. The guests had come with not only healthy appetites but healthy curiosity. They were to meet a notorious buccaneer. It was only natural that the fashionable folk of London should be keen to see what a buccaneer looked like, especially one who had made his name a symbol of terror all over the Spanish Main. His name was William Dampier.

But it was not only as a man of blood and iron that this Dampier had become a celebrity in the capital of the Merrie Monarch. He had brought back with him the manuscript of a book in which he had described, with unusual modesty, his travels and discoveries. That volume, *A New Voyage,* had become a sensation almost overnight. Men of learning had found in it a vast fund of information hitherto unknown about far-off lands and seas, winds and tides. Scholars of the Royal Society proclaimed it invaluable. Simpler folk, who just liked to read, were charmed by its simplicity and vivid adventures.

London had become curious about Dampier for other reasons, too. Naturally, there were enemies. They spread the most highly colored tales of his violence, the language he used, his generally swashbuckling, bloodthirsty character. Thus he had been made into a combination of literary sensation and ferocious Bad Man.

So Mr. Pepys's guests went to his dinner expecting to see some kind of strange monster—bluff, burly, bearded, swaggering. Instead they met a thin, slightly built man, about 46 years old. His hair was brown, his complexion ruddy and, of course, tanned by wind and sun. He had "strangely dark blue eyes." Between them jutted a nose curved almost like a sea-gull's beak. His portrait—which you can see for yourself in the National Portrait Gallery when you go to London—shows an unhappy, brooding expression on his face, somewhat pathetic.

Thus the appearance of this awesome buccaneer furnished surprise No. 1 for the guests of Mr. Pepys. His manners were still more astonishing. He was diffident, polite, soft-spoken. This is how he impressed

John Evelyn: "He seemed a more modest man than one would imagine by relation of the crew he assorted with." Then we get an idea why the notorious buccaneer had made such a hit with the learned men of England. In his quiet, bashful way he had come back with the information: "Gentlemen, all your charts of the Pacific are dead wrong." As John Evelyn wrote: "He brought a map of the course of the winds in the South Seas, and assured us that the maps hitherto extant were all false as to the Pacific Sea."

From all this we may paint for ourselves a pretty fair picture of this singular man. Among all the explorers you will hardly find a more contradictory character. Not much better than a pirate, he added invaluably to the knowledge of his times. He would step aside from the raiding of a peaceful town or the looting of a merchant vessel to make scientific observations. He associated with wild men who "drank brandy as liberally as Spaniards do clear water." But in his journals he confessed that he "did ever abhor drunkenness." He led bands of ruffians, "a savage and dirty people, fearing neither man nor God." Yet the tone and content of his journals show him to have been every whit as modest as Evelyn describes him.

He wrote so little about himself that we know almost nothing about his youth. He was born in Somersetshire, of a decent yeoman (small farmer) family. His parents sent him to school and wanted him to learn a trade. But he displayed so little stomach for Latin grammar that "they who had the disposal of me . . . placed me with the Master of a ship at Weymouth, complying with the inclinations I had very early of seeing the World."

Young William's first long voyage, before the mast, was to Newfoundland. He came home with a steady resolve never again to ship for such cold waters. The next time he sailed it was aboard an East Indiaman. He returned from the Dutch Spice Islands just in time to enlist for the second war with Holland. Able Seaman Dampier was wounded in the engagement off the Schooneveldt between the fleets of Prince Rupert, Admiral D'Estrées and the Dutch under the great Admiral De Ruyter. So he saw the fierce but indecisive Battle of the Texel from the deck of a hospital ship. As he related in after years, he never could comfortably adapt himself to the customs of the Royal Navy, even though he subsequently became a captain in that service.

When that inglorious war was over he wrote: "With my health I recovered my old inclination for the sea." So when a neighboring squire offered him a job on his plantation in Jamaica the lad, now in his early twenties, jumped at it. But he couldn't stand it for more than six months. Then he joined the company of a ship bound to Campeachy Bay for logwood. And that, although he didn't know it, was the real beginning of his career.

Those logwood cutters were as tough a bunch as the timber industry has ever seen. Compared to them the lumberjacks of the Michigan and Canadian forests were effeminate. The camps at Campeachy were, to a man, filled with ex-buccaneers. Some of them were former gorillas of Morgan's, out of a job since their erstwhile leader had become the respectable Sir Henry, Lieutenant-Governor of Jamaica. They were a constant thorn in the side of the near-by Spanish authorities. Though the logwood they cut was worth one hundred pounds sterling a ton, they drank all their profits away, paying fancy prices for Barbados rum.

Now young Dampier decided that a sober man could make money out of this logwood business. He took a job as a hired hand, worked ferociously in that Yucatan climate, became a partner of his employers. So far this sounds like a Horatio Alger story. But Destiny stepped into the picture. In June, 1676, a terrific hurricane swept the Caribbean, destroying every ship and wiping out everything that Dampier and his partners owned.

During this period he had started the journals which have been the admiration of the scientific world ever since. In them we find the first description of tarpon fishing. While a humble logwood cutter, he began making notes about birds, beasts, fishes. Wherever he went he made a point of learning as much about the inhabitants and their customs as possible. At the height of the hurricane that ruined him he took time to write down observations on tides, waves and winds.

That Caribbean hurricane was as much of a misfortune to the Spanish authorities as it was to Dampier and the logwood cutters. With the lumber industry at a standstill there was nothing for the last-named to do but go back to their old trade—buccaneering. Dampier, with some misgivings, joined them.

Now there is still a good deal of misunderstanding about those gentry. While they were every bit as ruthless and ruffianly as they have been described, they were not mere pirates. As their historian, Esquemeling, points out, the buccaneering movement, to begin with, was a rebellion against Spanish authority. The buccaneers originally were hunters, capturing or shooting the wild cattle, horses and boars on Hispaniola. The Spaniards claimed everything in that part of the world for themselves and tried to suppress and drive out the men of all other nations. The wild cattlemen on Hispaniola at first were mostly French. They derived their name from the *boucans*, where they salted their meat. It was the dog-in-the-manger policy of Spain that turned them into raiders and made the word buccaneer signify a savage sacker of towns and robber of merchant vessels. For a while they attacked none but Spanish ships. Later on they captured their prey first and inquired about nationality afterwards.

They considered themselves as belonging to an entirely honorable profession. Some of them, such as Sir Henry Morgan, became national heroes and were knighted. There were buccaneer captains who read Divine Service every Sabbath and allowed only essential work on all religious festivals.

But for the most part they were a desperate, godless lot. And such were the men with whom William Dampier started out to "singe the beard of the King of Spaine." His first venture does not appear to have been vastly profitable. His party captured the town of Alvarado, near Vera Cruz. But when they began looting they found all the inhabitants had escaped with their money and movable property. In this fashion Dampier roved and rambled up and down the Spanish Main for a twelvemonth. Then he went back to England for a short holiday.

On this visit he got married. His bride was "a young lady from the household of the Duke of Grafton." But he was soon back in the West Indies, this time with the most peaceable intentions. He made enough out of one enterprise to buy him a small estate in Dorsetshire. Just as he was about to return to England to inspect his property, a Captain Hobby offered him a share in a trading venture. But on this voyage the vessel ran into a harbor full of privateers' ships. Captain Hobby's crew deserted, to a man. A few days later Dampier also joined the buccaneers. It seemed as though Destiny kept pushing him in that sinister direction. The fleet of raiders set sail for Porto Bello. That hapless town was always being sacked!

For the next few years Dampier's story was one of raid after raid, frequent privations, constant fighting, desperate forced marches under various captains. He fought on land and on sea. He walked across the dangerous and pestilent Isthmus of Darien three times. From the battles he seems always to have escaped without a scratch. Also without much booty. He got forty pounds as his share of the sack of Porto Bello! He took part in the capture of many merchant vessels but apparently no fabulously rich prizes. One of the captains under whom he sailed was the redoubtable Watling. Dampier was with Watling in 1681 when, as we observed in an earlier story, a Mosquito Indian was left stranded on the island of Juan Fernandez. Watling was killed in an attack upon Arica. The English penetrated into the heart of the town, but were driven off "with heavy hearts that we should leave so much plate behind us."

After three years of such forays Dampier finally arrived in Virginia with a moderate amount of booty but voluminous notes. One year later he started on a voyage which, though he did not know it, was to take him all around the world and make him famous. He joined a party of buccaneers under Captain John Cook, for a buccaneering raid into the South Seas. They weighed anchor in August, 1683, setting their course first for Africa. Dampier by this time was an experienced man and had risen to be assistant-quartermaster. His shipmates were as tough a crowd as ever scuttled a ship. When they reached the mouth of the River Sherbro in Africa, south of Sierra Leone, they found a brand-new Danish craft of forty guns. Without the slightest hesitation or warning they boarded and captured her. She was re-christened *The Bachelor's Delight*. From Sierra Leone they sailed southwest, back across the Atlantic and rounded Cape Horn in February. On the 22nd of March they anchored off Juan Fernandez. The first thing they did was to send off a boat for Robin, the Mosquito Indian whom Watling had left there in 1681, three and a half years earlier. Captain Cook was taken ill at Juan Fernandez and died near Cape Blanco off the mainland of Mexico.

Soon after rounding "Cape Stiff," Cook had been overhauled by the *Nicholas* of London, commanded by Captain Eaton. They joined forces at Juan Fernandez and continued on up the coast together. Before long they were joined by the *Cygnet* of London, whose master was a corpulent fellow named Swan. He claimed to have been forced into buccaneering by his crew. But he proved an apt pupil, for he soon became as ruthless as any of them. So now the buccaneers formed quite a formidable force. They "jogged on" from island to island, taking ships, villages, towns. They even attacked the rich fleet of plate ships from

Lima, but were beaten off. However, they took and sacked the wealthy town of Leon, in Nicaragua. One of the Englishmen who fell was a veteran of eighty-four, one of Oliver Cromwell's old Ironsides.

In August, 1685, Dampier left Captain Davis, who had succeeded Cook and became navigating officer ("pilot" as it was then called) under the grampus-shaped Swan, on the *Cygnet*. His reason for the transfer was characteristic. He liked and respected Davis. But the latter wanted to return to the coast of Peru, whereas Swan wanted to sail north along the Mexican coast and thence to the East Indies. This was more in line with Dampier's incurable zest for high adventure, his ambition to see the world. Swan kept his plans a secret from everyone aboard except Dampier. As the cruise continued, many of the crew became mutinous. They wanted to cash their booty and enjoy life. It was Dampier's influence that kept them in line.

They set sail across the Pacific in March, 1686. There were now only two ships: the *Cygnet* and a smaller barque commanded by Teat, Swan's first mate. "We were 150 men, 100 aboard of the Ship and 50 aboard the Bark, besides Slaves." They made the island of Guam with just three days' provisions left. They had been on short rations for days, with a frightened and rebellious crew. Dampier learned that the men had plotted "first to kill Captain Swan and eat him when the Victuals were gone and after him all of us." To

DAMPIER WAS PERMITTED TO GO ASHORE WITH ALL HIS EFFECTS

which Swan replied: "Ah, Dampier, you would have made them but a poor meal!" Dampier was as lean as Swan was fat.

They refitted at Guam and sailed to Mindanao in the Philippines. There they remained six months. The commander-in-chief of the Sultan's army took a great fancy to the Englishmen. The comfortable life and his respectful treatment at the Sultan's court gave Swan a bad attack of the swelled head. He took to abusing his crew. They, in turn, were conspiring against their captain and drinking liquor in large quantities. It ended in open mutiny. Teat and another officer put to sea in the *Cygnet*, leaving Swan and thirty-six other Englishmen at Mindanao. Dampier sailed with Teat, becoming supercargo, though he was mistrusted at first because he had protested against deserting Swan. He was now, as Wilkinson observes, no longer a buccaneer, but just a plain pirate.

But the piratical cruise was as dull as it was unprofitable. Dampier was the only man aboard who got any benefit out of it: notes, knowledge, more notes. The *Cygnet* made for the Gulf of Siam to no purpose, thence north to the Pescadores, between Formosa and China. On the return voyage south by way of Mindanao, Dampier attempted to rescue Swan. But the ringleaders among the crew got wind of his plan and it failed.

The most important thing about the cruise was the

course set after the *Cygnet* left Celebes. They made for the land then known as "terra Australis incognita," the unknown land of the South. On the maps of the day it was called New Holland. The first man to discover it was the Dutchman Willem Janszoon, in 1606. But when Dampier sailed there nobody yet knew whether Australia was an island or a continent. Dampier did not solve the question. The spot where the *Cygnet* touched is shown on the map today as Dampier Land, near the rich Kimberley district. The group of islands near by is the Buccaneer Archipelago. Dampier's description of the part of Australia he saw is not flattering. He found the land barren and the natives such as to make the "Hodmadods" (Hottentots) seem gentlemen by comparison.

After the visit to Australia, Dampier asked Teat to put him ashore at the nearest English factory. The reply was a threat to maroon him. Conditions aboard the *Cygnet* must have been intolerable. In order to prevent desertions, Read, the second in command, made a practice of ill-treating the natives so that the crew might be afraid to land. They reached Sumatra without event. When they got to the Nicobar Islands, Dampier made a determined effort to get away. He was permitted to go ashore with all his effects. But an hour later Captain Teat, with an armed party, brought him back by force. Upon returning to the ship he found everything in an uproar. Three other men announced that they were determined to join Dampier. Almost the entire crew sympathized with the deserters, one of whom was the ship's surgeon. Finally Dampier and two others were permitted to land once more, but the surgeon was held by force. They were joined by four Malays and a Portuguese who had been prisoners aboard the *Cygnet*.

The deserters soon made friends with the natives. They were even able to trade an ax for a canoe. And in this craft, after one mishap, they set out on one of the most remarkable voyages in history. With all eight castaways in it, the gunwales were a bare three inches from the water!

"I have been in many imminent Dangers before now, some of which I have already related," wrote Dampier in his journal: "but the worst of them all was but a Play-game in comparison with this. . . . I made very sad Reflections on my former Life, and looked back with Horrour and Detestation on Actions which before I disliked, but now I trembled at the remembrance of. . . . I had long before this repented me of that roving Course of Life, but never with such concern as now." There were fierce storms in the middle of the nights, the sea "roaring in a white Foam about us." Dampier or one other Englishman steered, the rest bailing for dear life. Thunder crashed overhead, streaks of lightning crackled all around. At dawn on the fifth day out from Nicobar they made a small harbor on the island of Sumatra. They were one hundred miles east of Achin, the nearest English factory.

It was fortunate they had the Malays with them. It was all they could do to stagger into the huts of the nearest fishing village and throw themselves down on the beds hospitably offered. When they awoke, every European was racked with fever. "Natives would come to the door of the hut and stare at them in wonder." Finally the headman of the village sent them on by canoe around the coast to the English factory at Achin. There the Portuguese died and a couple of days later one of the Englishmen. As for Dampier, it left him with a case of dysentery that lasted months. But it did not curb his restless urge to keep moving.

He was now, for all his years of buccaneering, penniless. We don't know why, because he told so little about himself in his diary. It is another of the strange contradictions in the man. His name already was almost as feared on the Spanish Main as those of Watling, Davis, Swan or any of the raiding captains. Yet he had nothing to show for it all.

A captain who put in at Achin offered Dampier a trip to Persia, but he declined. Instead, he signed on for a voyage to Tonquin, weak and suffering as he was. But he did his work as capably as any healthy man aboard. And all the time he kept up his observations and notes. He got as far as Cachao, the capital of Tonquin, and made several expeditions further up the

river, alone save for a native guide. Out of his entire
Tonquin adventure he got no profit, but material for
one of his most popular books. He returned to Achin
as penniless as he had left. During the next year and
a half he made several other trading voyages, including
one to Madras and another to Bencoolen in Sumatra.
There the Governor gave him a job as chief gunner
and military engineer of the fort. It was a tedious
place and the Governor's "humours were brutish and
barbarous." By the end of 1690 the wanderer had
become actually homesick. The Governor refused him
permission to leave. So, early in January, he slipped
out at midnight, "creeping through one of the port-
holes of the fort" and escaped aboard a homeward
bound English ship. With him he took the famous
"Painted Prince," Jeoly. This was a captive native
chief, a prisoner of war. He represented Dampier's
sole venture as a showman. He had bought Jeoly, who
was elaborately tattooed, in the hope of making money
by exhibiting him in England, thus anticipating Barnum
by some 200 years.

It was a miserable voyage home. The ship was ill-
found and poorly provisioned. Thirty of the crew died
of a mysterious disease before they reached the Cape
of Good Hope. However, after a stay at St. Helena,
they cast anchor off the Downs on the 18th of September, 1691. As Clennell Wilkinson records, he returned to his unfortunate wife without a sou, after

twelve years of buccaneering and roving. What her life must have been in those twelve years we can only imagine.

We know practically nothing of what Dampier did or how he lived in the next five years. We read of his being at Corunna in 1694, so apparently he made at least one short voyage. Possibly he earned a few pounds from time to time as navigating officer of trading vessels. Wilkinson infers that most of the time he stayed on his Dorsetshire estate, resting and preparing his book for the printer's. It was not published until 1697 and, as we observed earlier, made him famous almost overnight. And if ever an author deserved success it was William Dampier. He had preserved his manuscript through fire and flood. He had carried it in hollow bamboo sticks as he swam rivers in Darien, sat up all night drying the leaves over a fire on the beach. This was after his canoe had overturned in the surf on his first attempt to leave Nicobar. While the other buccaneers were carousing to celebrate hard-fought battles, he had sat up in his cabin at night to keep his journal down to date.

His success brought Dampier both profit and advancement. The first book became a best-seller and his publisher clamored for a second. And, as Evelyn remarks, he was soon sent abroad again, this time "by the

King's encouragement." The Admiralty made him a captain in the Royal Navy and gave him a King's ship, H.M.S. *Roebuck*, of 250 tons and 12 guns. His orders were to explore "New Holland," as Australia was then known. This was, at the time, one of the principal objects of curiosity among European geographers. In England, not only the geographers, but the government, were deeply interested.

The ill-fated voyage began in January, 1699. There were quarrels aboard, even before Dampier set sail from the Downs. For his chief officer the Admiralty had given him a Lieutenant George Fisher, R.N. It was a fatal choice. Fisher resented Dampier, resented the fact that he, a "gentleman" and a regular officer of the King's Navy, should have to serve under a man who had not gained his rank in the usual way and who had been a buccaneer to boot. Fisher deliberately encouraged the crew to be insubordinate. In the presence of petty officers and the fo'c'sle hands he would refer to their captain as an "old Rogue, old Dog, old Cheat, a mere theaf." Unquestionably, as the records showed later, this Lieutenant Fisher, R.N., was conspiring against his commanding officer.

Mutiny was bound to break out, as it did when the *Roebuck* was some two weeks away from Bahia in Brazil. For all his qualities and experience, Dampier was not fitted to cope with such conditions. He had not the gift of leadership. He was probably the finest navigator of his day. But he was no commander. In the crisis he did the best he knew. He confined Fisher to his cabin, whence the chief officer continued to shout abuse of his captain. And three ringleaders among the crew were put in irons. Dampier sent Fisher ashore at Bahia and the Portuguese Governor threw the mutineer, manacled, into the common jail "among negros and mulattos," an outrageous thing to do to an "officer and gentleman." Fisher got back home eventually, where he gave most of his time and energy to preparing trouble for Dampier.

With his prickly lieutenant out of the way, Dampier contrived to "allay in some measure the ferment that had been raised among my men." After a month's stay at Bahia, where he wrote copious notes, he rounded the Cape of Good Hope on June 6, 1699. From there he made excellent time. He reached Australia on the 26th. Coasting along, he anchored in the bay named after him, but did not stay long. Following his instructions from the Admiralty, he sailed north. If he had disobeyed orders and gone south, as Wilkinson points out, he would have discovered a great deal more of Australia. But he had a discontented and timid crew. Moreover, he himself had no stomach for cold weather, which he thought he would encounter in southern waters.

On this cruise he made a correct guess at the location of a strait to the north of Australia. But he did not venture far enough to actually find it. He and his men had some encounters with Australian aborigines, and his observations enabled him to make another correct guess: that there was gold in those regions. Late in the nineteenth century he was proved to have been right.

From northwest Australia, Dampier sailed by way of Timor to New Guinea. He discovered many smaller islands: "the map is largely his about there." His most important exploit was the discovery of Nova Britannia (New Britain) and of Dampier Strait, between New Britain and New Guinea. While he was in those parts he learned that his old persecutor, the Governor of Bencoolen, had been killed. The *Roebuck* refitted at Batavia and sailed home the 17th of October, 1700. It was a painful, laborious voyage. The *Roebuck* was a crazy old tub to begin with and it became more and more difficult to keep her afloat. They did not reach the Cape of Good Hope until December 30th. After putting in at St. Helena, they sprang a perilous leak, just off the island of Ascension. With both chain pump and hand pump clanking for all they were worth they barely limped into Ascension harbor. There the old *Roebuck* sank. All hands were saved, with their effects and a handful of provisions. For five weeks they kept themselves alive on that bleak, uninhabited rock, eating little but turtle meat and eggs. It was not until

April 3, 1701, that four ships put in at Ascension and took them off.

"In those days they did not prepare public receptions for explorers who had lost their ships. They prepared courts-martial instead." For almost a year and a half Lieutenant Fisher had been busy in London, conspiring with Dampier's other enemies to make trouble for him. The worst of it was that, unlike some modern explorers I know, Dampier was a poor hand at defending himself from attack. Fisher turned out to be an excellent witness for himself, Dampier hopelessly weak. The verdict of the court-martial, headed by Admiral of the Blue, Sir Clowdisley Shovell, was against the ex-buccaneer. It found that he had been guilty of "very Hard and Cruel Usage of Lieutenant Fisher . . . and was not a fitt person to be employ'd as Commdr. of any of Her Majesty's ships." (Good Queen Anne was now on the throne.) Worse still, the court fined Dampier all his pay!

But public opinion took his side. And it was luck for him that the War of the Spanish Succession broke out. Privateers were equipped to raid French and Spanish shipping. Competent navigators were sorely needed. Ten months after that court-martial's scathing verdict Dampier "had the honour to kiss Her Majesty's hand, being introduced by His Royal Highness, the Lord High Admiral," Prince George of Denmark.

This occurred after Dampier had been appointed to the command of a privateer, with the official approval of the Lords of the Admiralty.

His new command was the *St. George,* twenty-six guns. He sailed April 20, 1703. Again he was unfortunate in the officers and crew who served under him. Perhaps it was just unlucky coincidence that trouble always broke out on his ships. In those days discipline was weak on every vessel that put to sea. But the truth seems to have been that Dampier, though he had been the "terror of the Spanish Main," had not the knack of handling men. His chief Lieutenant and the purser went ashore at St. Iago in the Cape Verde Islands and fought a duel. The Portuguese Governor put the Lieutenant under arrest. When he returned to his ship Dampier put his chief officer ashore with his clothes and his servant. This was a trick he had learned among the buccaneers. Their method of dealing with troublesome men was to maroon them, a practice not approved by the Lords of the Admiralty.

Dampier cruised around in the Atlantic some six months and seems to have captured no prizes of much value. Then, in company with Captain Thomas Stradling of a smaller privateer, the *Cinque Ports,* he steered south for "Cape Stiff." They made Juan Fernández in February. There Captain Stradling had such a violent row with his crew that forty-two of them deserted and went ashore. It was Dampier who arbitrated the

[303]

squabble and reconciled them. That illustrates the sea-going customs of the times.

Dampier and Stradling made an attack on the town of Santa Maria, near which were rich gold mines. They were beaten off without booty. Their luck changed somewhat when they took a Spanish "great ship." But they did not find the 80,000 dollars supposed to have been hidden in her hold. And now we come to a bit of literary history. The officer put in charge of this prize was Alexander Selkirk, Stradling's first mate. Thereby hangs a tale that has enthralled readers young and old for well-nigh two hundred years.

Dampier and Stradling parted company at Tobago. Stradling sailed south to Juan Fernández, where he had left five members of his crew the last time he was there. They were all gone, having been picked up by French ships. But while he was at the island, Stradling and Selkirk had a violent quarrel. The Scottish mate declined to sail another day with Stradling. He remained on Juan Fernández and, though he did not know it, provided the basis for one of the greatest books in all literature, *Robinson Crusoe*. There we will leave Alexander Selkirk for a matter of four years and a half. Let us continue our cruise with Captain Dampier.

His voyage continued with his usual poor luck. Captains of privateers had the same problem as buccaneers. If they took many prizes and much booty their crews wanted to go ashore and spend their money. If their loot was too small, the men wanted to go home. This was the case with Dampier's outfit. The crew of a privateer, to begin with, could never be described as the salt of the earth. When most of the Queen's ships were manned by the scum of England, what could you expect of the others? Dampier's lot were discontented, turbulent, unruly. Finally twenty-three of them seized one of the captured Spanish prizes and sailed off in her.

Dampier made a desperate effort to improve his own fortunes and restore the spirits of his fellows. He had captured a small Spanish barque and put a prize crew aboard her. Together they lay in wait for and attacked the "Manila ship," one of the richest of the Spanish plate fleet. They were beaten off with sore damage. Dampier was blamed for it, not without reason. This was the crushing blow. Thirty-five of his remaining men deserted him. That left him with one ship and twenty-eight mutinous followers. Then followed an amazing exploit. With his twenty-eight disgruntled, chicken-hearted roughs, in a leaking, crippled ship, he sailed boldly to the coast of South America, attacked the town of Puna, captured it and sacked it. It was the biggest coup he had achieved on the entire voyage. By this time the *St. George* was limping like a water-logged punt. At the crucial moment he captured another Spanish vessel. It was not a moment too soon, the poor old *St. George* sank shortly after Dampier had transferred himself and crew to their prize.

But it seems there was no defeating Dampier's bad luck. About the time he sacked Puna, his Letter of Marque as a privateer expired. Consequently, when he reached the Dutch East Indies in his prize, he had no legal standing. He and all his crew were arrested and thrown into prison. How long they suffered there we do not know. But eventually Dampier returned to England in precisely the same condition as from his previous voyages. He was exactly and literally broke once more.

And again he found that an enemy had gone ahead of him. The troublesome fellows whom he had put ashore at various places put in their licks against him. One of them was able to write and publish a book attacking Dampier. But though he was so poor in argument, though the official world condemned him, he was always able to keep the respect of the intelligent people in London. The gentlemen who were charmed by his manners at the dinner table of Mr. Secretary Pepys still realized that this was one of the great Englishmen of his time. After all, he had sailed around the world twice. That wasn't done so often in the dawn of the eighteenth century. Dampier again was commanded to kiss the Queen's hand and tell her all about his adventures. And again we must wonder: what sort of a life was that of Mistress Judith Dampier, the young lady from the household of the Duke of Grafton whom the buccaneer married in 1678 and promptly sailed away to be gone for twelve years, and who thereafter was separated from her for two long voyages during which she had not a word from him?

The next we hear of Captain William Dampier, he had taken a step down in rank. Financed by merchants of Bristol, two privateers under the command of Captain Woodes Rogers set sail on the 2nd of August, 1708. Aboard the flagship *Duke*, as navigating officer ("pilot"), was the former buccaneer. Though it was a step down in rank, it was not degrading. For illustration: today the navigator on one of the vessels of Uncle Sam's Navy, or any other navy, is an important, ranking officer. Dampier's name was a valuable contribution to any privateering expedition. "His reputation as a fighting man had become formidable. Every Spaniard [in South and Central America] was familiar with his name. It had become a terror in those waters unequaled since the days of Morgan." So writes his most impartial biographer.

Woodes Rogers had no more luck with his crews than had Dampier. Mutiny followed mutiny. And he sailed many a league before he took any booty worth talking about. As a matter of record, the most important thing that happened on that entire voyage had nothing to do with loot. It was the rescue of Alexander Selkirk, whom we left four and a half years before on Juan Fernández. Woodes Rogers made the landfall late in the afternoon of the 31st of January, 1709.

[307]

He sent a landing party, which saw a fire among the trees. What could that be? It might signify Spaniards, with a squadron of fighting ships lying out of sight around the headlands. Actually it was a signal fire lit by Selkirk. Imagine his feelings when the first English ship he had seen in four and a half years weighed anchor and sailed away upon seeing his beacon!

But on the following morning Woodes Rogers returned. This time, in the clear light of day, the landing party espied a lone, curious-looking creature running up and down the beach. He was waving a white flag. "He was clothed in a goatskin jacket, breeches and cap, sewed together with thongs of the same." A member of the crew describes him as talking "in a strange, stumbling voice." Curiously enough, if you will refer to Robert Louis Stevenson's *Treasure Island*, you will find the same symptoms in Ben Gunn, who had been marooned on Treasure Island by the ferocious Captain Kidd. There is another point in which we can see that Stevenson, as well as Defoe, took part of his material from the true story of Alexander Selkirk. When the castaway was invited to come aboard Woodes Rogers's ship, he first inquired whether a certain officer was a member of the expedition. Hearing the reply "yes" he declined to leave the island. He said he would rather stay where he was. But the crew of the boat shouted: "Come on, he ain't in command, he can't hurt you." And not until then did they learn that the man they were rescuing was Alexander Selkirk.

Four and a half years had passed since Captain Stradling had landed him from the *Cinque Ports*. He had built himself two huts, one for living and sleeping quarters, the other for a kitchen. Among the effects he had brought with him was a Bible. When not engaged in hunting, fishing or doing his chores, he passed most of his time reading the Scriptures, singing psalms and praying.

At first Selkirk found it difficult to eat because he had no salt. Presently, however, he got used to that. (Some Arctic explorers tell us that to them salt has become positively obnoxious.) For a while his meals consisted principally of seals and sea-food. The waters around Juan Fernández have always abounded and still abound in palatable fish and lobsters.

But after a few months the castaway was able to vary his menus with goat's meat. This he did not obtain by the methods described in *Robinson Crusoe*. He had neither ammunition nor firearms. Alexander Selkirk got his goats by catching them with his bare hands. He became so nimble and fleet of foot that he could run the animals down over even the rockiest ground. In four and a half years he consumed five hundred goats. Incidentally, they had been brought there by Juan Fernández, the original discoverer and owner.

Whenever Spaniards came to the island, as they did from time to time, Selkirk hid in the woods. The real

Crusoe had no "Man Friday."

Rogers nicknamed Selkirk the "Governor" of Juan Fernández. You may recall that this was the title which Robinson Crusoe gave himself. The crew tested Selkirk's speed. They matched him against the ship's dog. Whether in a sprint or a distance run, the maroon outran the dog every time. They also set him to catching them a full supply of goat's meat. "What about this Selkirk?" asked Woodes Rogers of his pilot. "One of the best men who ever sailed these waters," replied Dampier. Rogers made Selkirk one of his officers.

The two English privateers then sailed north, taking prizes as they went. Rogers took full advantage of the terror inspired by Dampier's name. He tried an assault on Guayaquil, which so many English buccaneers had attempted. He found the garrison waiting for him. Dampier advised him not to attack. Nevertheless the captain sent in a messenger to demand ransom. The Spaniards argued, while they strengthened their fortifications. Woodes Rogers was not fooled. While the Dons were stalling, he swooped down with seventy men. Dampier was in command of the guns and turned them on the streets of the town. It was a complete victory for the English privateers. The Spaniards bought themselves off for thirty thousand pieces of eight. That did not include personal loot in the shape of jewelry taken from the women.

Rogers's next feat was the capture, after a desperate

engagement, of a rich Spanish ship off the coast of Lower California. Five days later he came up with the "admiral" of the Manila fleet. The Spaniards beat him off, though for two days it was touch and go. That was the last real adventure worth recording from that cruise. Woodes Rogers, with William Dampier as navigating officer, cast anchor off the Sussex Downs on October 14, 1711. They had been on the high seas more than three years.

Consider poor Mistress Judith Dampier. If ever there was a "sailor's widow" it was she. Perhaps the strange, soft-spoken buccaneer and man of science she married so impetuously was all the more romantic and fascinating because she saw so little of him. Twice he had returned to her without a cent to show for one absence of twelve years and another of three years. Once more he came home, this time with a respectable sum of money. Mistress Judith had given it up. She was dead, buried. William Dampier himself died three years later, obscure, forgotten by his generation.

It is worth remarking that on his one profitable voyage, under Woodes Rogers, he made none of the scientific observations and notes that left his name unforgettable. In fact, as a geographer he ceased to exist after the leaky old *Roebuck* foundered in Ascension harbor. Maybe the loss of his first command did something to him.

He remains the great contradiction among explorers.

You will find him summed up on a brass tablet under that picture in the National Portrait Gallery:

"Captain William Dampier:
Pirate and Hydrographer."

The diary of Mistress Dampier might be interesting.

XII

THE MYSTERY OF LAPEROUSE

XII

THE MYSTERY OF LAPÉROUSE

"My entire history has been a romance."

When you hear a man talking like that you are inclined to put him down as an impostor. Usually that sort of thing is said only by somebody whose actual life is so drab that he has to make up for it by pretense.

But the man who wrote the particular words quoted above was Jean François Galaup, Comte de Lapérouse, one of the most gallant gentlemen who ever came out of France. He said, if anything, less than the truth. No novelist ever related a more picturesque career. He was even more romantic a figure than he thought he was. He did not know that he was destined to leave behind him a mystery about which historians and geographers are still puzzling.

Jean François was of the old nobility of Languedoc. He was born in 1742, fourteen years after James Cook, Cook the Circumnavigator, whom in after years the young Frenchman took for his model. It also happened that Lapérouse and Cook fought on opposite sides in the Seven Years' War. Jean François was only fifteen years old when he entered the French navy in the rank corresponding to midshipman. As would any other lad, he thought he was tremendously lucky when the war broke out a few weeks after he had joined his ship. He was hardly dry behind the ears when he smelled gunpowder in action and took part in the spectacular maneuvers of naval engagements in the days of sail.

He was barely seventeen when he fought and was wounded in the crucial Battle of Quiberon Bay in November, 1759. It was the battle which the naval historian, Admiral Mahan, has termed the "Trafalgar of the Seven Years' War." Incidentally it resulted in a peerage for the English Admiral Hawke. The adolescent Comte de Lapérouse was aboard Admiral du Verger's flagship, the *Formidable*. She bore the brunt of the British cannonading and was the first ship in that battle to strike her colors.

All this was precocious experience for a seventeen-year-old youth. No wonder he declared more than once: "My life has been one long romance."

During the next twenty-five years Lapérouse fought all over the world. He was in naval engagements in the East Indies, in the West Indies, in Canadian waters and in the home waters. By the time the American War of Independence broke out he was a hardened veteran. Hardened, that is, physically and in point of experience. Inside he remained tender and gentle to the day of his mysterious death.

As a matter of fact, Lapérouse's history should have a particular interest for Americans. When France jumped in to help the American revolution, Jean François, now a captain, commanded the *Amazon* in D'Estaing's fleet. Though there were no important engagements between the French and the British, and D'Estaing was not an excessively lucky admiral, nevertheless the aid of King Louis' men-o'-war was invaluable to General Washington. For by 1781 the British had lost command of the sea. Mahan and other experts claim that this was one of the principal factors which contributed to the capitulation at Yorktown. It also enabled Washington to drive the English out of New York.

About this time Captain the Comte de Lapérouse was transferred to the command of the *Sceptre*, a 74-gun frigate under Admiral La Touche Tréville. This is a particularly significant part of the story. It led to an incident which better than anything else illustrates the chivalry of the man's character.

Though the British had been driven out of New York, numbers of loyalists among the colonials still held out in forts up the Hudson River. They constituted a serious menace to Washington's forces. Not because of their own strength, but because they held the waterway from Canada by which the English and their Indian allies could attack the revolutionary armies from the North. Lapérouse was detailed to sail the *Sceptre* up the Hudson to wipe out the loyalist posts. He did the job efficiently and completely, dislodged the Tory garrisons, dismantled the forts.

Then comes the significant gesture. The defeated loyalists were now at the mercy of hostile Indians, Washington's allies. They stood an excellent chance of losing, not merely their hair, but their wives, children and lives. Lapérouse equipped them with food, ammunition and clothing. He reported what he had done to La Touche Tréville with the words: "An enemy conquered should have nothing to fear from a civilized foe: he then becomes a friend."

In that action and that message we see clearly what kind of a knight he was. It enables us to understand better the subsequent life of this Jean François Galaup, Comte de Lapérouse.

We now come to the romance of his heart. I venture to say you will find it as touching a tale as you ever read. The scene in which it was laid is also the locale of another romance that hitherto has been still more famous.

For the next thing we hear of Lapérouse he is at the island of Mauritius, then owned by King Louis XVI and known as the Isle de France. To the world at large it is perhaps more familiar as the scene of the love story of Paul and Virginia.

That is where Jean François met Louise Eléonore Broudon. She was a beautiful thing, with a magnolia white skin, blue-black hair and dark blue eyes, a rare combination. She was as gentle and lovable as she was beautiful. Accomplished, also, by the standards of the times.

During an official reception at the Governor's residence she was introduced to the noble and distinguished officer of the navy of the Most Christian King. They danced, he talked, she replied, in language as modest as her manner and voice were charming. He had met women all over the world. He had trod the minuet with ladies at Versailles and at Philadelphia, in the ports of the East Indies and the West Indies. But none captivated him so completely as this nineteen-year-old girl of the Isle de France.

We have observed what sort of a man he was, as an officer, gentleman and fighter. But what sort of a fellow was he to look at? When Louise Eléonore Broudon met him, he was no chicken. He was in his fortieth year. Somewhat portly, with a slight double chin. Nose and mouth of average dimensions, though made to appear smaller than they actually were by his chubby cheeks. But the most important feature of all was the kindly, humorous expression of the eyes. As you stare at his portrait you can imagine him saying to a lieutenant, over-excited in the heat of battle: "Take it easy, *mon brave*, take it easy; let's give them a broadside from the port guns." In short, the man whom Louise Eléonore Broudon met was no Adonis. But he was brave, courtly, well poised and witty.

The upshot was that she fell as hard as he did. They

had ideal surroundings for it. If you read your *Paul et Virginie* again you will be able to conjure up a pretty accurate picture of the courtship of Mlle. Broudon.

They became engaged. Father and Mother Broudon were, of course, flustered, bewildered, glad but also a bit dubious. For Eléonore's father was only a subordinate civil official of the government of the Isle de France. Practically, of the lower middle classes. Her lover, on the other hand, was not only captain of a frigate in His Majesty's navy, he was also Comte de Lapérouse, of the ancient nobility of Languedoc.

Papa Broudon's misgivings were justified. The letter from Jean François announcing his engagement to his parents, the Marquis and Marquise, was a bombshell. When he returned home he had to face unpleasant music. His father tut-tutted, his mother stormed and wept. Jean François was forty years old, a veteran of several wars, a ranking officer. But by the laws of France he could not marry without his parents' consent. That consent was flatly and unequivocally refused. "For the Honor of the Family, you cannot do this thing. Your mother and I have betrothed you to the daughter of our old friend and neighbor, the Sieur de Vésian." While Jean François had been away, fighting the King's battles, his father and mother had affianced him to a girl he had never even seen!

A less gentle son would have told his father to go jump into the Rhone. He would at least have made himself excessively disagreeable about the business. Jean François somehow kept the balance between a true lover and an affectionate son. For all his seniority and experience, as a nobleman of France he owed respect and obedience to his parents. He pleaded with tears in his eyes. In the end, he wrote sadly and pitifully to Eléonore and told her he could not disobey his father and mother. Papa Broudon, of course, said: "I thought so. Do not weep, my child. We cannot go against the laws of France."

Eléonore collapsed, pined, then recovered. She kept her suffering to herself and said nothing. If Jean François had given up hope, she had not. Her father was due to return home shortly because his term of service in the colony had almost expired. She had an opportunity to marry one or two young men in her own class and remain on the Isle de France. She declined, kindly but firmly. The love for her brilliant captain was rooted deep in her heart. Before many months had passed, she was in Paris. And, somehow, she contrived to break the information to her lover.

Parents or no parents, laws or no laws, that was too much for him. He was resting on his father's estate in Languedoc, waiting for orders from the Minister of Marine, when he received Eléonore's letter. Riding on relays of horses, he was in Paris in two days and a few hours later had Eléonore in his arms.

On the following day he had two difficult letters

to write. One was to his father and mother. The other was to Mlle. de Vésian, whom even yet he had never set eyes on. Mlle. de Vésian and her parents accepted the situation with dignity and common sense—three months later she married somebody else. The Marquis de Lapérouse and his Marquise were not so philosophical. "What will your Admiral think? What will the Minister of Marine think? What will the KING think? Your career is at an end." But they yielded, prophesying ruin. Jean François married his Eléonore.

What *did* the Minister of Marine say? He wrote a kindly letter of good wishes and advised the bridegroom that he was about to be given an important commission. What did the King say? He had been reading the Journal of Captain Cook's first voyage. It had been translated into French and made a tremendous success. Furthermore, King Louis was struck with alarm when he observed that England was discovering and annexing so much new territory. France, he decided, must have her place in the southern sun. The King called in the Court Geographer, the Comte de Fleurieu. Between them they outlined the plan of a French voyage of discovery. Two of the finest frigates in His Majesty's navy were put into commission for the expedition. And who was assigned to command it? The captain who had been warned that his ill-advised marriage would ruin his career, Captain Jean François

Galaup, Comte de Lapérouse.

For several reasons he was selected as the man best fitted for the job. In the first place, he was a first-class seaman, an expert navigator. In the second place, he knew geography. He, too, had read all about Cook and acquired an enormous admiration for the great Englishman who went before him. As he wrote: "M. Cook will always be in my eyes the first of navigators. It is he who has determined the precise position of those islands, who has explored their shores. Chance might enable the most ignorant man to discover islands. But it belongs only to great men like him to leave nothing to be done regarding the coasts they have found." In the third place, Lapérouse's conduct during the war had made him respected and liked by the English, an important factor in such an expedition.

Lapérouse hoisted his flag on the *Boussole*. His second-in-command was the Vicomte de Langle, aboard the *Astrolabe*. Astronomers, zoologists, botanists and mineralogists accompanied them. Their instructions, in the King's handwriting, were amazingly complete. In addition to scientific observations, they were to report on the commercial possibilities and political conditions of the lands they visited, also the lay-out from a military standpoint. Knowing Lapérouse, it was hardly necessary for the King to add:

"The Sieur de Lapérouse will invariably show the utmost kindness and humanity towards the different peoples visited in the course of the voyage. He will study with zeal and interest every means of improving their condition, by supplying them with the vegetables, fruits and useful trees of Europe. . . . If the force of circumstances should ever compel the Sieur de Lapérouse to assert the superiority of his arms over those of the savages, in order to procure, in spite of opposition, the necessities of life, he must use force with the greatest moderation and punish with the utmost rigor any of his people who may exceed his orders. He will resort to arms only in the last extremity."

Lapérouse sailed from Brest on August 1, 1785. His married life with Eléonore had been short but without a flaw. He rounded Cape Horn successfully and cruised around among the islands of the Pacific for a few months. Then he went north and sighted Mt. St. Elias, in Alaska, on June 23, 1786. In those waters he encountered his first disaster. Both his ships came within a hairsbreadth of being wrecked. As it was, two boats were capsized while taking soundings. Twenty-one men were drowned. Saddened by the loss, he carried on and surveyed the west coast of America, from Alaska to California. At that point he sailed west for Kamchatka. There he landed a messenger with dispatches for the King. That messenger bore the historic name of the Vicomte de Lesseps, of the same family as the De Lesseps who one hundred years later made such a tragic failure of the attempt to

LAPÉROUSE SURVEYED THE WEST COAST OF AMERICA, FROM ALASKA
TO CALIFORNIA

dig a canal across the Isthmus of Panama. Lapérouse made elaborate hydrographic surveys along the Asiatic coast, proved that Sakhalin is an island and discovered the strait that now bears his name. In December, 1787, Lapérouse was at Samoa. There the expedition ran into a second calamity. The Vicomte de Langle was sent ashore in charge of four boats to get fresh water. The natives were most friendly and furnished all the water they wanted. Trouble started when De Langle trotted out a few presents for the chiefs. This excited those islanders who did not get any. Hundreds of them massed together and mobbed the Frenchman. De Langle's men made for the boats. The Samoans grabbed the grapnel ropes and tried to stop them. De Langle ordered his marines to fire over the heads of the crowd. The answer was a shower of stones. In the end the French escaped with the loss of two boats, of the Vicomte de Langle, of one of the scientists and ten of the crew.

Lapérouse then set sail for Australia. He arrived there just too late to claim any territory for the King of France. Barely a day before he came, a fleet of eleven British ships under Captain Arthur Phillip had cast anchor in Botany Bay. On January 26, 1788, Phillip, who had been sent out as governor of the new colony of New South Wales, formally founded the city of Sydney on the shores of Port Jackson. Phillip was still selecting the site when a cry went up: "Another sail!" Presently two vessels of considerable size were seen standing in for the mouth of the bay. There was keen alarm. The fear was that they might be Dutchmen sent to dispossess the English. The Hollanders still maintained a claim on Australia. But as soon as the French ensigns were seen fluttering from the mastheads the panic subsided. Presently Lapérouse's ships were swinging to their anchors. Phillip sent an officer aboard and the French commander returned the call. Thus Lapérouse in a sense took part in the founding of Sydney. In those parts the tradition still lingers of the charming impression left behind by the ill-fated explorer. A monument to his memory stands there today overlooking the harbor.

He entrusted Governor Phillip with dispatches to be sent home to the King of France. Phillip's chief lieutenant, Philip King—later governor of the colony—was one of the last Europeans to talk to Lapérouse before he vanished. He often quoted the Frenchman's words: "M. Cook has done so much that he has left me nothing to do but admire his work." After a month's stay at Botany Bay the French ships weighed anchor. His last message to his king told of his intention to run to the Friendly Islands. One of his main objects was to ascertain whether the land discovered by Bougainville and called La Louisiade was a part of New Guinea. Also to discover a new strait between New Guinea and New Holland, after which he intended to sail down the west coast of Australia as far as Tasmania. He hoped to be at the Isle de France on his way home by December, 1788.

Unfortunately, by December, 1788, he was nowhere. The message he sent to his king through Governor Phillip was the last word from him. And we may well imagine that a long letter to his Eléonore went with it. As his ships disappeared over the horizon from Botany Bay they disappeared as completely as though they had sailed over the edge of the world. No white man ever again set eyes on Lapérouse or any one else aboard.

Meanwhile a tremendous thing happened at home— the French Revolution. The King and his family went to prison. The nobility, the class to which Lapérouse belonged, went to the guillotine or over the frontiers. Those who stayed home lived in hourly fear for their lives.

You might suppose that in all that upheaval an explorer at the other end of the world would have been forgotten. But the scientists of France did not forget him. Neither did his colleagues of the navy. After three years the National Assembly set aside two ships to go out and search for him. A temporary parliament that could give time and consideration to such a matter, in such disturbed times, could not have been as bad as it was painted. Napoleon, as we shall see, was far too selfish to pay any attention to a lost explorer. The expedition was put under the command of Admiral

Bruni d'Entrecasteaux. The naturalist, Labillardière, was aboard and it was he who wrote the story of the cruise.

D'Entrecasteaux took with him a copy of Lapérouse's last dispatch. He was instructed to follow the route which the missing explorer had outlined in it. But when the relief ships reached the Isle de France the admiral heard a vague rumor. Natives on the Admiralty Islands were reported to be wearing French naval uniforms. So D'Entrecasteaux altered his course. He made straight for those islands and found the rumor to be a myth. From this time on, ill fortune haunted the expedition. Scurvy broke out. The second-in-command died of it and a few months later D'Entrecasteaux himself. Nevertheless, the two ships continued to cruise vainly around the south Pacific. Once they were within gunshot of finding traces of Lapérouse, but they didn't know it. Nevertheless they made valuable discoveries and added names to the map. Several spots in that part of the world are still called after D'Entrecasteaux, and the officers who survived him brought back a set of charts which even today are considered models of excellence.

But there seemed to be no end to the expedition's bad luck. Riddled with disease, both vessels sorely in need of refitting, the survivors put in at Soerabaya, the principal port of the Dutch colony of Java. And what did they find there? War had broken out between

France and Holland. The French ships were seized as prizes and the crews thrown into prison, much to the discredit of Dutch chivalry. Other civilized nations, even in wartime, regarded vessels sent out for scientific purposes as immune from interference and capture. Many a month of suffering passed before the Frenchmen were allowed to return home. For all this, the expedition of D'Entrecasteaux made important contributions to geography and to the honor of French science and enterprise.

But it ended all official attempts to solve the mystery of Lapérouse. Napoleon and his wars blotted out the memory of the gallant explorer. As a mystery it continued for forty years. An extraordinary series of adventures finally brought some curious information to light. We now have to consider the romantic life of a sailor named Peter Dillon. In 1813 this Irishman was mate of a vessel in the sandalwood trade. It was attacked by natives on one of the Fiji Islands. Most of the crew were massacred. Dillon escaped and with him a German named Martin Bushart. The latter was married to a native woman. As she was about to have a baby, Martin persuaded the captain to land them on a small island called Tucopia in the New Hebrides.

Thirteen years later Peter Dillon was on a voyage from Valparaiso to Bengal. Passing the New Hebrides, he suddenly decided to put in at Tucopia and visit Martin Bushart. Dillon became curious about a silver sword-guard in Bushart's possession. He learned that the German had obtained it in exchange for a handful of fishhooks. The silver guard was engraved. Bushart told Dillon that the natives had a number of articles of European origin: silver forks, knives, axes and other things. They all came from the near-by island of Vanikoro.

Dillon investigated. He found out that two large ships had anchored off those islands many years before. A terrific hurricane blew up. Both vessels were driven ashore and soon were battered to pieces by the waves. One crew took to the boats, landed in the heavy surf and were wiped out by the natives, massacred. The other ship, however, grounded on a sandy beach. By dint of gifts her crew made friends with the savages. Thus they were able to establish themselves ashore. They built a boat out of the timber from their wrecked ship. It was not large enough to hold them all. But most of them sailed away in that boat, promising to return for their shipmates. They never were seen again. The remaining castaways, apparently, were still on Vanikoro.

Dillon was not a learned man. Yet the tale he heard brought to his mind the legend, current in all those waters, of the two French ships that had sailed away from Botany Bay in 1788 and vanished. He determined to sail to Vanikoro and rescue the survivors, if any. But he was becalmed several days, his ship was leaky and he was short of provisions. So when the wind sprang up again he made for Calcutta and reported his information to the Government of Bengal.

The directors of the East India Company, which then ruled Hindustan, acted promptly. They commissioned Dillon to go to Vanikoro and rescue the castaways, if any were left. They gave him their surveying vessel, the *Research*. And they sent a Dr. Tytler with him as medical officer and naturalist.

It must have been a turbulent voyage. Dillon was no dove. When the *Research* put in at Tasmania, Dr. Tytler had the captain arrested for assault. Dillon was convicted, fined fifty pounds and thrown into prison for two months. Evidently that did not cool the Irishman's temper. He had a quarrel with his chief officer, who left him and returned to Calcutta. The purser absconded with a large part of the ship's funds and the crew mutinied at Port Jackson.

However, Dillon sighted Vanikoro on September 7, 1827. He made a thorough investigation into the wreck of the two large ships. He found that the story he had heard the year before was true. In the spirit house on one of the islands were the skulls of sixty white men. He also came upon a quantity of silver plate, engraved with monograms and crests. Likewise the stern of a ship decorated with the *fleur-de-lys*, the emblem of the kings of France. But there were no survivors. The last of these who remained on Vanikoro had died six years previously, except one who had put out in a canoe with a native chief and never returned.

Of the men who had sailed away from Vanikoro in the boat they made from the timbers of the wreck, he could find no trace. There were vague reports in some of the neighboring islands, but nothing definite. Dillon sailed home with his relics. He was presented to King Charles X of France and made a Chevalier of the Legion of Honor. He also received an annuity of 4,000 francs.

Meanwhile, there was one survivor from the two ships' companies that had sailed with Lapérouse in the *Boussole* and the *Astrolabe*. That was the Vicomte de Lesseps, whom we last left on the coast of Kamchatka where Lapérouse had landed him to carry dispatches to the King. He was able positively to identify the relics the Irishman had brought home.

While Dillon was on his way back from Vanikoro, the French Government had sent Captain Dumont d'Urville to help in the search for traces of Lapérouse. He was in command of a frigate named the *Astrolabe*, after one of the ill-fated ships wrecked with Lapérouse. Dumont d'Urville made some discoveries and supplemented the world's information about southern waters. He also found more relics of the Lapérouse expedition, as well as the exact spot where one of his ships had sunk. He put up a small memorial on the shore and came home.

And so we observe that the mystery of Lapérouse is

only partially solved. Was he among the ship's company who were instantly massacred? Was his one of these sixty skulls adorning the savages' spirit house? Or was he one of the boat's crew that sailed away never to return? There are a round dozen questions we should like to have answered.

Above all, we should like to know more about the beautiful Louise Eléonore, Comtesse de Lapérouse. She was still practically in the ecstasies of her honeymoon when her gallant and romantic captain left her. We can only guess at her feelings as the years dragged on without a word from the brave and lovable Jean François.

THE END